WEBSTER'S
CONCISE WORLD ATLAS

WEBSTER'S
CONCISE WORLD ATLAS

DEALERFIELD

Published by arrangement with De Agostini Editions Limited,
Griffin House, 161 Hammersmith Road, London W6 8SD

This edition specially printed for Dealerfield Ltd 1995

ISBN 1 85927 078 6

© Istituto Geografico De Agostini 1995

Printed in the EU, Officine Grafiche De Agostini - Novara 1995

CONTENTS

WORLD: Key to map pages

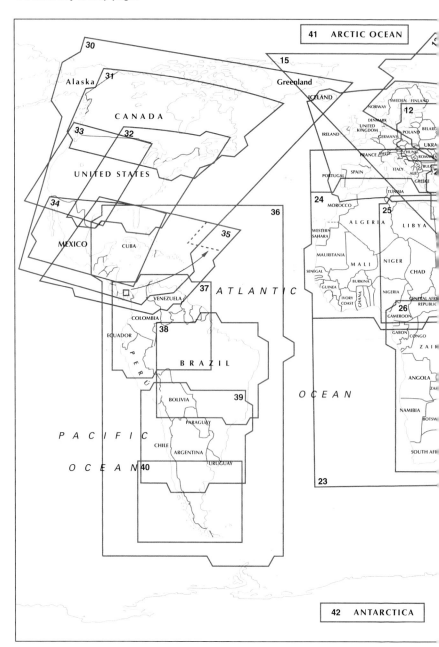

41 ARCTIC OCEAN

30

15

31 Alaska

Greenland

ICELAND

SWEDEN FINLAND

NORWAY

12

CANADA

DENMARK
UNITED
KINGDOM POLAND BELARU
IRELAND GERMANY

33 32

FRANCE SWITZ CZECH HUNG ROMANIA
BULG
UNITED STATES PORTUGAL SPAIN ITALY ALB
GREECE

TUNISIA

34

24 MOROCCO 25

36

ALGERIA LIBYA
WESTERN
SAHARA

35

MEXICO CUBA

MAURITANIA
MALI NIGER
SENEGAL CHAD

37 ATLANTIC

GUINEA BURKINA
IVORY NIGERIA CENTRAL AFR
COAST GHANA REPUBLIC

26
VENEZUELA CAMEROON

COLOMBIA
38 GABON CONGO

ECUADOR
ZAIR

BRAZIL

ANGOLA
ZA

BOLIVIA 39 OCEAN

PARAGUAY NAMIBIA BOTSW

PACIFIC

CHILE
ARGENTINA SOUTH AFR

OCEAN 40 URUGUAY

23

42 ANTARCTICA

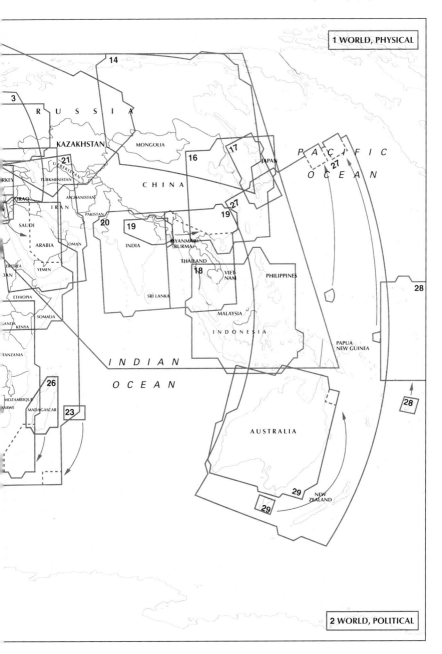

EUROPE: Key to map pages

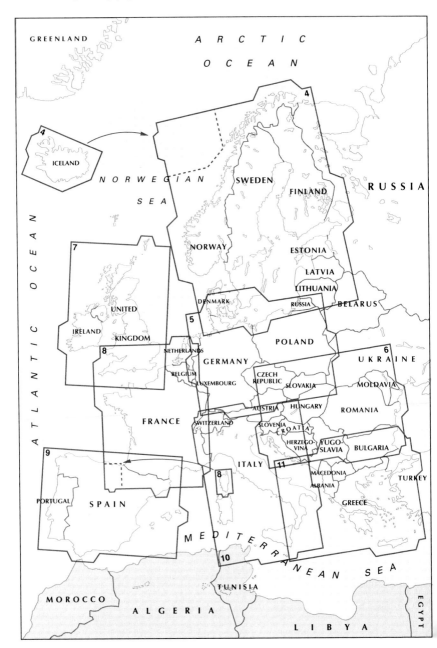

GREENLAND

A R C T I C

O C E A N

4

4

ICELAND

N O R W E G I A N

SWEDEN

FINLAND

R U S S I A

S E A

NORWAY

ESTONIA

LATVIA

LITHUANIA

7

DENMARK

RUSSIA

BELARUS

5

POLAND

O C E A N

UNITED

6

IRELAND

KINGDOM

NETHERLANDS

U K R A I N E

8

GERMANY

BELGIUM

CZECH
REPUBLIC

LUXEMBOURG

SLOVAKIA

MOLDAVIA

AUSTRIA

HUNGARY

ROMANIA

A T L A N T I C

FRANCE

SWITZERLAND

SLOVENIA

CROATIA

9

HERZEGO-
VINA

YUGO-
SLAVIA

BULGARIA

ITALY

11

MACEDONIA

TURKEY

ALBANIA

PORTUGAL

S P A I N

8

GREECE

M E D I T E R R A N E A N   S E A

10

TUNISIA

E G Y P T

MOROCCO

A L G E R I A

L I B Y A

© ISTITUTO GEOGRAFICO DE AGOSTINI S. p. A. - NOVARA

A GEOGRAPHICAL DICTIONARY OF COUNTRIES, CONTINENT BY CONTINENT

STATE (official name/ English translation)	CAPITAL ① inhabitants	AREA (sq km)	POPULATION	DENSITY (inhab/sq km)	LIFE EXPECTANCY (in years) M
ALBANIA (Republika e Shqipërisë/ Republic of Albania)	Tirana (Tiranë) 243 000	28 748	3 256 000	113	69.6 75
ANDORRA (Principat d'Andorra/ Principauté d'Andorre/ Principality of Andorra)	Andorra la Vella (Andorre-la-Vieille) 15 600	453	52 000	115	74.0 81
AUSTRIA (Republik Österreich/ Republic of Austria)	Vienna (Wien) 1 533 000	83 859	7 712 000	92	72.1 78
BELGIUM (Koninkrijk België/ Royaume de Belgique/ Kingdom of Belgium)	Brussels (Brussel/Bruxelles) 960 000	30 518	9 950 000	326	70.0 76
BOSNIA-HERZEGOVINA (Republika Bosnia i Hercegovina)	Sarajevo 526 000	51 129	4 350 000	85	68.0 73
BULGARIA (Republika Bulgarija/ Republic of Bulgaria)	Sofia (Sofiya) 1 221 000	110 994	8 990 000	81	68.3 74
CROATIA (Republika Hrvatska/ Republic of Croatia)	Zagreb 763 000	56 538	4 750 000	84	67.0 74
CZECH REPUBLIC (Ceská Republika)	Prague (Praha) 1 212 000	78 864	10 365 000	131	68.1 75
DENMARK (Kongeriget Danmark/ Kingdom of Denmark)	Copenhagen (København) 467 000	43 093	5 140 000	119	71.9 77
ESTONIA (Eesti Vabariik/ Republic of Estonia)	Tallinn 484 000	45 100	1 578 000	35	65.8 75
FINLAND (Suomen Tasavalta/ Republiken Finland/ Republic of Finland)	Helsinki (Helsingfors) 491 000	338 145	4 986 000	15	70.7 78
FRANCE (République Française/ French Republic)	Paris 2 152 000	543 965	56 600 000	104	72.7 80
GERMANY (Bundesrepublik Deutschland/Federal Republic of Germany)	Berlin 3 410 000	356 957	79 479 000	223	72.2 78

GROSS NATIONAL PRODUCT ②	LANGUAGES	RELIGIONS	ECONOMY
740	Albanian (Gheg and Tosc [off.])	Muslim 70%; Orthodox 20%	**Economy** Mainly agriculture (cereals, potatoes, sugar beet, olives, fruit), animal farming and industry (food processing, textile and tobacco production, building materials). **Mineral resources** Substantial reserves of chromite and petroleum.
17 600	Catalan (off.); Spanish; French	Catholic	**Economy** As a free-trade (duty-free) zone, considerable income is generated by tourism, trade and banking. **Agriculture** Another main economic activity. Cattle and pigs are the chief livestock, cereals, potatoes and tobacco the principal crops.
17 360	German	Catholic 84%; Protestant 6%	**Industry** Dominates the economy (mechanical, chemical, wood, paper, textile and food production). **Mineral resources** Iron, magnesite, petroleum, lignite, lead. **Agriculture** Almost self-sufficient (cereals, sugar beet).
16 390	Flemish; French	Catholic	**Economy** Relies mainly on manufacturing. Brussels profits from being the HQ of the EC. **Agriculture** Main crops: cereals, potatoes, beet. Dairy farming is thriving. **Industry** Coal mining and the production of machinery, textiles, chemicals, food, diamonds.
1 741	Serbo-Croat	Muslim; Christian	**Economy** Based on agriculture (cereals, tobacco, fruit) and animal farming. **Mineral resources** Copper, lead, zinc, gold and iron. **Industry** Mechanical, electronics, chemical, textile and food industries.
2 320	Bulgarian	Orthodox 80%; Muslim 13%	**Economy** Essentially agricultural (cereals, potatoes, beet, vines, tobacco). Roses are traditionally grown too. **Mineral resources** Coal, iron, copper, lead and zinc. **Industry** The food, mechanical and electronic sectors are well established.
3 226	Croat	Catholic 76%; Orthodox 11%	**Agriculture** Principal crops: cereals, potatoes, beet, vines, olives. Animal farming is productive. **Principal resources** Timber from the large forests, coal, bauxite, hydrocarbons. **Industry** Mechanical, chemical, food, textiles and wood.
7 200	Czech	Catholic	**Economy** Dominated by heavy industry, although the country has profited from its considerable timber and coal reserves. **Agriculture** Cereals, hops and beet are cultivated widely. **Industry** Food, textile, mechanical and chemicals.
20 510	Danish	Protestant	**Agriculture** Animal farming (dairy products, meat) is important to domestic and export markets. Also fishing and arable farming (cereals, potatoes, sugar beet). **Industry** Primarily food, mechanical, chemical and ceramic production.
5 849	Estonian	Lutheran	**Economy** Dominated by agriculture (cereals, potatoes, animal fodder crops), animal farming (pigs, cattle), forestry and mineral resources (bituminous shale, phosphorites, peat). **Industry** Food processing, wood- and metalworking.
22 060	Finnish; Swedish	Protestant	**Economy** Dense forestation provides great quantities of timber, much for export, the rest for wood and paper factories. **Agriculture** Dairy farming and fishing are significant. **Industry** Metalworking, shipbuilding and food processing.
17 830	French	Catholic	**Agriculture** Extensive fishing, arable (cereals, potatoes, beet, grapes for wine) and animal farming. **Principal resources** Coal, petrol, natural gas, timber. **Industry** Food, machinery, vehicles, chemicals, electronics, textiles, fashion, rubber.
20 750	German	Protestant 41%; Catholic 41%	**Economy** Very strong, notably industry (metals, mechanical, chemicals, electronics) and services. **Agriculture** Main crops: potatoes, cereals, beet, hops for brewing. Animal farming. **Mineral resources** Coal, lignite, potassium salts.

STATE (official name/ English translation)	CAPITAL ① inhabitants	AREA (sq km) POPULATION		DENSITY (inhab/sq km)	LIFE EXPEC ANCY (in year M
GREECE (Elliniki Dimokratia/ Hellenic Republic)	**Athens** (Athinai) 885 000	131 957	10 123 000	77	72.2 7
HUNGARY (Magyar Köztársaság/ Hungarian Republic)	**Budapest** 2 016 000	93 033	10 364 000	111	65.4 7
ICELAND (Lyðveldið Ísland/ Republic of Iceland)	**Reykjavík** 96 700	102 819	255 000	2	75.7 8
IRELAND (Poblacht na h'Éireann/ Republic of Ireland)	**Dublin** (Baile Átha Cliath) 503 000	70 283	3 503 000	50	71.0 7
ITALY (Repubblica Italiana/ Republic of Italy)	**Rome** (Roma) 2 693 000	301 302	56 800 000	187	73.2 7
LATVIA (Latvija)	**Riga** 916 000	64 500	2 683 000	41	64.2 7
LIECHTENSTEIN (Fürstentum Liechtenstein/ Principality of Liechtenstein)	**Vaduz** 4 900	160	29 000	181	66.1 7
LITHUANIA (Lietuva)	**Vilnius** 582 000	65 200	3 725 000	57	66.9 7
LUXEMBOURG (Grand-Duché de Luxembourg/Grand Duchy of Luxembourg)	**Luxembourg** 76 000	2 586	381 000	147	70.6 7
MACEDONIA (Republika Makedonija)	**Skopje** 406 000	25 713	2 030 000	79	68.0 7
MALTA (Republic of Malta/ Repubblika ta' Malta)	**Valletta** 9 200	316	354 000	1120	73.8 7
MONACO (Principauté de Monaco/ Principality of Monaco)	**Monaco** 1 234	1.9	30 000	15 789	—
THE NETHERLANDS (Koninkrijk der Nederlanden/Kingdom of the Netherlands)	**Amsterdam** 695 000	41 574	14 893 000	358	73.7 80

GROSS NATIONAL PRODUCT ②	LANGUAGES	RELIGIONS	ECONOMY
5 340	Greek	Orthodox	**Agriculture** Important economically. Main crops: cereals, olives, vines, citrus fruits, cotton, tobacco. Livestock and fishing also important. **Industry** Tourism highly profitable; also food processing, petrochemicals, textiles, metals and chemicals.
2 560	Hungarian	Catholic 64%; Protestant 23%	**Agriculture** Among the major crops are cereals, potatoes, sugar beet and grapes. Animal farming is significant. **Mineral resources** Bauxite, petroleum and coal. **Industry** Machinery, textiles, chemicals and food.
21 240	Icelandic	Protestant	**Economy** Fishing (cod, herrings) is vital. **Agriculture** Small-scale: the inhospitable climate is most suitable for grazing and sheep rearing. **Industry** Mainly fish storage and processing; hydroelectricity fuels the profitable aluminium-smelting plants.
8 500	Irish (off.); English	Catholic 93%; Anglican 3%	**Economy** Essentially agricultural, with livestock (sheep and cattle) of primary importance. Main crops: cereals, potatoes and sugar beet. **Principal resources** Peat, zinc and natural gas. **Industry** Food processing, machinery and brewing.
15 150	Italian	Catholic	**Agriculture** Important to the domestic economy (cereals, olives, vines, citrus fruits, tomatoes, beet). Also animal farming (cattle, pigs) and fishing. **Industry** Cars, machinery, chemicals, food, textiles, clothing and tourism.
6 176	Lettish	Lutheran; Orthodox	**Economy** Heavily industrialized, specializing in metals, food, electronics, textiles, chemicals and wood. **Agriculture** Of secondary importance. Cereals, potatoes, flax, beet and fodder are the main crops. Also dairy farming and fishing.
21 000	German	Catholic	**Economy** Dominated by tourism and industry (particularly precision instruments, chemicals, pharmaceutics, food, textiles, ceramics). **Agriculture** Relatively modest. Main crops: cereals, potatoes, vegetables. Main livestock: cattle, pigs, sheep.
4 796	Lithuanian	Catholic	**Agriculture** Dominates the economy (cereals, potatoes, flax, beet, vegetables). Animal farming and forestry are also important activities. **Industry** Major industries are food, machinery, textiles, wood and chemicals.
24 860	Letzeburgish; French; German	Catholic	**Agriculture** The leading products are cereals, potatoes and grapes. Animal farming is widespread. **Industry** The most developed sector of the economy, particularly iron and steel, machinery, chemicals, rubber and plastics.
1 697	Macedonian	Orthodox	**Economy** Industry and mining (of iron, chromite, copper and lignite) predominate. **Agriculture** Main crops: cereals, tobacco, cotton, fruit. Also sheep breeding and forestry. **Industry** Chiefly food, metals, chemicals and textiles.
5 820	Maltese; English	Catholic	**Agriculture** Cereals, potatoes, vegetables, fruit and flowers. Animal farming and fishing are important. **Industry** Main sectors: clothing, food, electronics, shipbuilding, publishing and tobacco. Tourism is a major source of foreign revenue.
9 636	French; Monegasque	Catholic	**Economy** Light industry, banking, casinos and tourism are the main sources of revenue. **Industry** Textiles, clothing, electronics, chemicals, pharmaceutics and paper are among the chief manufactured goods.
16 010	Dutch	Catholic 36%; Protestant 26%	**Agriculture** Main crops: cereals, potatoes, fruit, beet, flowers (tulips, hyacinths). Animal farming and fishing are important. **Mineral resources** Natural gas, petrol. **Industry** Food, chemicals, electronics and rubber are manufactured.

STATE (official name/ English translation)	CAPITAL ① inhabitants	AREA (sq km) POPULATION DENSITY (inhab/sq km)			LIFE EXPECT ANCY (in year M
NORWAY (Kongeriket Norge/ Kingdom of Norway)	Oslo 461 000	323 878	4 242 000	13	73.3 7
POLAND (Polska Rzeczpospolita/ Republic of Poland)	Warsaw (Warszawa) 1 656 000	312 683	38 180 000	122	66.8 7
PORTUGAL (República Portuguesa/ Portuguese Republic)	Lisbon (Lisboa) 830 000	91 191	10 251 000	112	70.6 7
ROMANIA (România)	Bucharest (Bucureşti) 2 127 000	237 500	23 207 000	98	66.5 7:
SAN MARINO (Serenissima Repubblica di San Marino/Most Serene Republic of San Marino)	San Marino 2 300	60.6	23 000	379	73.2 7
SLOVAKIA (Slovenská Republika Republic of Slovakia)	Bratislava 441 000	49 036	5 297 000	108	66.9 7
SLOVENIA (Republika Slovenija Republic of Slovenia)	Ljubljana 267 000	20 251	1 950 000	96	67.0 7
SPAIN (Reino de España/ Kingdom of Spain)	Madrid 3 121 000	498 507	36 950 000	74	73.6 7
SWEDEN (Konungariket Sverige/ Kingdom of Sweden)	Stockholm 674 000	449 964	8 559 000	19	74.2 8(
SWITZERLAND (Schweizerische Eidgenossenschaft; Confédération Suisse)	Berne (Bern) 134 000	41 285	6 712 000	162	74.0 8(
UNITED KINGDOM (United Kingdom of Great Britain and Northern Ireland)	London 6 378 000	244 100	55 487 000	227	72.2 7
VATICAN CITY (Stato della Città del Vaticano/ State of the Vatican City)		0.44	1 000	—	—
YUGOSLAVIA (Federativna Republika Jugoslavija/Federal Republic of Yugoslavia)	Belgrade (Beograd) 1 554 000	102 173	10 300 000	101	68.1 7

ROSS TIONAL ODUCT ②	LANGUAGES	RELIGIONS	ECONOMY
1 850	Bokmaal; Nynorsk	Protestant	**Agriculture** Main crops: cereals, potatoes. Animals are profitably reared for dairy products (sheep), meat (reindeer), fur. Fishing is a major industry. **Principal resources** Timber, petrol, natural gas. **Industry** Mechanical, chemical and wood-processing.
1 760	Polish	Catholic	**Agriculture** Main crops: cereals, potatoes, beet, tobacco, flax, hops, hemp. Animal farming and fishing are practiced. **Mineral resources** Coal, lignite, copper, silver, sulphur. **Industry** Iron, steel, machinery, food and textiles are important.
4 260	Portuguese	Catholic	**Agriculture** Cereals, potatoes, tomatoes and grapes (for prosperous wine industry) are the chief crops. Fishing (sardines). **Principal resources** Cork, pyrethrum and tungsten. **Industry** Textiles, clothes, chemicals and ceramics.
2 540	Romanian	Orthodox	**Agriculture** Cereals, potatoes, beet, fruit and grapes are the main crops. Animal farming and forestry are important. **Mineral resources** Petroleum, natural gas, lignite, coal, iron. **Industry** Metallurgy, food and chemical production.
8 590	Italian	Catholic	**Economy** Tourism and the sale of postage stamps are the backbone of the economy. **Agriculture** Principal crops: cereals, grapes and olives. **Industry** Principal products: food, textiles, leather goods, ceramics and other local crafts.
5 960	Slovak	Catholic	**Agriculture** An important sector of the economy (cereals, potatoes, sugar beet, vines, tobacco). Cattle, pigs and sheep are reared. **Mineral resources** Copper, iron, lead and zinc. **Industry** Food, textile and metal industries.
6 307	Slovene	Catholic	**Agriculture** Dairy and arable farming (cereals, potatoes, beet, vegetables, fruit). **Principal resources** Timber, iron, lead, zinc, copper, lignite, mercury. **Industry** Iron, steel and textile production, mechanical and chemical engineering.
9 150	Spanish (Castilian); Catalan; Basque; Galician	Catholic	**Agriculture** Dairy farming and fishing are widespread. Main crops: cereals, grapes, citrus fruits, olives. **Principal resources** Cork, coal. **Industry** Main products: consumer goods, chemicals, food, textiles. Tourism is also important.
?1 710	Swedish	Protestant	**Agriculture** Limited (cereals, potatoes, beet). Animal farming and fishing at a modest level. **Principal resources** Plentiful timber, iron, lead, zinc, copper and hydroelectricity. **Industry** Motor vehicles, machinery, food, paper and wood.
30 270	German; French; Italian; Romansch	Catholic 48%; Protestant 44%	**Economy** Rich, as a result of its status as an international financial centre and its plentiful hydroelectricity. **Agriculture** Mainly dairy farming. **Industry** Main products: food, textiles, chemicals, pharmaceutics, precision instruments. Tourism.
14 570	English	Protestant; Catholic 9%	**Agriculture** Mainly dairy farming (sheep, cattle) and fishing. **Mineral resources** Rich reserves of petrol, natural gas, coal. **Industry** Services, banking, tourism and manufacturing (metals, chemicals, food, textiles and bricks).
—	Italian and Latin (both off.)	Catholic	**Economy** The City attracts pilgrims and tourists from all over the world. Its revenue derives from charitable donations and income from investments.
2 490	Serbo-Croat	Orthodox	**Economy** Agriculture-based, with cereals, tobacco, fruit and grapes among the main crops. Animal farming and forestry are profitable. **Industry** Major concerns are machinery, textiles, food and paper.

THE COMMONWEALTH OF INDEPENDENT STATES (CIS)

STATE (official name/ English translation)	CAPITAL ① inhabitants	AREA (sq km) POPULATION		DENSITY (inhab/sq km)	LIFE EXPEC ANC (in yea M
ARMENIA (Haikakan Hanrapetoutioun)	**Yerevan** 1 199 000	29 800	3 335 000	112	69.0 7
AZERBAIJAN (Republik Azarbaijchan)	**Baku** 1 150 000	86 600	7 134 000	82	66.6 7
BELARUS (BYELORUSSIA) (Respublika Belarus)	**Minsk** (Mensk) 1 589 000	207 600	10 260 000	49	66.8 7
GEORGIA (Sakartvelos Respublika/ Republic of Georgia)	**Tbilisi** 1 260 000	69 700	5 460 000	78	63.9 7
KAZAKHSTAN (Kazak Respublikasy)	**Alma-Ata** 1 128 000	2 717 300	16 740 000	6	63.9 7
KYRGYZSTAN (Kyrgyz Respublikasy)	**Bishkek** (Biškek) 616 000	198 500	4 394 000	22	64.3 7
MOLDOVA (Republika Moldovenească)	**Chişinău** 665 000	33 700	4 362 000	129	65.5 7
RUSSIA (Rossiya/Rossiyskaya Federativnaya Respublika)	**Moscow** (Moskva) 8 769 000	17 075 400	148 288 000	8	64.2 7
TAJIKISTAN (Respublika i Tojikiston)	**Dushanbe** (Dušanbe) 595 000	143 100	5 303 000	37	66.8 7
TURKMENISTAN (Türkmenostan)	**Ashkabad** 398 000	488 100	3 668 000	7	61.8 6
UKRAINE (Ukraïna)	**Kiev** (Kyiv) 2 587 000	603 700	51 889 000	86	66.1 7
UZBEKISTAN (Ozbekiston Respublikasy)	**Tashkent** 2 073 000	447 400	20 514 000	46	66.0 7
CIS (Commonwealth of Independent States)		22 100 900	281 347 000	13	
EUROPE Total ⓐ		10 396 569	709 019 000	68	

GROSS NATIONAL PRODUCT ②	LANGUAGES	RELIGIONS	ECONOMY
4 710	Armenian	Orthodox	**Agriculture** Chief crops are wheat, potatoes, vegetables, fruit, grapes, cotton and tobacco. Livestock includes cattle, sheep and goats. **Industry** Metalwork, machinery, chemicals, food and bricks.
3 750	Azerbaijani	Muslim (Shiite 75%; Sunni 25%)	**Economy** Depends mainly on its reserves of oil (plus natural gas) and manufacturing (machinery, chemicals, petrochemicals). **Agriculture** Arable (cereals, cotton, tobacco, tea, grapes, fruit) and animal farming are significant.
5 960	Belarussian	Orthodox; Catholic	**Economy** Based on agriculture (cereals, potatoes, sugar beet, vegetables, fruit, flax), animal farming (cattle, pigs) and industry (metals, electronics, chemicals, food, textiles).
4 410	Georgian	Orthodox	**Agriculture** Cereals, citrus fruits, grapes, tea, flowers and tobacco. Animals are kept for meat and wool. **Principal resources** Manganese ore, hydroelectricity. **Industry** Developing rapidly. Main products: metals, chemicals and bricks.
3 720	Kazakh	Muslim (Sunni); Orthodox	**Economy** Plentiful resources (coal, petrol, iron, natural gas, tungsten, copper, lead, zinc) aid industrial growth (metals, chemicals, textiles). **Agriculture** Animal farming; much of the population grows crops (cereals, cotton, sugar beet).
3 030	Kyrgyz	Muslim (Sunni); Orthodox	**Agriculture** Cereals, potatoes, sugar beet and fruit are the principal crops, with sheep, goats and cattle the main livestock. **Industry** Textiles, tanning, metallurgy, machinery, electronics, mining (coal, uranium).
3 830	Romanian	Orthodox	**Agriculture** Arable farming – cereals, potatoes, beet, fruit, grapes (for wine), vegetables, sunflower seeds – and animal herding are vital to the economy. **Industry** The major products are machinery, textiles, chemicals and processed food.
5 810	Russian	Orthodox	**Economy** Owing to abundant resources (hydrocarbons, combustibles, timber, minerals) all industrial sectors are highly developed. **Agriculture** Large-scale. Main crops: cereals, potatoes. Animal farming and fishing are also practiced.
2 340	Tajik	Muslim (Sunni)	**Agriculture** The main products are cotton, vegetables, fruit and seeds. Sheep, goats and cattle are raised. **Mineral resources** Uranium, gold, iron and lead. **Industry** Concentrates on food and textiles (carpets).
3 370	Turkmen	Muslim (Sunni)	**Agriculture** Cotton is one of the chief exports; animal breeding (especially karakul sheep) is also important. **Principal resources** Plentiful petroleum and natural gas. **Industry** Machinery, textiles (especially carpets) and petrochemicals.
4 700	Ukrainian	Christian	**Agriculture** Animal and arable farming (cereals, potatoes, sunflower seeds, beet) are widespread. **Economy** Rich deposits of minerals (coal, iron) have helped the development of the iron and steel, mechanical and chemical industries.
2 750	Uzbek	Muslim (Sunni)	**Agriculture** Cotton, cereals, vegetables and fruit are the main crops, sheep and goats the main livestock. **Mineral resources** Large reserves of natural gas, petrol, coal, lead, zinc and gold. **Industry** Machinery-building and chemicals.

Includes the Azores Is (Portugal), Asian Greek Islands, the European parts of Turkey and the CIS; excludes the Canary Is (Spain) and Madeira (Portugal).

① The local form is given in brackets only when it differs from the English form

② Per inhabitant, in US$.

STATE (official name/ English translation)	CAPITAL ① inhabitants	AREA (sq km) POPULATION		DENSITY (inhab/sq km)	LIFE EXPECTANCY (in year) M
AFGHANISTAN (Da Afghānistān Jamhuriat Republic of Afghanistan)	**Kābul** 1 424 000	652 225	16 922 000	26	41.0	42
BAHRAIN (Dawlat al-Bahrain)	**Manama** (Al Manāmah) 151 500	678	516 000	761	71.0	7
BANGLADESH (Gana Praja Tantri Bangladesh/People's Republic of Bangladesh)	**Dhaka** 6 105 000	143 998	105 000 000	729	56.9	55
BHUTAN (Druk-Yul/ Realm of the Dragon)	**Thimphu** 30 000	47 000	1 476 000	31	49.2	4
BRUNEI (Negara Brunei Darussalam/Sultanate of Brunei)	**Bandar Seri Begawan** 55 100	5 765	264 000	46	72.6	7
CAMBODIA (Roat Kâmpŭchéa/ State of Cambodia)	**Phnom Penh** 564 000	181 035	8 781 000	48	47.0	4
CHINA (Zhonghua Renmin Gongheguo/People's Republic of China)	**Peking** (Beijing) 5 770 000	9 536 499	1155 790 000	121	68.4	7
CYPRUS (Kypriaki Dimokratia/ Kibris Cumhuriyeti/ Republic of Cyprus)	**Nicosia** 187 000	9 251	710 000	77	73.9	78
INDIA (Bhārat Juktarashtra/ Republic of India)	**Delhi** 294 000	3 287 782	849 638 000	258	58.1	5
INDONESIA (Republik Indonesia/ Republic of Indonesia)	**Jakarta** 7 829 000	1 529 072	180 910 000	118	58.5	62
IRAN (Jomhurī-e-Islāmī-e-Irān/ Islamic Republic of Iran)	**Tehran** 6 620 000	1 648 196	56 250 000	34	64.0	65
IRAQ (Al Jumhūrīya al-'Irāqīya/ Republic of Iraq)	**Baghdād** 3 844 600	434 128	17 903 000	41	63.0	6
ISRAEL (Medinat Yisra'el/ State of Israel)	**Jerusalem** 524 000	20 700	4 975 000	240	74.5	78
JAPAN (Nihon or Nippon/ Land of the Rising Sun)	**Tōkyō** 8 163 000	372 819	123 921 000	332	75.9	8

GROSS NATIONAL PRODUCT ②	LANGUAGES	RELIGIONS	ECONOMY
160	Dari; Pushto	Muslim (Sunni) 80%	**Economy** Mainly agricultural (cereal crops); cotton is widely cultivated for the textile industry. Animal farming is the basic livelihood of nomads. **Mineral resources** Rich, under-exploited reserves of natural gas and iron ore.
6910	Arabic	Muslim 85%	**Economy** Relies on petroleum, refined locally for export. An important financial centre. **Industry** Booming, particularly food, cement, chemicals, aluminium. **Agriculture** Fishing (fish, pearls) and agriculture are the traditional activities.
220	Bengali (off.); English	Muslim 86.6%; Hindu 12.1%	**Economy** Agriculture-based. Rice is the main crop, followed by jute, tea, sugar-cane, cotton and tobacco. Animal farming is widespread and fishing is important. **Industry** Food processing and textile manufacturing are developing.
180	Dzongkha	Buddhist; Hindu	**Economy** Extremely poor. Agriculture (cereals, potatoes, fruit), stock-raising (mainly cattle, then pigs, sheep and goats) and lumbering (firewood) employ virtually the whole population of this rural country. Local crafts are exported.
27 860	Malay; English; Chinese	Muslim 63%; Buddhist 14%	**Economy** Rich reserves of petroleum and natural gas make Brunei one of the wealthiest countries in Asia. **Agriculture** Rice, bananas and citrus fruits; forestry and fishing. **Industry** Chiefly petrochemicals, food, wood and rubber.
200	Khmer (off.); French	Buddhist	**Agriculture** Dominates the economy, especially rice. Fishing and animal farming are traditional livelihoods. Forests are particularly rich (rubber and timber). **Industry** Primarily food processing, textiles, tobacco and mechanical industries.
370	Chinese; Uighur; Tibetan; Mongol	Confucian 19%; Budd. 14%; Mus. 5%; Christ.	**Economy** Essentially agricultural. The largest rice producer in the world. Pig farming, fishing and silk-worm breeding are important. **Principal resources** China is rich in minerals and fuel. **Industry** All sectors are developing rapidly.
8640	Greek; Turkish	Christian; Cypriot 81%; Mus. 19%	**Economy** Based on agriculture (wine, olives, citrus fruits and potatoes). Sheep and goat farming are practiced on a modest scale, as is fishing. **Industry** Principally mineral extraction (of pyrite, chromite, asbestos) and tourism.
330	Hindi (off.); English; Telugu; Bengali; Marathi; Urdu	Hindu 80%; Muslim 11%	**Economy** Agriculture-based. Cereals and rice are the most profitable crops. Livestock are reared extensively, although mainly to meet subsistence needs. Some income raised through fishing and forestry. **Industry** Growing rapidly.
610	Bahasa Indonesia (off.); Javanese	Muslim 87%; Christian 9.6%	**Economy** Almost half the population is involved in agriculture (rice, tea, coffee, sugar-cane, palm-oil, coconuts, tobacco). Second largest rubber producer. **Principal resources** Rich mineral reserves (oil) contribute to developing industry.
2320	Persian (Farsi)	Muslim (Shia)	**Principal resources** Profits from international sales of oil and natural gas are being used to enhance all sectors of the economy. **Industry** The mining, petrochemical, mechanical and textile (carpet) industries are flourishing.
3650	Arabic; Kurdish	Muslim (Sunni, Shia)	**Economy** Petroleum is a major source of foreign revenue. **Agriculture** Employs a third of the population, thanks to fertile river basins. Cereals grown for domestic market; dates for export. **Industry** Textiles, chemicals, cement, food, paper.
11 330	Hebrew (off.); Arabic	Jewish; Muslim	**Economy** Structurally modern and well organized. All sectors are flourishing, especially agriculture. **Industry** Manufacturing (chemical, mechanical, textiles), mining (diamonds) and tourism are particularly lucrative.
26 920	Japanese	Shintoist; Buddhist	**Economy** Most industrialized in Asia, third world-wide. All manufacturing sectors well developed (mechanics, electronics, chemicals, textiles and paper). **Agriculture** Mainly rice; fishing is important to domestic and export markets.

STATE (official name/ English translation)	CAPITAL ① inhabitants	AREA (sq km)	POPULATION	DENSITY (inhab/sq km)	LIFE EXPEC ANCY (in year M
JORDAN (Al Mamlaka al Urdunīyah al Hāshemīyah/Hashemite Kingdom of Jordan)	**Ammān** 936 000	97 740	3 285 000	34	64.2 6
KUWAIT (Dawlat al-Kuwait/ State of Kuwait)	**Kuwait City** 44 400	17 818	2 241 000	126	71.2 7!
LAOS (Satharanarath Pasathipatai Pasason Lao/Lao People's Democratic Republic)	**Vientiane** (Viengchane) 377 400	236 800	4 262 000	18	47.8 5!
LEBANON (Al-Jumhūriya al-Lubnānīya)	**Beirut** (Bayrūt) 474 900	10 400	2 965 000	285	65.1 6
MALAYSIA (Persekutuan Tanah Malaysia/ Federation of Malaysia)	**Kuala Lumpur** 1 103 000	329 758	18 239 000	55	68.8 7
THE MALDIVES (Divehi Jumhuriya/ Republic of Maldives)	**Malé** 55 100	298	222 000	745	62.2 5'
MONGOLIA (Mongol Uls/ Mongolian Republic)	**Ulan Bator** (Ulaanbaatar) 548 000	1 566 500	2 140 000	1	61.2 6
MYANMAR (BURMA) (Pyidaungsu Myanma Naingngandaw/ Union of Myanmar)	**Rangoon** (Yangon) 2 459 000	678 033	42 561 000	63	60.0 6!
NEPAL (Nepàl Adhiràjya/ Kingdom of Nepal)	**Kathmandu** 393 500	147 181	19 379 000	131	55.4 52
NORTH KOREA (Chosun Minchu-chui Inmin Konghwa-Guk/Democratic People's Republic of Korea)	**P'yŏngyang** 2 639 000	120 538	22 937 000	190	66.2 7!
OMAN (Sulțanat 'Umān/ Sultanate of Oman)	**Muscat** 50 000	212 457	1 559 000	7	62.2 6!
PAKISTAN (Islāmi Jamhūrīya e-Pakistān/ Islamic Republic of Pakistan)	**Islāmābād** 204 400	796 095	115 520 000	145	59.3 6(
PHILIPPINES (Republika ñg Pilipinas/ Republic of the Philippines)	**Manila** 1 599 000	300 000	62 000 000	207	62.5 6(
QATAR (Dawlat al-Qațar/ State of Qatar)	**Doha** (Ad Dawhah) 217 000	11 437	455 000	39	66.9 7!

GROSS NATIONAL PRODUCT ②	LANGUAGES	RELIGIONS	ECONOMY
1120	Arabic	Muslim	**Economy** Quite poor; the arid soil yields only vegetables, citrus fruits and cereals. **Principal resources** Phosphates and potash (the main export). **Industry** Food processing, chemical, cement and tobacco manufacture.
6 160	Arabic	Muslim	**Economy** Rich oil reserves make Kuwait one of the world's wealthiest countries. **Agriculture** Fishing is traditionally strong; irrigation is used to expand arable land. **Industry** Chemical, mechanical and cement plants supplied by natural gas.
230	Lao (off.); French	Buddhist	**Economy** The least developed in Indochina. Agriculture, forestry and fresh-water fishing are almost the only economic activities. **Agriculture** Rice is the principal crop. **Industry** Largely limited to the production of local crafts.
350	Arabic (off.); French	Christian 42%; Muslim 29%	**Agriculture** Olives, citrus fruits, grapes, fruit and vegetables are the main yields. Minimal animal farming and fishing. **Industry** The principal employers in this sector are the oil-refineries, cotton-mills, and cigarette and cement factories.
2490	Malay (off.); English; Chinese	Mus. 53%; Buddhist; Taoist; Christian	**Agriculture** Mainly rice, coconuts, palm-oil, coffee, tea, pineapples and rubber (of which Malaysia is the world's largest exporter). **Mineral resources** Abundant tin, petrol, bauxite, copper. **Industry** Tourism is being promoted.
460	Dhivehi	Muslim	**Agriculture** The majority of the population is involved in fishing or cultivating coconuts (fish and coconut fibre being the principal exports). Most staple foods have to be imported. **Industry** Tourism is growing rapidly.
473	Mongolian	Buddhist	**Economy** Depends mainly on animal herding (sheep, goats, cattle, horses, camels). Some cereals are cultivated. **Industry** Centres on food processing. **Principal resources** The country has deposits of copper and coal.
200	Birmano (off.); English	Buddhist 88%	**Agriculture** Dominates. Teak and forestry products have replaced rice as the principal export. Crops for industrial use include sugar-cane, tobacco, jute and cotton. **Mineral resources** The country has considerable reserves of oil.
180	Nepali (off.); Bihari	Hindu 89%; Buddhist 5%	**Economy** Dominated by cultivation (cereals, potatoes, jute, sugar-cane, tobacco) and animal farming (yak, cattle, buffalo, goats). **Industry** Small-scale, mainly processing industries. Tourism is flourishing and brings in foreign revenue.
1040	Korean	Buddhist; Confucian; Shintoist	**Economy** Dominated by mining (coal, iron, copper, lead). **Industry** Iron and steel production, mechanical and chemical engineering and textile manufacture all well established. **Agriculture** Principal crops are rice, maize and potatoes.
5650	Arabic (off.); English	Muslim (Sunni)	**Economy** Depends on the export of petrol and natural gas. Of lesser importance: agriculture (vegetables, fruit, dates), animal farming (goats, sheep), and fishing. **Industry** Metal-lurgical (copper), petrochemical and cement production.
400	Urdu (nat.); English	Muslim	**Economy** Expanding. **Agriculture** Flourishing, the main crops being cereals, sugar-cane and cotton. Cotton is the principal export, and also supplies a productive textile industry. **Mineral resources** Petroleum, natural gas and coal.
740	Tagalog (Filipino); English	Catholic 84%	**Agriculture** Fundamental to the economy (rice, maize, coconuts, sugar-cane, bananas). Fishing is also important. **Industry** Mining growing rapidly (gold, copper) along with food processing, electronics, chemicals and textiles.
15 870	Arabic	Muslim (Sunni)	**Economy** Relies on its plentiful reserves of petroleum and natural gas. **Industry** Petrochemicals and cement are the chief industrial products. **Agriculture** Fishing and nomadic animal herding are traditional livelihoods.

STATE (official name/ English translation)	CAPITAL ① inhabitants	AREA (sq km) POPULATION		DENSITY (inhab/sq km)	LIFE EXPECTANCY (in years) M	F
SAUDI ARABIA (Al Mamlaka al'Arabīya as-Saʽūdīya/Kingdom of Saudi Arabia)	Riyadh (Ar Riyād) 1 308 000	2 153 168	15 267 000	7	61.7	65
SINGAPORE (Republik Singapura/ Republic of Singapore)	Singapore	639	2 763 000	4324	70.3	75
SOUTH KOREA (Daehan-Minkuk/ Republic of South Korea)	Seoul (Sŏul) 10 628 000	99 237	43 530 000	438	66.9	74
SRĪ LANKA (Srī Lanka Prajatantrika Samajawadi Janarajaya)	Colombo 615 000	65 610	17 247 000	263	69.1	73
SYRIA (Al Jumhūrīya al ʽArabīya as Sūrīya)	Damascus (Dimashq) 1 326 000	185 180	12 524 000	67	65.2	69
TAIWAN (REPUBLIC OF CHINA) (Chung-hua Min Kuo)	Taipei 2 718 000	36 202	20 489 000	566	71.3	76
THAILAND (Prathet Thai/ Kingdom of Thailand)	Bangkok 5 876 000	513 115	55 884 000	109	63.8	68
TURKEY (Türkiye Cumhuriyeti/ Republic of Turkey)	Ankara 2 553 000	755 688	51 277 000	69	68.0	72
UNITED ARAB EMIRATES (Al Imārāt al ʽArabīya al-Muttahida)	Abu Dhabi 243 000	83 600	1 945 000	23	68.6	72
VIETNAM (Công Hòa Xã Hôi Chu' Nghiã Viêt Nam/Socialist Republic of Vietnam)	Hanoi 1 089 000	329 566	67 589 000	205	63.7	67
YEMEN (Al-Jumhūrīya al-Yamanīyah/ Republic of Yemen)	Sana'ā 427 000	524 342	11 843 000	22	49.0	51

ASIA   27 140 550   3 121 179 000   115
ASIA   Total Ⓐ   44 032 038   3 210 194 000   73

GROSS NATIONAL PRODUCT ②	LANGUAGES	RELIGIONS	ECONOMY
7070	Arabic	Muslim (Sunni)	**Economy** Petroleum is the most valuable resource (Saudi Arabia is the world's third biggest producer of crude oil). **Industry** Mainly petrochemical. Tourism is also flourishing (many pilgrims visit the sacred cities of Mecca and Medina).
12 890	Chinese; Malay; Tamil; English	Tao. 29%; Bud. 27%; Mus. 16%; Christ. 10%	**Economy** Dominated by industrial sector (electronics, ship-yards, textiles, chemicals, rubber, metallurgical and petro-chemical plants). A major international financial and com-mercial centre, the island also has a thriving fishing industry.
6340	Korean (off.)	Budd.40%; Christ. 28%; Conf. 17%	**Agriculture** Mainly rice, potatoes, cotton and tobacco. Also fishing. **Mineral resources** Rich in coal, iron, gold and tungsten. **Industry** Well developed mechanical, electronic, textile and petrochemical sectors .
500	Sinhalese; Tamil (off.); English	Bud. 69%; Hindu 15%; Christ. 7%; Mus. 8%	**Economy** Essentially agricultural (rice, coconuts, tea, cinnamon, coffee). The forests yield caoutchouc. **Industry** Precious stones are mined; textiles, cement, rubber and chemicals are manufactured. Tourism is increasing.
1110	Arabic	Muslim (Sunni) 75%; Christ. 10%	**Economy** Based on agriculture (wheat, cotton, grapes, olives, vegetables and fruit). Sheep farming is widespread. **Industry** Mining (petroleum, phosphates), textiles, food, leather, cement and glass industries are all developing.
8810	Chinese	Confucian; Buddist	**Agriculture** Well-organized; rice, sugar-cane, tea and sweet potatoes are the main crops. Little animal farming, but fishing is profitable. **Industry** Textiles are the primary pro-duct, plus electronics, machinery, petrochemicals and toys.
1580	Thai	Buddist	**Economy** Still fundamentally agricultural: rice, maize, cassava and sugar-cane are the chief products. Fishing, forestry (timber, caoutchouc) and mining (tin) are important. Tourism is now the primary foreign exchange earner.
1820	Turkish (off.); Kurdish	Muslim	**Agriculture** Employs almost half the population (cereals, cotton, vine, olive, fruit, sugar beet, tobacco). Animal farming is widespread. **Industry** The food, textile, chemical and machinery sectors are expanding; tourism is flourishing.
19 870	Arabic (off.); English	Muslim 95%	**Economy** One of the wealthiest countries in the world due to extensive on- and off-shore reserves of petroleum and natural gas. Fishing and pearl cultivation are traditional livelihoods. **Industry** Petrochemical, metallurgical and cement.
110	Vietnamese	Buddist; Taoist	**Economy** Much of the work force is employed in cultivating rice. Cassava, sweet potatoes, coconuts, tea and tobacco are also grown. Fishing is important. **Industry** Mining (coal, petrol), metal, food and chemical sectors are well developed.
540	Arabic	Muslim	**Economy** Agriculture (cereals, dates, vegetables, fruit, cotton, coffee) and fishing employ most of the population, while sheep, goats and cattle are herded. **Industry** Oil is mined; chemical, textile and cement production is increasing.

Includes Christmas and Cocos Is, Hong Kong, Macao, Sinai Peninsula, Gaza Strip and the Asian parts of the CIS, but excludes Irian Jaya and Socotra.

① The local form is given in brackets only when it differs from the English form

② Per inhabitant, in US$

STATE (official name/ English translation)	CAPITAL ① inhabitants	AREA (sq km) POPULATION		DENSITY (inhab/sq km)	LIFE EXPECTANCY (in years)	
					M	F
ALGERIA (Al Jumhūrīya al Jazā'iriya ad Dīmūqrātīya ash-Sha'bīya)	**Algiers** (Al Jazair) 1 687 600	2 381 741	25 660 000	11	65.0	67
ANGOLA (República de Angola/ Republic of Angola)	**Luanda** 1 136 000	1 246 700	10 303 000	8	44.9	48
BENIN (République du Bénin/ Republic of Benin)	**Porto-Novo** 164 000	112 622	4 889 000	43	49.0	52
BOTSWANA (Republic of Botswana)	**Gaborone** 134 000	600 372	1 320 000	2	52.7	59
BURKINA FASO (République de Burkina Faso/ Republic of Burkina Faso)	**Ouagadougou** 442 200	274 200	9 242 000	34	47.6	50
BURUNDI (République du Burundi/ Republika y'Uburundi/ Republic of Burundi)	**Bujumbura** 235 400	27 834	5 600 000	201	50.0	54
CAMEROON (République du Cameroun/ Republic of Cameroon)	**Yaoundé** 653 700	475 442	11 932 000	25	53.5	56
CAPE VERDE (República de Cabo Verde/ Republic of Cape Verde)	**Praia** 61 700	4 033	341 000	84	63.0	67
CENTRAL AFRICAN REPUBLIC (République Centrafricaine)	**Bangui** 597 000	622 436	3 015 000	5	48.0	53
CHAD (République du Tchad/ Republic of Chad)	**N'djamena** 594 000	1 284 000	5 819 000	4	45.9	49
COMOROS (République Fédérale Islamique des Comores)	**Moroni** 22 000	1 862	481 000	258	54.0	59
CONGO (République Populaire du Congo/People's Republic of the Congo)	**Brazzaville** 760 000	342 000	2 346 000	7	52.1	57
DJIBOUTI (République de Djibouti/ Jumhūrīya Jībutī/ Republic of Djibouti)	**Djibouti** 220 000	23 200	541 000	23	47.4	50
EGYPT (Jumhūrīyat Mişr al 'Arabīya/ Arab Republic of Egypt)	**Cairo** (Al Qāhirah) 6 069 000	942 247	54 688 000	58	59.0	60

GROSS NATIONAL PRODUCT ②	LANGUAGES	RELIGIONS	ECONOMY
2020	Arabic (off.); French; Berber	Muslim	**Agriculture** Supplies processing industry (vines, vegetables, olives, citrus fruit) and satisfies subsistence needs. **Mineral resources** Hydrocarbons. **Industry** Developing gradually; traditional crafts bring in foreign revenue.
620	Portuguese (off.); Bantu languages	Cath. 65%; Animist; Protestant	**Agriculture** One of the country's main economic activities; coffee, cotton, tobacco, palm-oil, sugar-cane and sisal are the principal crops. **Mineral resources** Mining (petroleum, diamonds and iron) generates considerable income.
380	French (off.); Fon; Yoruba; Adja	Animist 63%; Cath. 18%; Mus. 15%	**Agriculture** Dominates the economy. Cereals, cassava, cotton and palm-oil are the main products. Animal farming and fishing are widely practiced. **Industry** Limited to the processing of agricultural goods.
2590	English (off.); Setswana	Animist; Christian 30%	**Economy** Traditionally based on animal farming (especially cattle) and subsistence agriculture (cereals, legumes, groundnuts, citrus fruit). **Principal resources** Diamonds, coal, copper and nickel are the main mineral exports.
350	French (off.); Mossi; Fulani	Animist; Mus. 30%; Christ. 10%	**Economy** Very poor and with few natural resources. **Agriculture** Cereals, sugar-cane and cotton are the only crops of any importance. Cattle rearing is becoming more widespread.
210	French and Kirundi (both off.); Swahili	Cath. 65%; Animist; Protestant	**Economy** Principally agrarian. **Agriculture** The main source of employment. The most important subsistence crops are sweet potatoes and cassava; coffee, tea and cotton are exported.
940	French and English (both off.); Fulani; Sao; Bamileke	Animist 40%; Mus. 22%; Cath. 21%	**Agriculture** A major sector of the domestic economy. Crops include cereals, cocoa, coffee, sugar-cane, palm-oil, cotton and bananas. Forests provide timber and caoutchouc. **Industry** The oil industry is of growing importance.
750	Portuguese (off.); Crioulu	Catholic	**Agriculture** Yields a variety of products, but in quantities insufficient to sustain the local population. **Economy** Export trade is boosted by the production of sea salt and fishing (tuna, lobster).
390	French (off.); Sangho (nat.); Sudanese dialects	Animist 57%; Prot. 15%; Mus. 8%	**Agriculture** Cereals, cassava and bananas are cultivated for domestic consumption; cotton, groundnuts, palm-oil and coffee for export. **Principal resources** Diamonds and gold are sold internationally. **Industry** Largely food processing.
220	French and Arabic (off.); other local languages	Muslim 50%; Animist 44%	**Agriculture** Cotton plantations are a highly profitable part of the economy. Cereal crops are also significant, as is fishing (on Chad's internal rivers and lakes). Animal farming is quite advanced. **Industry** Very limited.
500	French and Arabic (both off.); other local languages	Muslim	**Agriculture** The main economic activity, producing vanilla, cloves, ylang-ylang, copra, coffee, cocoa and bananas for export. Some fishing. **Industry** Generally quite undeveloped although the islands are beginning to attract tourists.
1120	French (off.); local languages	Animist 47%; Catholic 38%	**Economy** Oil is a major source of foreign revenue, thanks to reserves of petroleum and natural gas. **Agriculture** Well organized (mainly sugar-cane, coffee, cocoa, palm-oil and cassava); the forests provide timber for export.
600	Arabic and French (both off.); other local languages	Muslim	**Economy** Impoverished, largely as the land is so arid and infertile. Relies mainly on service industries, particularly the capital's port and airport. **Agriculture** Low rainfall restricts agriculture to nomadic animal grazing (sheep, goats, camels).
620	Arabic (off.); French and English used commercially	Muslim 90%; Christian 7%	**Agriculture** Concentrated along the banks of the Nile. Main crops: cereals, cotton and sugar-cane. **Mineral resources** Petrol, natural gas, iron, phosphates. **Economy** Tourism and tolls on the Suez Canal bring in foreign currency.

STATE (official name/ English translation)	CAPITAL ① inhabitants	AREA (sq km) POPULATION		DENSITY (inhab/sq km)	LIFE EXPECTANCY (in years)	
					M	F
EQUATORIAL GUINEA (República de Guinea Ecuatorial/Republic of Equatorial Guinea)	**Malabo** 30 700	28 051	356 000	13	44.4	47
ERITREA (Eritrea)	**Asmara** (Àsmera) 331 000	121 143	3 325 000	27	–	–
ETHIOPIA (Ityopya)	**Addis Ababa** 1 673 000	1 130 139	50 058 000	44	42.4	45
GABON (République Gabonaise/ Gabonese Republic)	**Libreville** 352 000	267 667	1 350 000	5	49.9	53
GAMBIA (Republic of the Gambia)	**Banjul** 44 500	11 295	884 000	78	41.4	44
GHANA (Republic of Ghana)	**Accra** 949 000	238 538	15 509 000	65	52.2	55
GUINEA (République de Guinée/ Republic of Guinea)	**Conakry** 705 000	245 857	7 052 000	28	42.0	43
GUINEA-BISSAU (República da Guiné-Bissau/ Republic of Guinea-Bissau)	**Bissau** 125 000	36 125	984 000	27	41.9	45
IVORY COAST (République de la Côte d'Ivoire/ Republic of the Ivory Coast)	**Yamoussoukro** 120 000	322 463	10 820 000	33	52.8	56
KENYA (Jamhuri ya Kenya/ Republic of Kenya)	**Nairobi** 1 429 000	582 646	23 183 000	40	56.5	60
LESOTHO (Muso oa Lesotho/ Kingdom of Lesotho)	**Maseru** 109 400	30 355	1 806 000	59	51.5	60
LIBERIA (Republic of Liberia)	**Monrovia** 465 000	111 369	2 520 000	23	53.9	56
LIBYA (Al Jamāhīrīya al 'Arabīya al-Lībīya ash Sha'bīya al-Ishtir ākīya)	**Tripoli** (Tarābulus) 591 000	1 775 500	4 325 000	2	59.1	62
MADAGASCAR (Repoblika demokratika n'i Madagaskar/République démocratique de Madagascar)	**Antananarivo** (Tananarive) 1 050 000	587 041	11 493 000	19	54.0	57

ROSS TIONAL ODUCT ②	LANGUAGES	RELIGIONS	ECONOMY
330	Spanish (off.); Bubi; Fang; Pidgin English	Catholic 80%	**Agriculture** Cocoa and coffee are the most common plantation crops, followed by sugar-cane, bananas, palm-oil and coconuts. The country's main resource is its valuable timber (rosewood, ebony). **Industry** Almost none.
–	Tigrinya and Arabic (both off.); Italian	Coptic; Muslim	**Economy** Based on agriculture (cereals, citrus fruits, oilseed, cotton, tobacco, coffee), animal farming (sheep and goats), fishing and extracting sea salt. **Industry** Undergoing reconstruction.
120	Amharic (off.); Arabic; Oromo; other local languages	Coptic 55%; Muslim 35%	**Agriculture** The most profitable sector of the economy (coffee, tobacco, cotton, bananas and sugar-cane). Animals are reared extensively for their skins and leather. **Industry** Food processing and textile manufacture predominate.
3780	French (off.); Bantu (Fang)	Christian	**Economy** Depends on the forests, which provide valuable timber. **Agriculture** Practiced only at subsistence level. **Principal resources** Petroleum, natural gas, uranium, manganese and gold are lucratively mined and exported.
360	English (off.); Wolof; Mandinka; Fula	Muslim 95%; Christ. 4%	**Economy** Depends on the cultivation of groundnuts. Other crops include cotton, cereals and palm nuts. **Industry** Manufacturing centres on processing groundnuts. Tourism is a rapidly growing industry.
400	English (off.); Asante; Ewe; Ga	Christ. 52%; Animist 35%; Mus. 13%	**Economy** Ghana is the third leading producer of cocoa, which it exports worldwide. Fishing, forestry and mining (diamonds, gold, bauxite, petroleum and manganese) are also important.
450	French (off.); Sudanese languages	Muslim 85%; Animist 5%	**Economy** Most of the workforce is employed in agriculture. Groundnuts, citrus fruits, bananas, pineapple, coffee and palm-oil are exported. **Mineral resources** Guinea has large reserves of bauxite, which is exported in considerable bulk.
190	Portuguese (off.); Creole; Sudanese languages	Animist 65%; Muslim 30%	**Economy** Agricultural: the main products are groundnuts, palm-nuts, cashew nuts and cotton, which are processed locally and then exported. Cereals are widely cultivated. Many inhabitants engage in fishing and lumbering.
690	French (off.); local languages	Animist 37%; Mus. 34%; Cath. 22%	**Economy** Most revenue comes from agriculture (especially from coffee and cocoa, followed by oil and palm-nuts), lumbering (valuable wood and caoutchouc) and mining (petroleum, diamonds). **Industry** Expanding.
340	Swahili (off.); Kikuyu; Kamba; English	Animist; Cath. 21%; Prot. 15%	**Agriculture** Flourishing: the broad range of crops include cereals, coffee, tea, sugar-cane, pyrethrum, cotton and sisal. Animal farming is widespread. **Industry** Productive, especially food processing. Tourism brings in substantial revenue.
580	English; Sesotho	Christian 90%; Animist 6%	**Economy** Very impoverished. **Agriculture** Barely above subsistence level (cereals, legumes, fruit). Animal farming is widespread; wool and mohair are exported. **Industry** Some mining (precious stones). Tourism is profitable.
400	English (off.); Sudanese languages	Christian; Animist 20%; Mus. 15%	**Agriculture** Coffee, cocoa, rice, citrus fruits and cassava; plantation crops such as palm-oil and caoutchouc are significant. **Mineral resources** Iron ore, diamonds and gold are mined. **Industry** Manufacturing industries are developing.
5310	Arabic; other local languages	Muslim	**Economy** Depends on reserves of petroleum and natural gas. **Agriculture** Cereals, olives, grapes, citrus fruits and dates are among the main crops; animal farming is also practiced. **Industry** Centres on oil production.
210	Malagasy; French	Anim. 50%; Cath. 25%; Prot. 20%; Muslim 5%	**Economy** The island depends largely on agriculture; coffee, vanilla, cloves and pepper are the principal exports. Rice and cassava are cultivated for domestic consumption. **Industry** Mainly food processing.

STATE (official name/ English translation)	CAPITAL ① inhabitants	AREA (sq km) POPULATION DENSITY (inhab/sq km)			LIFE EXPECTANCY (in years) M F
MALAWI (Mfuko la Malaŵi/ Republic of Malawi)	Lilongwe 220 000	118 484	8 556 000	72	48.4 49
MALI (République du Mali/ Republic of Mali)	Bamako 646 200	1 240 142	8 299 000	6	45.0 47
MAURITANIA (Jumhūrīyat Mūrītānīya al-Islāmīya/Islamic Republic of Mauritania)	Nouakchott 393 000	1 030 700	2 036 000	2	45.0 48
MAURITIUS (Republic of Mauritius)	Port Louis 143 000	2 045	1 069 000	523	65.0 72
MOROCCO (Al Mamlakah al Maghribīya/ Kingdom of Morocco)	Rabat 556 000	458 730	25 698 000	56	61.6 65
MOZAMBIQUE (República de Moçambique/ Republic of Mozambique)	Maputo 1 070 000	799 380	16 084 000	20	46.9 50
NAMIBIA (Republic of Namibia/ Republiek van Namibie)	Windhoek 115 000	824 292	1 400 000	2	55.0 57
NIGER (République du Niger/ Republic of Niger)	Niamey 399 000	1 186 408	7 984 000	6	42.9 46
NIGERIA (Federal Republic of Nigeria)	Abuja 379 000	923 768	88 500 000	96	50.8 54
RWANDA (Republika y'u Rwanda/ République Rwandaise)	Kigali 234 000	26 338	7 150 000	271	48.8 52
SAO TOME E PRINCIPE (República Democrática de São Tomé e Príncipe)	São Tomé 35 000	964	123 000	127	64.0 67.
SENEGAL (République du Sénégal/ Republic of Senegal)	Dakar 1 490 000	196 722	7 433 000	38	54.0 56
SEYCHELLES (Republic of Seychelles)	Victoria 24 300	453	68 000	150	65.3 74
SIERRA LEONE (Republic of Sierra Leone)	Freetown 470 000	71 740	4 260 000	59	41.4 44.

GROSS NATIONAL PRODUCT ②	LANGUAGES	RELIGIONS	ECONOMY
230	English (off.); Chichewa (nat.); other local dialects	Animist; Catholic 19%	**Economy** Relatively poor. Tobacco, cotton, sugar-cane and tea are cultivated for export; maize is the principal subsistence crop. **Industry** Growing modestly, particularly the food processing, cement manufacture and tobacco sectors.
280	French (off.); Bambara; local languages	Muslim 90%; Animist 9%	**Economy** Extremely poor, and based almost entirely on agriculture. Cotton, rice, cassava and groundnuts are the main crops. Fishing is important, and sheep, goat and cattle farming is well developed (droughts notwithstanding).
510	Arabic (off.); French; Poular; Wolof; Soninke	Muslim	**Agriculture** Severe droughts have hampered arable farming: cereals and dates are almost the only crops. Deep-sea fishing and nomadic animal farming (cattle, sheep) are widespread. **Principal resources** Rich reserves of iron ore.
2420	English (off.); French; Creole; Hindi	Christ. 30%; Hindu 52%; Mus. 13%	**Economy** Depends on the production and export of sugar-cane, although there are also large plantations of tea, coffee and coco-palm. Fishing is profitable. **Industry** Mainly manufacturing; tourism is a significant source of revenue.
1030	Arabic (off.); Berber; French	Muslim	**Agriculture** Cereals, grapes, vegetables and fruit are cultivated. Animal farming is widespread (sheep, goats, cattle). **Principal resources** Phosphates. **Industry** Food manufacturing, textile and tanning industries. Tourism is important.
70	Portuguese (off.); other local languages	Animist 48%; Cath. 14%; Mus. 16%	**Agriculture** The main crops are cotton and sugar-cane; also tea, sisal, cassava, cashew nuts, cereals, bananas. **Mineral resources** Rich but under-exploited deposits of coal, diamonds and bauxite. **Industry** Largely food manufacturing.
1120	Afrikaans (off.); English; other local languages	Christian	**Economy** Depends on rich deposits of diamonds and uranium (plus copper, lead, zinc, silver and tin) which are exported internationally. **Agriculture** Animal farming and fishing are practiced widely. **Industry** Mainly food processing.
300	French (off.); Hausa; Tamashek; Poular; Djerma; Kanuri	Muslim; Animist 15%	**Economy** Uranium, the main mineral resource, is mined in substantial quantities, but agriculture employs the bulk of the population. Millet, sorghum, rice and cassava are the chief crops. Animals are farmed for their skins and leather.
290	English (off.); Sudanese languages (Hausa, Ibo, Yoruba)	Muslim 45%; Christian 38%	**Economy** In the past, agriculture predominated (cocoa, palm-oil, coconuts, groundnuts, caoutchouc and bananas), but oil is now the main source of revenue. **Industry** Mining (tin as well as oil) and food processing.
260	French; Kinyarwanda	Catholic 56%; Anim. 17%; Prot. 13%	**Agriculture** Coffee, tobacco, tea, pyrethrum and groundnuts are grown for cash; maize, rice, sorghum, sweet potatoes, cassava and bananas for subsistence. Some animal herding. **Principal resources** Tin, gold and tungsten.
350	Portuguese (off.); Creole	Catholic	**Agriculture** The mainstay of the economy. Cocoa, coffee, walnuts, palm-oil, coconuts, copra and bananas are the most important crops. Fishing is another source of revenue. **Industry** Scarcely developed.
720	French (off.); Sudanese languages (Wolof, nat.)	Muslim 85%	**Economy** Largely agrarian (groundnuts, cotton, cereals). Senegal is a leading producer of groundnuts. Fishing is important. **Principal resources** Phosphates. **Industry** Mainly groundnuts processing, oil production and tourism.
5110	Creole (off.); English; French	Catholic	**Agriculture** Coconut palms, cinnamon and vanilla are the principal crops. Fishing is also an important aspect of the economy. **Industry** About a third of the labour force is employed in the highly successful tourist industry.
210	English (off.); Krio; Sudanese languages	Animist 51%; Muslim 39%	**Mineral resources** The chief exports, particularly diamonds, rutile and bauxite. **Agriculture** Mainly at a subsistence level, the principal crops being cocoa, coffee and palm kernels. **Industry** Processing industries.

	STATE (official name/ English translation)	CAPITAL ① inhabitants	AREA (sq km) POPULATION		DENSITY (inhab/sq km)	LIFE EXPECT ANCY (in year M	
	SOMALIA (Jamhuuriyadda Diimoqraadiga Soomaaliya/ Somali Democratic Republic)	Mogadishu (Muqdisho) 500 000	637 657	6 760 000	11	43.4	46
	SOUTH AFRICA (Republic of South Africa/ Republiek van Suid-Afrika)	Pretoria/Cape Town (Kaapstad)* 443 000/777 000	1 224 641	38 191 000	31	57.5	63
	SUDAN (Jamhūrīyat es Sūdān/ Republic of Sudan)	Khartoum (Al Kharṭūm) 557 000	2 505 813	25 941 000	10	52.0	54
	SWAZILAND (Umbuso we Swatini/ Kingdom of Swaziland)	Mbabane 38 000	17 364	798 000	46	56.2	59
	TANZANIA (Jamhuri ya Muungano wa Tanzania/United Republic of Tanzania)	Dodoma 204 000	939 470	26 353 000	28	51.3	54
	TOGO (République Togolaise/ Togolese Republic)	Lomé 400 000	56 785	3 643 000	64	51.3	54
	TUNISIA (Al Jumhūrīyah at Tūnisīyah/ Republic of Tunisia)	Tunis 626 000	163 610	8 293 000	51	64.9	66
	UGANDA (Republic of Uganda)	Kampala 651 000	241 038	16 830 000	70	51.4	54
	ZAIRE (République du Zaïre/ Republic of Zaïre)	Kinshasa 3 741 000	2 344 885	36 672 000	15	50.3	53
	ZAMBIA (Republic of Zambia)	Lusaka 982 000	752 614	8 023 000	10	54.4	56
	ZIMBABWE (Republic of Zimbabwe)	Harare 863 000	390 759	10 130 000	26	57.9	61

AFRICA   29 981 681   630 136 000   21
AFRICA   Total   Ⓐ   30 249 096   632 915 000   21

ROSS TIONAL ODUCT ②	LANGUAGES	RELIGIONS	ECONOMY
150	Somali (off.); Arabic; Italian; English (adm.)	Muslim (Sunni)	**Economy** Depends on animal farming (cattle, sheep, goats, camels) and agriculture (cereals, cotton, sugar-cane, bananas). Both are major sources of employment. Fishing is on the increase.
2530	Afrikaans and English (both off.); other local languages	Protestant; Animist; Cath. 8%	**Economy** The most prosperous in Africa. The mining sector (gold, diamonds, uranium, platinum, coal, iron), industry (mechanical, chemical and textile) and agriculture (cereals, vegetables, fruit) are all flourishing.
400	Arabic (off.); other local dialects	Mus. 73%; Animist 17%; Cath. 6%	**Agriculture** Cotton is the most important crop; cereals, dates, sugar-cane and oilseed are also cutivated. Nomadic herding is widespread. Sudan is one of the world's largest producers of gum arabic. **Industry** Relatively undeveloped.
1060	English and siSwati	Christian 47%; Animist 40%	**Economy** Arable and animal farming, timber felling and mining are the main activities. **Agriculture** Sugar-cane and citrus fruits are cultivated widely. **Mineral resources** The country is quite rich in asbestos, carbon, diamonds and iron.
100	Swahili; English	Muslim; Christ. 30%; Hindu; Animist	**Agriculture** Coffee, tea, cotton, tobacco, sugar, sisal and cloves are grown for export. Animal farming and fishing are common. **Mineral resources** Diamonds and gold. **Industry** Food processing and textile production.
410	French (off.); Ewe; Poular; Hausa; Gour; Assirelii	Animist; Muslim 17%; Cath. 26%	**Agriculture** The population largely comprises subsistence farmers; coffee, cocoa, cotton, groundnuts and palm-oil are grown for export. **Mineral resources** Phosphates are the main export; iron ore is also mined. **Industry** Modest.
1510	Arabic (off.); French; Berber	Muslim	**Economy** Based on agriculture (cereals, olives, grapes, citrus fruits, dates) and mining; phosphates and petrol account for over a third of exports. Fishing is profitable. **Industry** Mainly food processing and metallurgy. Tourism is increasing.
160	English and Swahili (both off.); Luganda	Cath. 40%; Prot. 20%; Muslim 6%	**Agriculture** Coffee, tea, cotton, tobacco, cocoa and sugarcane are cultivated for export, while maize, millet, sorghum and cassava are the main subsistence crops. **Industry** Well developed in the food and metallurgical fields.
220	French (off.); other local dialects	Cath. 48%; Prot. 29%; Animist	**Agriculture** Cassava, rice, maize and bananas are the chief subsistence crops; coffee, cotton, cocoa, tea, caoutchouc and palm-oil are exported. **Mineral resources** Tin, copper, diamonds, petroleum and zinc are mined for export.
420	English (off.); local languages include Lozi, Nyanja, Tonga	Prot. 34%; Cath. 26%; Animist 27%	**Economy** Depends on mining (copper, cobalt, manganese, lead, zinc, tin) and the related industries of metal and chemical processing. **Agriculture** Limited; maize, cassava, groundnuts and tobacco are the most common crops.
620	English (off.); local languages include Chishona and Sindebele	Animist; Prot. 17%; Cath. 12%	**Agriculture** Wheat, maize, cotton, sugar, coffee, soya and tobacco are the principal crops. **Mineral resources** Gold, asbestos, coal, iron, silver, tin, nickel, copper and cobalt are exported. **Industry** Manufacturing is developing slowly.

Includes Saint Helena, Comoros Is., Réunion I., Madeira, Canary Is, Ceuta, Melilla, Socotra, Western Sahara.

Pretoria (administrative); Cape Town (legislative)

① The local form is given in brackets only when it differs from the English form

② Per inhabitant, in US$

STATE (official name/ English translation)	CAPITAL inhabitants	AREA (sq km)	POPULATION	DENSITY (inhab/sq km)	LIFE EXPECTANCY (in years) M	
AUSTRALIA (Commonwealth of Australia)	**Canberra** 302 500	7 682 300	17 086 000	2	73.3	7
FIJI (Matanitu Ko Viti/ Republic of Fiji)	**Suva** 70 000	18 272	736 000	40	68.3	7
KIRIBATI (Republic of Kiribati)	**Bairiki** 2 100	849	72 000	85	50.6	5
MARSHALL ISLANDS (Republic of the Marshall Islands)	**Dalap-Uliga-Darrit** 17 600	181	44 000	243	61.0	6
MICRONESIA (Federated States of Micronesia)	**Palikir** —	707	111 000	157	64.0	6
NAURU (Republic of Nauru)	**Yaren** —	21	9 000	428	64.0	6
NEW ZEALAND (New Zealand)	**Wellington** 147 800	270 534	3 390 000	12	72.0	7
PALAU	**Koror** 10 500	487	15 000	31	—	
PAPUA NEW GUINEA (Papua New Guinea)	**Port Moresby** 152 100	462 840	3 600 000	8	54.0	5
SOLOMON ISLANDS (Solomon Islands)	**Honiara** 35 300	28 369	319 000	11	59.9	6
TONGA (Pule'anga Tonga/ Kingdom of Tonga)	**Nuku'alofa** 28 900	748	96 000	128	61.0	6
TUVALU (The Tuvalu Islands)	**Fongafale** —	24	9 000	375	60.0	6
VANUATU (Ripablik Blong Vanuatu/ Republic of Vanuatu)	**Port-Vila** 19 300	12 189	147 000	12	61.1	5
WESTERN SAMOA (Malo Tuto'atasi/ Independent State of Western Samoa)	**Apia** 33 200	2 831	164 000	58	64.0	6
AUSTRALIA AND OCEANIA		8 480 352	25 798 000	3		
AUSTRALIA AND OCEANIA Total Ⓐ		8 942 252	29 128 000	3		

© ISTITUTO GEOGRAFICO DE AGOSTINI S.p.A. - NOVARA

GROSS NATIONAL PRODUCT ①	LANGUAGES	RELIGIONS	ECONOMY
440	English	Protestant; Catholic 26%	**Economy** Based on agriculture (cereals, fruit, sugar-cane, cotton) and animal farming (sheep, cattle). **Mineral resources** Vast reserves of coal, natural gas, oil, nickel, gold, iron ore and bauxite. **Industry** All sectors expanding.
640	English, Fijian; Hindi	Methodist; Hindu 38%; Muslim	**Economy** Sustained by agriculture (sugar-cane, bananas, coconuts and potatoes) and fishing. Tourism also generates considerable revenue. **Mineral resources** Subsoil is rich in gold and silver. The island is heavily forested.
700	English (off.); I-Kiribati	Protestant; Catholic	**Agriculture** Most of the population is involved in agriculture and fishing. The principal crop is the coconut palm. **Industry** The tourist industry is expanding.
500	English (off.); Marshallese	Protestant; Catholic 8.5%	**Economy** Based on subsistence agriculture and fishing. Main crops are coconuts, copra, cassava and fruit. **Industry** Tourism is well developed.
500	English	Protestant; Catholic	**Economy** Most islanders are involved in fishing and cultivation (coconuts, copra, sweet potatoes, cassava, bananas). **Industry** The tourist industry is growing fast.
000	Nauruan (off.); English	Protestant; Catholic 24%	**Economy** Nauru is the wealthiest country in Oceania thanks to its rich phosphate deposits (which cover nearly 75% of the island). Phosphate mining accounts for three-quarters of the country's GDP.
800	English	Protestant; Catholic 15%	**Economy** Dominated by livestock farming, particularly sheep (for wool and meat) and cattle (dairy products and beef). **Agriculture** Well established. **Industry** Expanding, due in part to inexpensive hydroelectricity.
—	English; Palauan	Christian	**Economy** At subsistence level. The archipelago relies mainly on agriculture (potatoes, coconuts, cassava and bananas) and fishing. **Industry** Tourism is beginning to develop.
900	English (off.); Pidgin-English; Motu; other local dialects	Animist; Catholic 27%	**Economy** Essentially agricultural; sweet potatoes, cocoa, coffee and coconuts are the main crops. **Principal resources** Mining (especially gold, silver, copper) generates considerable revenue. The island is richly forested.
570	English (off.); Pidgin-English; Melanesian and Polynesian languages	Protestant; Catholic 18%	**Economy** The population is largely employed in cultivating coconut palms and sweet potatoes. Timber, fish and copra are the main exports. **Industry** Fishing is a major concern; a modest food processing industry has been established.
910	English; Tongan	Protestant; Catholic 13%	**Economy** Some 58% of the population is involved in agriculture (coconuts, potatoes, cassava and groundnuts). The chief exports are copra and coconuts. Fishing is also profitable. **Industry** Tourism is well established.
530	Tuvaluan; English	Protestant	**Economy** The two main sources of income are coconuts and fishing. The country relies on revenue from emigrants and foreign aid.
860	Bislama; English (off.); French (off.); other local dialects	Animist; Catholic 14%	**Economy** Based on subsistence agriculture and fishing. Main crops are coconut palm, cocoa, groundnuts and maize. The islands are densely forested. **Mineral resources** Primarily manganese.
720	Samoan (off.); English	Protestant; Catholic 22%	**Economy** Agriculture is the country's main resource, the principal crops being bananas, coconuts and cocoa. Fishing and pig farming are also well developed. **Industry** Confined to the manufacture of agricultural products.

Includes Norfolk I., Macquarie I., Cook Is. Niue I., Tokelau I., Pitcairn Is, New Caledonia, Wallis and Futuna, Polynesia, Clipperton, Guam, Hawaii, Midway Is, American Samoa, Wake Is, Mariana Is, Irian Jaya, Chilean Is.

① Per inhabitant, in US$ 1 million

ANTARCTICA has an area of 14 107 637 sq km, including the islands and ice-shelf (13 176 727 sq km without the ice-shelf).

© ISTITUTO GEOGRAFICO DE AGOSTINI S.p.A. NOVARA

STATE (official name/ English translation)	CAPITAL ① inhabitants	AREA (sq km) POPULATION DENSITY (inhab/sq km)			LIFE EXPECTANCY (in years) M
ANTIGUA AND BARBUDA (Antigua and Barbuda)	**Saint John's** 36 000	442	64 000	145	70.0 7
BAHAMAS (The Commonwealth of the Bahamas)	**Nassau** 172 000	13 939	259 000	18	69.0 7
BARBADOS (Barbados)	**Bridgetown** 7 600	431	258 000	598	72.9 7
BELIZE (Belize)	**Belmopan** 3 700	22 965	189 000	8	67.0 7
CANADA (Canada)	**Ottawa** 300 800	9 970 610	27 300 000	3	73.3 8
COSTA RICA (República de Costa Rica/ Republic of Costa Rica)	**San José** 297 000	51 100	3 064 000	60	72.4 7
CUBA (República de Cuba/ Republic of Cuba)	**Havana** (La Habana) 2 119 000	110 922	10 736 000	97	73.0 7
DOMINICA (Commonwealth of Dominica)	**Roseau** 15 900	751	71 000	94	73.0 7
DOMINICAN REPUBLIC (República Dominicana)	**Santo Domingo** 1 600 000	48 442	7 313 000	151	63.9 6
EL SALVADOR (República de El Salvador/ Republic of El Salvador)	**San Salvador** 481 000	21 041	5 392 000	256	63.0 6
GRENADA (State of Grenada)	**Saint George's** 7 500	344	101 000	293	69.0 7
GUATEMALA (República de Guatemala/ Republic of Guatemala)	**Guatemala City** 1 114 000	108 889	9 197 000	84	59.7 6
HAITI (République d'Haïti/ Republic of Haiti)	**Port-au-Prince** 514 000	27 400	6 625 000	242	53.1 5
HONDURAS (República de Honduras/ Republic of Honduras)	**Tegucigalpa** 608 000	112 088	4 708 000	42	61.9 6

GROSS NATIONAL PRODUCT ②	LANGUAGES	RELIGIONS	ECONOMY
4770	English (off.); Creole	Protestant	**Economy** Domestic economy relies primarily on tourism and secondarily on agriculture (cotton, sugar-cane, coconuts, vegetables and fruit). Fishing is well developed. **Industry** Limited to the manufacture of agricultural products and rum.
1 720	English (off.); Creole	Protestant; Catholic 22%	**Economy** The tourist industry is the main source of revenue. Agriculture (sugar-cane, tomatoes, pineapple), fishing (shellfish and turtles) and the production of sea-salt are also important.
6630	English	Protestant; Catholic 5%	**Economy** The island's economy is based entirely on sugar-cane. Maize, potatoes and cassava are produced for domestic consumption. Fishing is profitable. **Industry** Expanding. The tourist industry is highly developed.
2050	English (off.); Spanish; Creole	Catholic 58%; Protestant 28%	**Economy** Agriculture-based; citrus fruits, cereals (rice and maize), coconuts, bananas and sugar-cane are the main cash crops. Other activities include fishing, animal farming and lumbering (cedar, mahogany, pine and rosewood).
1 260	English; French	Catholic 46%; Protestant 41%	**Economy** Cereal crops dominate (wheat, oats, rye, barley, maize). Cattle and animal-fur farming are widely practiced. **Principal resources** The vast forests are a rich asset. **Industry** All sectors are well established.
1930	Spanish	Catholic	**Economy** Primarily plantation agriculture (coffee, bananas, cocoa, sugar-cane, cotton and tobacco). Tuna-fishing and animal farming also generate considerable revenue. **Industry** Food processing is a principal industry.
2000	Spanish	Catholic	**Economy** The national wealth depends on sugar-cane (the main export), tobacco, coffee and fruit. Also, animal farming and fishing. **Industry** Nickel-mining, food processing, and the textile and tobacco industries are the chief industries.
2440	English (off.); French patois	Catholic	**Economy** Based on agriculture (bananas, citrus fruits, coconuts) and fishing. **Industry** The processing of agricultural products is developing rapidly. Tourism is also growing.
950	Spanish	Catholic	**Agriculture** Based on plantation crops (cocoa, sugar-cane, coffee, tobacco, coconuts). Also animal farming and fishing. **Mineral resources** Gold, silver and nickel are major exports. **Industry** Tourism brings in foreign revenue.
1070	Spanish; Nahua; Maya	Catholic	**Economy** The main resource of this agricultural country is maize, followed by rice, beans, coffee, sugar-cane, cotton and sesame. Forests yield cedar, mahogany and rosewood. **Industry** Modestly developed.
2180	English (off.); Creole; French patois	Catholic; Protestant 34%	**Economy** Agriculturally based. Citrus fruits, bananas, cocoa, coconuts, cotton, sugar-cane and nutmeg are cultivated. Fishing is an important pursuit. **Industry** Tourism is developing.
930	Spanish (off.); Mayan languages	Catholic; Protestant 25%	**Economy** Depends on plantation agriculture (bananas, coffee, sugar-cane, cotton, tobacco, and cocoa). Forests provide valuable wood, in particular mahogany and cedar. Sheep and cattle farming are profitable.
370	French; Creole	Catholic	**Economy** Essentially agricultural. The main crops are coffee, bananas and sisal, followed by cotton, sugar-cane, cocoa, citrus fruits and tobacco. **Principal resources** Bauxite is the sole mining resource of any significance.
570	Spanish (off.); other local languages	Catholic	**Agriculture** Bananas, coconuts, coffee and tobacco. **Principal resources** Timber (mahogany, cedar and pine). Gold, silver, lead, zinc and antimony are mined on a large scale. **Industry** Processing yields a high income.

	STATE (official name/ English translation)	CAPITAL ① inhabitants	AREA (sq km) POPULATION		DENSITY (inhab/sq km)	LIFE EXPECTANCY (in years) M
	JAMAICA (Jamaica)	**Kingston** 104 100	10 991	2 375 000	216	70.4 7
	MEXICO (Estados Unidos Mexicanos/United Mexican States)	**Mexico City** (Ciudad de México) 8 237 000	1 972 547	82 151 000	41	66.5 7
	NICARAGUA (República de Nicaragua/ Republic of Nicaragua)	**Managua** 682 000	130 682	3 999 000	31	64.8 6
	PANAMA (República de Panamá/ Republic of Panama)	**Panama City** 411 000	77 082	2 466 000	32	70.1 7
	SAINT CHRISTOPHER (KITTS) AND NEVIS (Federation of Saint Christopher and Nevis)	**Basseterre** 18 500	269	44 000	163	65.9 7
	SAINT LUCIA (Saint Lucia)	**Castries** 51 200	616	153 000	248	68.0 7
	SAINT VINCENT AND THE GRENADINES (Saint Vincent and the Grenadines)	**Kingstown** 26 500	389	108 000	277	68.0 7
	UNITED STATES OF AMERICA (United States of America)	**Washington** 607 000	9 355 855	250 928 000	27	72.0 7

NORTH & CENTRAL AMERICA Ⓐ 22 037 795 417 501 000 19
NORTH & CENTRAL AMERICA Total 24 227 189 422 159 000 17

GROSS NATIONAL PRODUCT ②	LANGUAGES	RELIGIONS	ECONOMY
1380	English	Protestant	**Economy** A leading producer of bauxite. **Agriculture** Plantation agriculture (tobacco, coffee, cocoa, bananas, sugar-cane, spices) is well developed. **Industry** Expanding. Tourism generates substantial foreign currency.
2870	Spanish (off.); Nahua; Maya	Catholic 90%	**Economy** Oil, silver, lead, gold and sulphur are the mainstays of the domestic economy. **Agriculture** A third of the population is in agriculture and animal farming. **Industry** Rapidly expanding. Tourism is well developed.
340	Spanish (off.); other local languages	Catholic	**Economy** Principally plantation agriculture (coffee, cotton, cocoa, sugar-cane, and bananas). The forests are rich in valuable wood (mahogany, cedar, rosewood). **Industry** Relatively undeveloped.
2180	Spanish (off.)	Catholic	**Economy** Sustained mainly by revenue raised by granting access to the Panama Canal. **Agriculture** Subsistence agriculture is practiced; large plantations growing bananas, coffee and cocoa also exist.
3960	English (off.); Creole	Protestant	**Agriculture** The economy's main source of revenue, with cotton and sugar-cane the chief crops. **Industry** Agricultural processing is developing modestly while the tourist industry is undergoing rapid expansion.
2500	English (off.); French patois	Catholic	**Agriculture** Domestic economy dominated by agriculture (potatoes, bananas, cocoa, coconuts and copra). Animal farming and fishing are developed. **Industry** Principally food processing and the production of fertilizers.
1730	English (off.); Creole	Protestant; Catholic 19%	**Agriculture** Plantation agriculture yields potatoes, bananas, coconuts, cotton and exotic fruit, largely for the overseas market. **Industry** Industry in general is developing; tourism is well established.
22 560	English	Protestant 53%; Catholic 26%	**Economy** The economy of the United States is the most developed in the world. It is founded on highly specialized agriculture, substantial mineral reserves and power resources, and impressive industrial organization.

Includes the Virgin Is, Puerto Rico, Anguilla, Cayman Is, Turks and Caicos, Bermuda, Montserrat, Guadeloupe, Martinique, St Pierre and Miquelon, North American Antilles, Greenland. Excludes the 16 759 sq km and 1 135 000 inhabitants of Hawaii, which is included in Oceania.

① The local form is given in brackets only when it differs from the English form

② Per inhabitant, in US$

STATE (official name/ English translation)	CAPITAL inhabitants	AREA (sq km)	POPULATION	DENSITY (inhab/sq km)	LIFE EXPECTANCY (in years) M F
ARGENTINA (República Argentina/ Argentine Republic)	**Buenos Aires** 2 961 000	2 780 092	32 713 000	12	68.0 74
BOLIVIA (República de Bolivia/ Republic of Bolivia)	**Sucre (legal); La Paz (admin.)** 101 000/126 000	1 098 581	7 612 000	7	50.9 55
BRAZIL (República Federativa do Brasil/Federative Republic of Brazil)	**Brasília** 1 596 000	8 511 996	146 000 000	17	63.5 69
CHILE (República de Chile/Republic of Chile)	**Santiago** 5 134 000	756 626	13 386 000	18	68.1 75
COLOMBIA (República de Colombia/ Republic of Colombia)	**Santa Fe de Bogotá** 4 922 000	1 141 748	33 613 000	29	66.4 72
ECUADOR (República del Ecuador/ Republic of Ecuador)	**Quito** 1 094 000	283 561	9 819 000	34	63.4 67
GUYANA (Cooperative Republic of Guyana)	**Georgetown** 200 000	214 970	760 000	3	61.0 68
PARAGUAY (República del Paraguay/ Republic of Paraguay)	**Asunción** 608 000	406 752	4 004 000	10	64.4 68
PERU (República del Perú/ Republic of Peru)	**Lima** 6 115 000	1 285 216	21 998 000	17	62.9 66
SURINAME (Republiek van Suriname/ Republic of Suriname)	**Paramaribo** 67 900	163 820	417 000	2	66.4 71
TRINIDAD AND TOBAGO (Republic of Trinidad and Tobago)	**Port of Spain** 50 900	5 123	1 253 000	244	69.7 74
URUGUAY (República Oriental del Uruguay/Eastern Republic of Uruguay)	**Montevideo** 1 248 000	176 215	3 112 000	17	68.9 75
VENEZUELA (República de Venezuela/ Republic of Venezuela)	**Caracas** 1 290 000	912 050	19 733 000	21	67.0 73
SOUTH AMERICA		**17 736 750**	**294 420 000**	**16**	
SOUTH AMERICA	Total Ⓐ	**17 833 382**	**294 762 000**	**16**	

GROSS NATIONAL PRODUCT ①	LANGUAGES	RELIGIONS	ECONOMY
2780	Spanish (off.); Guarani; Quechua	Catholic 91%	**Economy** Traditionally farming (crops and animals) and the manufacture of pastoral and agricultural goods. **Industry** Petroleum output is rising; iron and steel, mechanical goods, textiles and food also of importance.
650	Spanish; Quechua; Aymará	Catholic 94%	**Principal resources** Minerals, including tin, gold, silver, bismuth, lead, zinc, tungsten, antimony and oil. **Agriculture** Currently at subsistence level, but animal husbandry (cattle, sheep) is developing rapidly.
2920	Portuguese (off.); Carib; Tupi	Catholic 88%	**Economy** Based on plantation crops (coffee, cocoa, sugar-cane, tobacco, cotton). **Industry** Food processing (by large, specialized companies) is the main activity. Industry is prosperous. The country is densely forested.
2160	Spanish (off.); Araucanian	Catholic 89%	**Economy** The most profitable sector is mining, particularly of copper, nitrates, oil, gold, silver, iron ore and coal. **Agriculture** Agronomy, animal farming and fishing are booming. **Industry** In a good position to grow.
1280	Spanish (off.); other local languages	Catholic 94%	**Economy** Principal export is coffee; other profitable cash crops include tobacco, cotton and sugar-cane. **Mineral resources** Gold, silver, platinum, emeralds and oil. **Industry** Relatively undeveloped.
1020	Spanish (off.); Quechua	Catholic 90%	**Economy** Relies on plantation crops: cocoa, coffee, sugar-cane, bananas, tobacco, cotton. **Mineral resources** Of considerable importance, principally oil, gold, silver and iron. **Industry** Developing modestly.
290	English (off.); Creole; Hindu; Urdu	Hindu 37%; Prot. 31%; Cath. 11%; Mus. 9%	**Agriculture** Mainly cane, rice, coffee, cassava and citrus fruits. **Mineral resources** Large quantities of bauxite (Guyana's main export), as well as gold and diamonds. **Industry** Limited to the production of agricultural goods.
1210	Spanish (off.); Guaraní	Catholic	**Economy** Essentially agricultural. Cotton, tobacco and fruit are the main exports, and timber. Cattle ranching also a major concern. **Industry** Growing as a result of inexpensive hydroelectric power.
1020	Spanish, Quechua, Aymará (all off.)	Catholic 92%	**Economy** Agriculture-based. Principal crops are cotton, sugar-cane, coffee and fruit. Animal farming is an important economic activity, and fishing even more so. **Mineral resources** Oil, copper and silver. **Industry** Prosperous.
3610	Dutch (off.); Carib; Creole	Hindu 26%; Cath. 22%; Mus. 19%; Prot. 18%	**Economy** Depends on agricultural products (especially rice, sugar-cane, coffee, citrus fruits, bananas and coconuts) and mining (bauxite, gold). **Industry** Limited to the production of agricultural goods.
3620	English (off.); Spanish; Hindu; Creole	Cath. 32%; Prot. 28%; Hindu 24%	**Economy** Industry has superseded agriculture as the main source of revenue due to rich deposits of oil, natural gas and asphalt. Other major industrial activities include refining and the production of petrochemicals and fertilizers.
2860	Spanish	Catholic	**Economy** Rearing livestock (sheep and cattle) and food processing are the chief economic activities in Uruguay, with wool, meat and hides the principal exports. **Agriculture** Also developing.
2610	Spanish (off.); Carib	Catholic 92%	**Economy** Previously relied on plantation crops, but petroleum production and the petrochemical industry now account for most export earnings. Fishing is also profitable. The country has considerable forest resources.

Includes the Falkland Is, South American Antilles, Aruba and French Guiana

① Per inhabitant, in US$

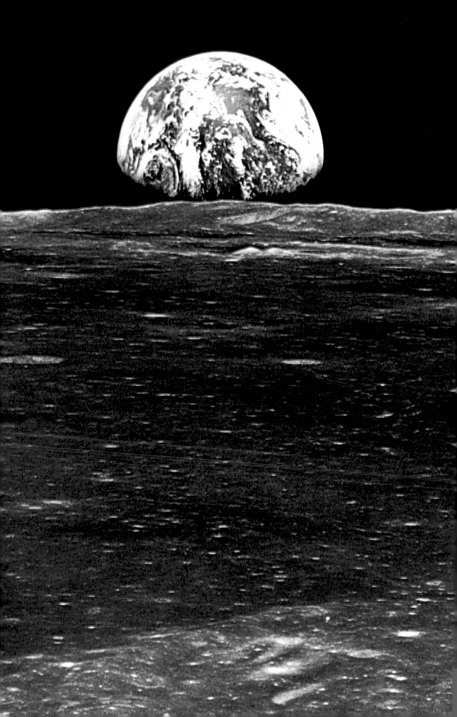

WORLD MAPS

Earth seen from the Moon
(image taken by astronauts aboard "Apollo 10" in May 1969)

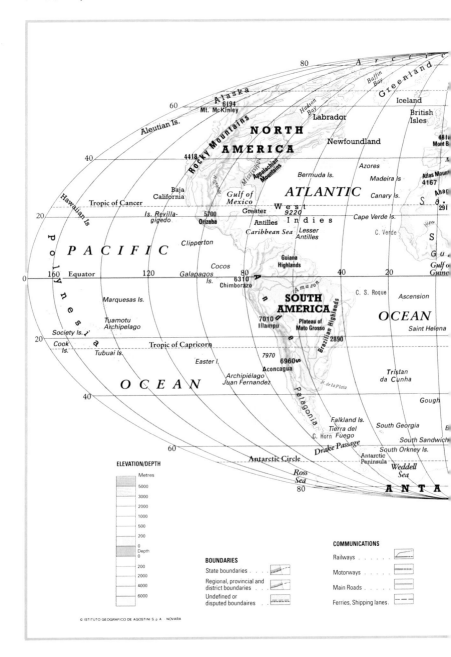

ELEVATION/DEPTH

Metres
5000
3000
2000
1000
500
200
0
Depth
0
200
2000
4000
6000

© ISTITUTO GEOGRAFICO DE AGOSTINI S.p A. NOVARA

BOUNDARIES

State boundaries . . . .

Regional, provincial and
district boundaries . . .

Undefined or
disputed boundaires . .

COMMUNICATIONS

Railways . . . . . .

Motorways . . . . .

Main Roads . . . . .

Ferries, Shipping lanes .

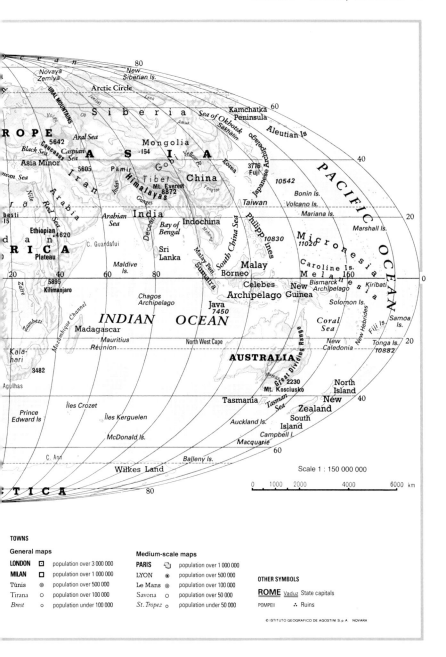

TOWNS

General maps

LONDON	⬒	population over 3 000 000
MILAN	☐	population over 500 000
Tùnis	◉	population over 500 000
Tirana	○	population over 100 000
Brest	○	population under 100 000

Medium-scale maps

PARIS	⬒	population over 1 000 000
LYON	◉	population over 500 000
Le Mans	◉	population over 100 000
Savona	○	population over 50 000
St. Tropez	○	population under 50 000

OTHER SYMBOLS

ROME	Vaduz	State capitals
POMPEII	∴	Ruins

© ISTITUTO GEOGRAFICO DE AGOSTINI S.p.A. NOVARA

1 GUYANA
2 SURINAME
3 French Guiana
4 UNITED KINGDOM
5 IRELAND
6 NETHERLANDS
7 BELGIUM
8 FRANCE
9 LUXEMBOURG
10 GERMANY
11 POLAND
12 ESTONIA
13 LATVIA
14 LITHUANIA
15 BELARUS
16 CZECH REPUBLIC
17 SLOVAKIA
18 AUSTRIA
19 HUNGARY
20 MOLDOVA
21 ROMANIA
22 SWITZERLAND
23 ITALY
24 SLOVENIA
25 CROATIA
26 BOSNIA-HERZEGOVINA
27 YUGOSLAVIA
28 MACEDONIA
29 ALBANIA
30 BULGARIA
31 GREECE
32 PORTUGAL
33 SPAIN
34 BURKINA
35 BENIN
36 CENTRAL AFRICAN REPUBLIC
37 CAMEROON
38 EQUATORIAL GUINEA
39 UGANDA
40 RWANDA
41 BURUNDI
42 MALAWI
43 ZIMBABWE
44 DJIBOUTI
45 ERITREA
46 OMAN
47 UNITED ARAB EMIRATES
48 QATAR
49 BAHRAIN
50 ARMENIA
51 GEORGIA
52 AZERBAIJAN
53 TURKMENISTAN
54 UZBEKISTAN
55 TAJIKISTAN
56 KYRGYZSTAN
57 BANGLADESH
58 CAMBODIA
59 British Indian Ocean Territory

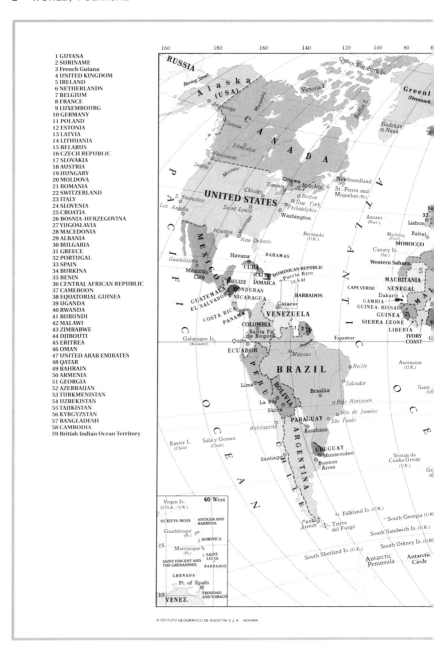

© ISTITUTO GEOGRAFICO DE AGOSTINI S p A   NOVARA

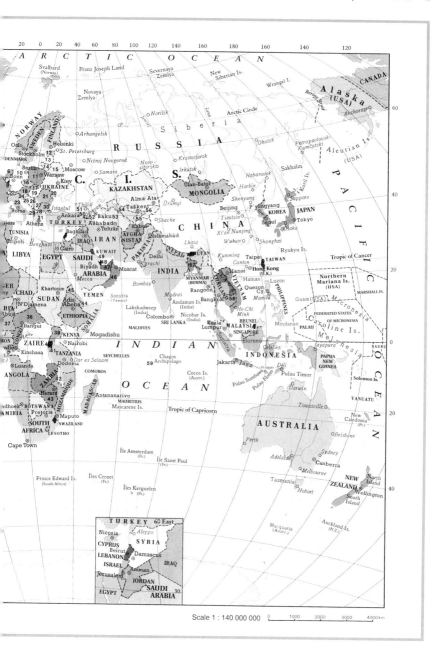

Scale 1 : 140 000 000

Scale 1 : 24 000 000

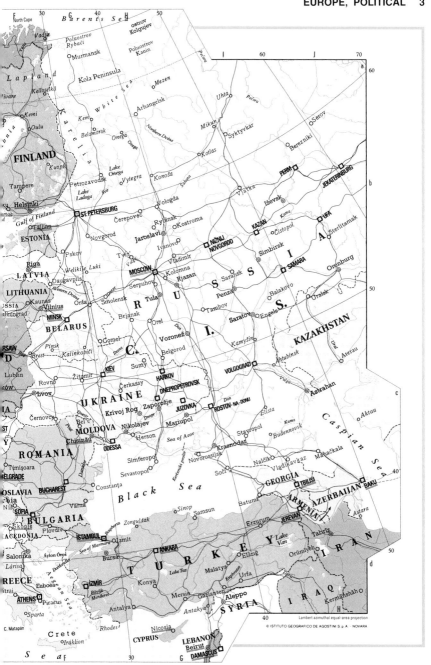

Lambert azimuthal equal-area projection
© ISTITUTO GEOGRAFICO DE AGOSTINI S.p.A. NOVARA

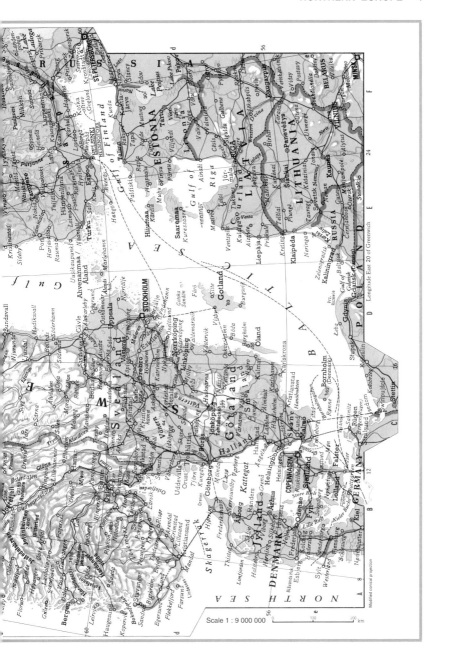

Scale 1 : 9 000 000

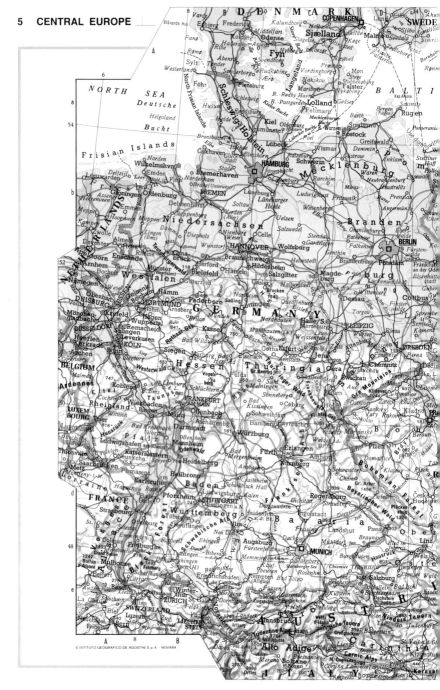

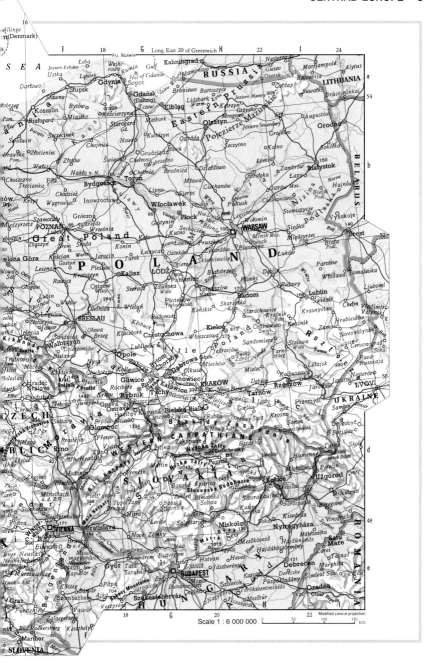

Scale 1 : 6 000 000   Modified conical projection

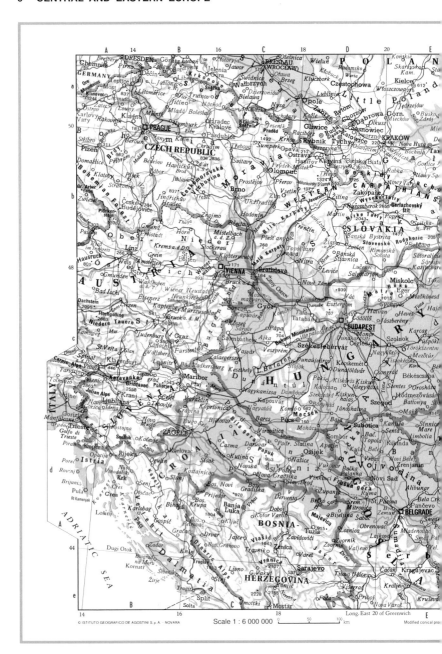

Scale 1 : 6 000 000

Long. East 20 of Greenwich

© ISTITUTO GEOGRAFICO DE AGOSTINI S.p.A. - NOVARA

Modified conical pro

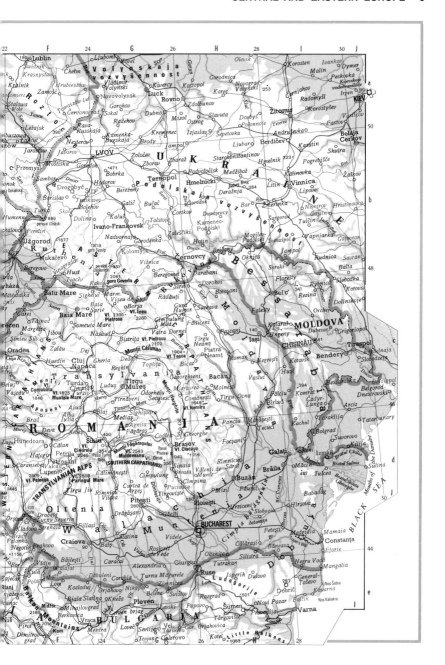

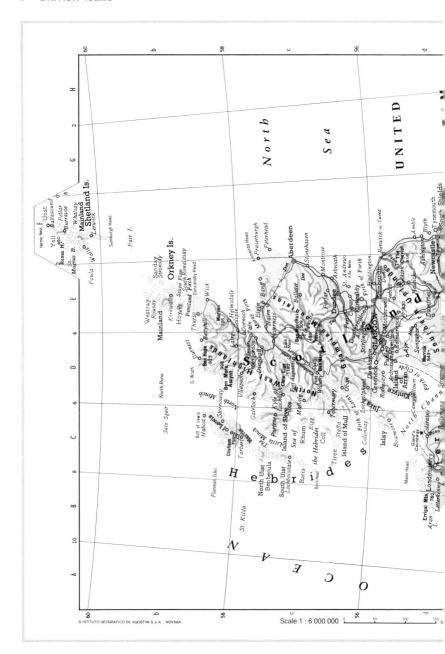

Scale 1 : 6 000 000   0   50   100   150 km

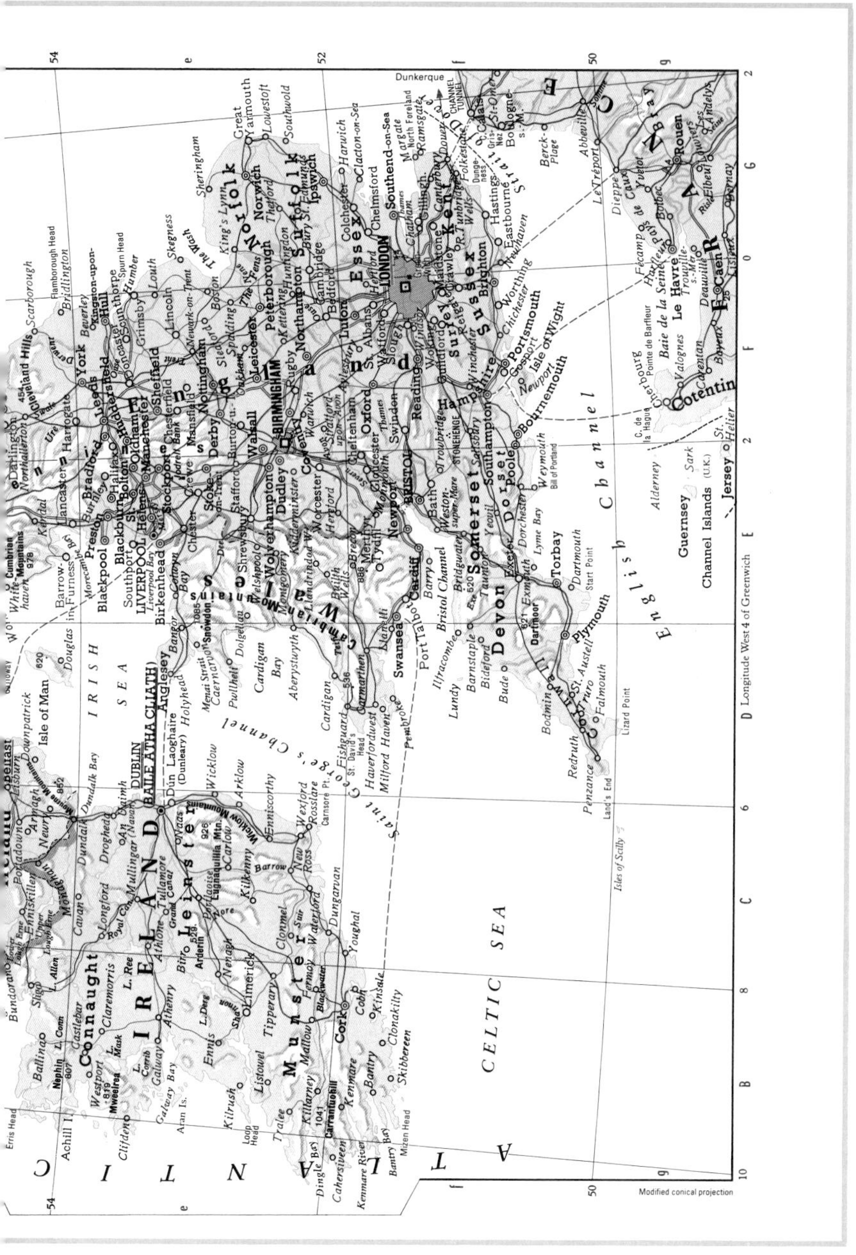

Dunkerque

54 · 52 · 50

Great Yarmouth
Lowestoft
Southwold
Sheringham
Norwich
NORFOLK
King's Lynn
SUFFOLK
Ipswich
Harwich
Clacton-on-Sea
Colchester
Chelmsford
ESSEX
Southend-on-Sea
Margate
Ramsgate
North Foreland
CHANNEL
Dover
Folkestone
Dungeness
Hastings
Eastbourne
Newhaven
Brighton
Worthing
Chichester
Portsmouth
Isle of Wight
Bournemouth
Poole
DORSET
Weymouth
Bill of Portland

Boulogne
Berck-Plage
Le Tréport
Dieppe
Fécamp
Le Havre
ROUEN
CAEN
Deauville
Cherbourg
Cap de la Hague
Pointe de Barfleur
Barneville
Valognes
COTENTIN
Alderney
Guernsey
Sark (U.K.)
Jersey St. Helier
Channel Islands

LONDON
St. Albans
Watford
Reading
Oxford
Swindon
BIRMINGHAM
Coventry
Leicester
Nottingham
Derby
Sheffield
Leeds
Bradford
York
Hull
Grimsby
Lincoln
Skegness
Boston
Peterborough
Northampton
Cambridge
Luton

ENGLAND

Scarborough
Bridlington
Flamborough Head
Spurn Head
Bridlington

LIVERPOOL
Birkenhead
Southport
Blackpool
Preston
Blackburn
Bolton
MANCHESTER
Chester
Stoke
Stafford
Wolverhampton
Dudley
Worcester
Gloucester
Cheltenham
Bristol
Bath
Weston-super-Mare
Bridgwater
SOMERSET
Taunton
DEVON
Exeter
Exmouth
Torbay
Dartmouth
Start Point
Plymouth
Lyme Bay
Dorchester

Cardiff
Newport
Swansea
Port Talbot
WALES
Carmarthen
Pembroke
Milford Haven
Haverfordwest
Fishguard
St. David's Head
Cardigan
Cardigan Bay
Aberystwyth
Snowdon
Anglesey
Holyhead
Menai Strait
Carnarvon
Pwllheli
Barmouth

Barrow-in-Furness
Lancaster
Cumbrian Mountains
Isle of Man
Douglas

IRISH SEA

Wicklow
Wexford
Rosslare
Carnsore Pt.
Waterford
Enniscorthy
New Ross
Kilkenny
Carlow
Arklow
Dún Laoghaire (Dunlaoghaire)
DUBLIN (BAILE ÁTHA CLIATH)
Drogheda
Dundalk
Dundalk Bay
Newry
Armagh
Downpatrick
BELFAST
Carrickfergus

IRELAND
Leinster
Munster
Connaught
Mullingar (Muileann)
Athlone
Tullamore
Portlaoise
Grand Canal
Naas
Tipperary
CORK
Cobh
Kinsale
Clonakilty
Skibbereen
Bantry
Bantry Bay
Kenmare River
Killarney
Tralee
Listowel
Limerick
Ennis
Galway
Galway Bay
Aran Is.
Clifden
Westport
Castlebar
Ballina
Sligo
Donegal
Enniskillen
Cavan
Longford

Caher
Charleville
Mallow
Dingle Bay
Dingle
Cahersiveen
Mizen Head
Mine Head
Loop Head
Kilrush

CELTIC SEA

ENGLISH CHANNEL

Saint George's Channel

Lundy
Barnstaple
Bideford
Bude
Bodmin
Bodmin Moor
Redruth
Penzance
Land's End
Isles of Scilly
St. Austell
Falmouth
Truro
Lizard Point

D Longitude West 4 of Greenwich F
Modified conical projection

Famborough Head
Cumberland Hills

Berwick-upon-Tweed

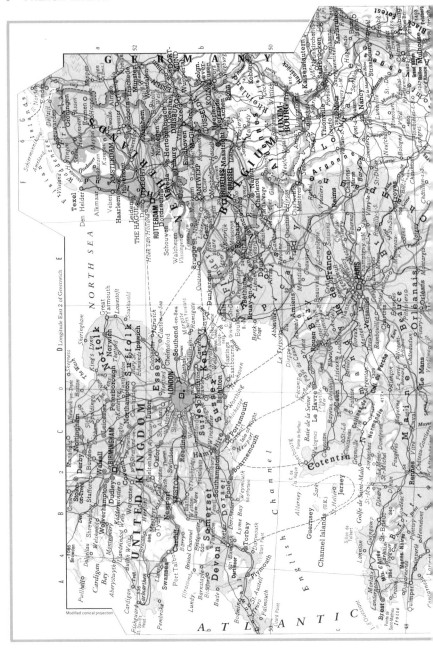

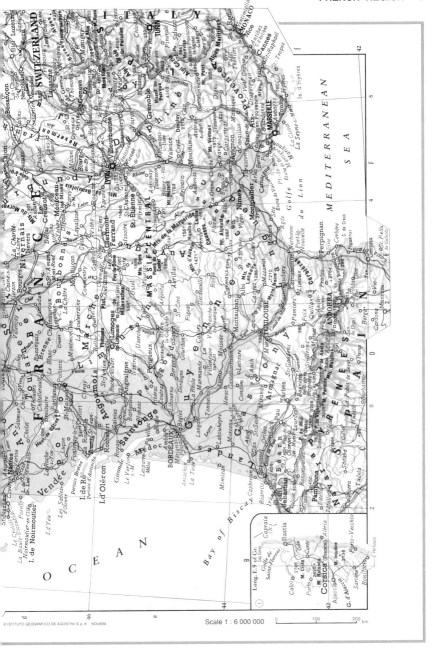

Scale 1 : 6 000 000

© ISTITUTO GEOGRAFICO DE AGOSTINI S.p.A. NOVARA

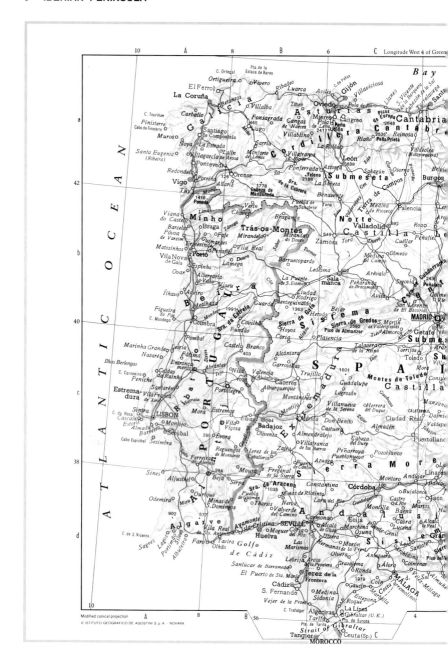

Scale 1 : 6 000 000

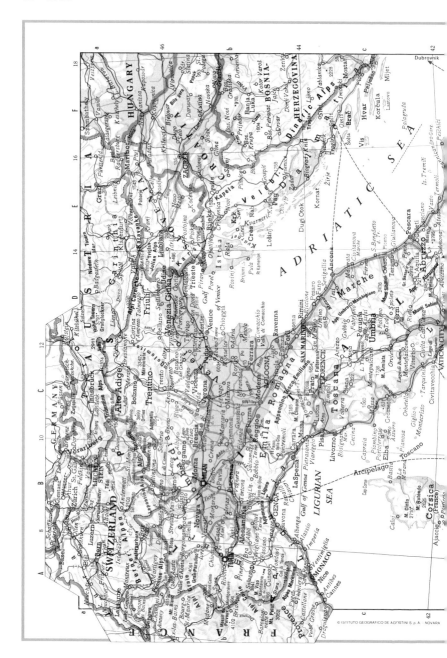

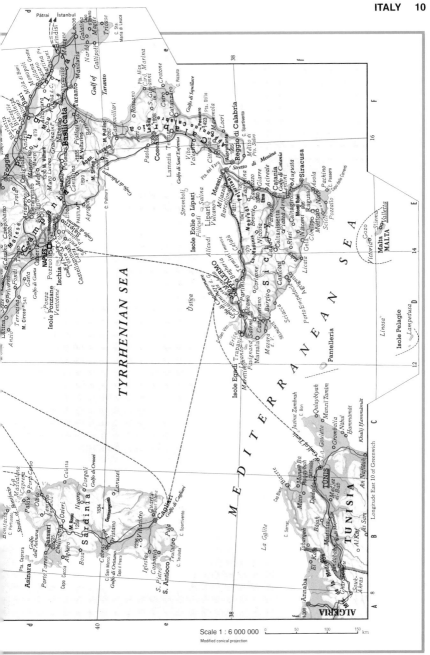

TYRRHENIAN SEA

MEDITERRANEAN SEA

Scale 1 : 6 000 000

Modified conical projection

0   50   100   150 km

Scale 1 : 6 000 000

0   50   100   150
km

Modified conical projection

© ISTITUTO GEOGRAFICO DE AGOSTINI S.p.A. - NOVARA

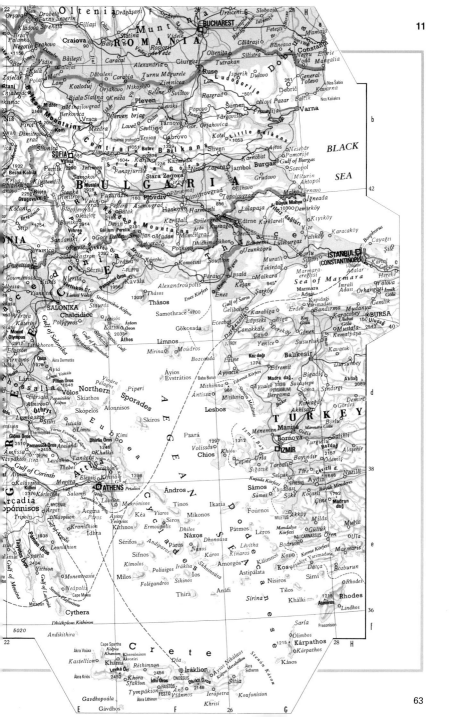

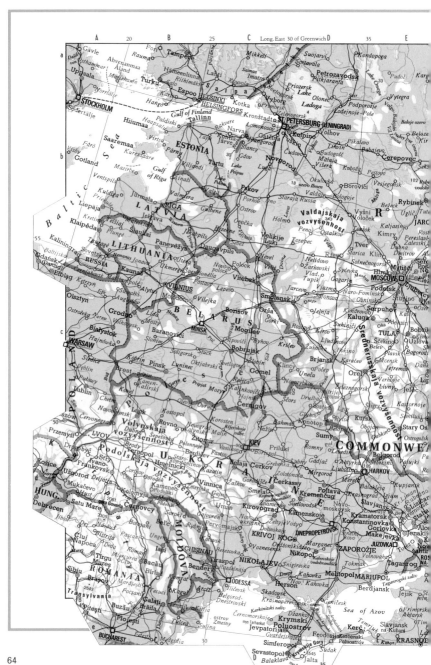

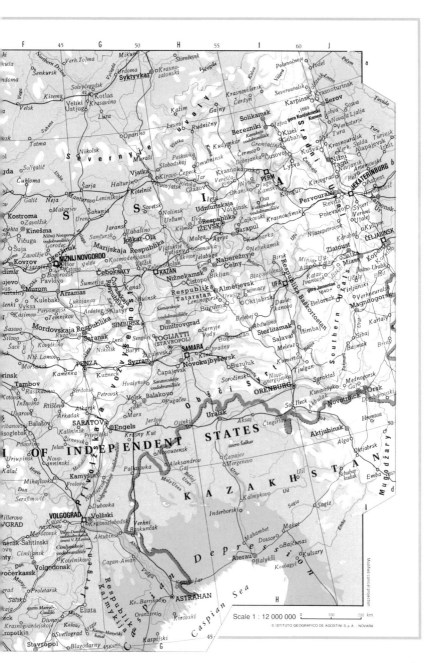

COMMONWEALTH OF INDEPENDENT STATES

KAZAKHSTAN

Caspian Depression

Caspian Sea

Scale 1 : 12 000 000

© ISTITUTO GEOGRAFICO DE AGOSTINI S.p.A. · NOVARA

Modified conical projection

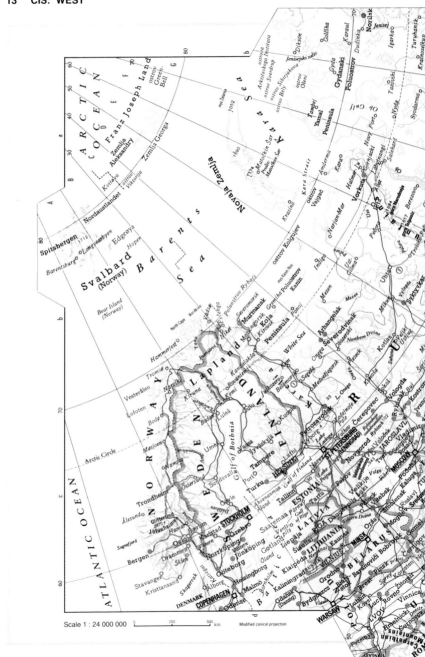

Scale 1 : 24 000 000   0   250   500 km   Modified conical projection

AUTONOMOUS
REPUBLICS

RUSSIA
1 - Karelia
2 - Komi
3 - Mordovia
4 - Chuvash
5 - Mari
6 - Udmurt
7 - Tatar Aut. Rep.
8 - Bashkir
9 - Kalmyk
10 - Karbardino-Balkar
11 - North Ossetia
12 - Checheno-Ingush
13 - Dagestan

GEORGIA
1 - Abkhasia
2 - Aszhar

AZERBAIJAN
1 - Naxhichevan

UZBEKISTAN
1 - Kara-Kolpak

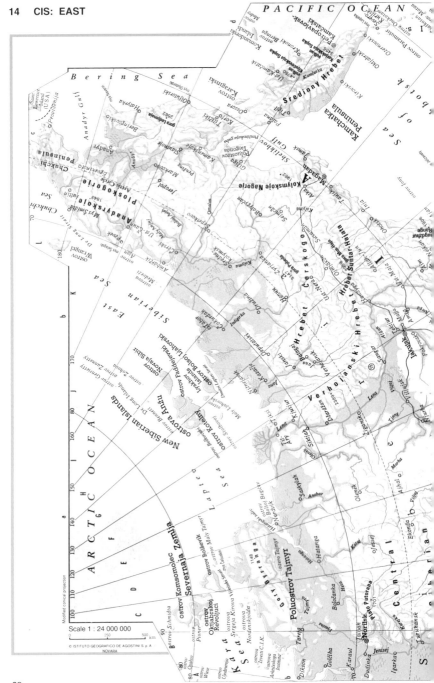

Scale 1 : 24 000 000

© ISTITUTO GEOGRAFICO DE AGOSTINI S.p.A
NOVARA

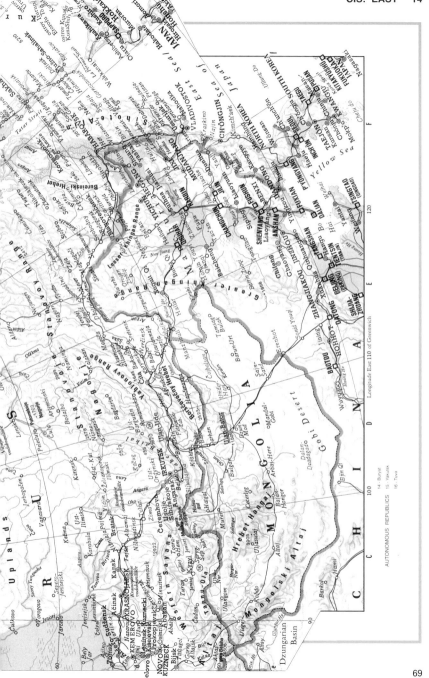

AUTONOMOUS REPUBLICS   14 Buryat   15 Yakutsk   16 Tuva

Scale 1 : 50 000 000 0   500   1000   1500 km

Lambert azimuthal equal-area projection

© ISTITUTO GEOGRAFICO DE AGOSTINI S.p.A
NOVARA

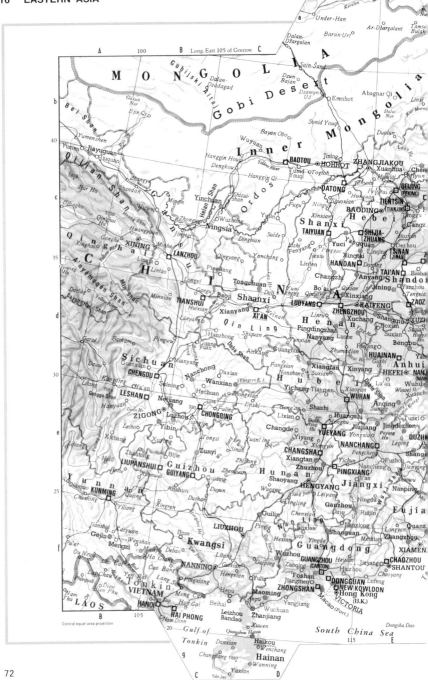

© ISTITUTO GEOGRAFICO DE AGOSTINI S.p.A   NOVARA   Conical equal-area projection   Scale 1 : 9 000 000   0   100   200 km

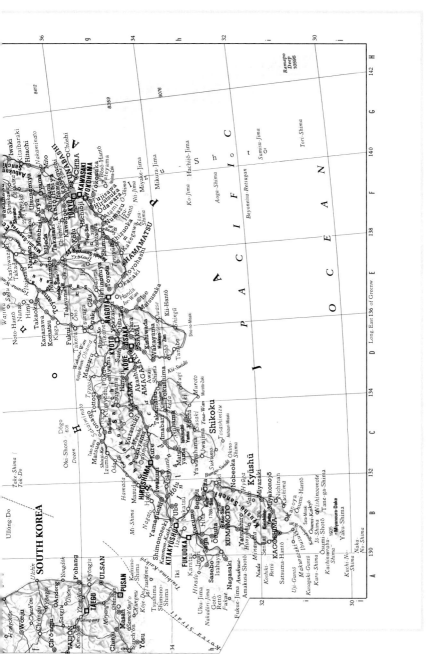

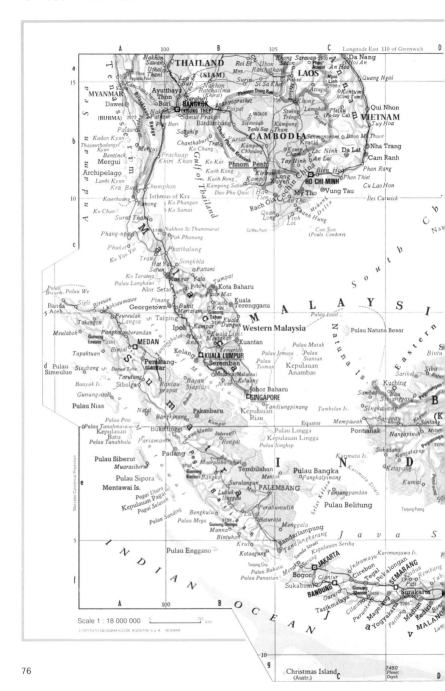

Scale 1 : 18 000 000

© ISTITUTO GEOGRAFICO DE AGOSTINI S.p.A. NOVARA

PHILIPPINES

Calayan
Dalupiri
Babuyan Is.
Babuyan Channel
Escarpade Point
Bangui
Laoag
Aparri
Tuguegarao
Vigan
Bangued
Bontoc
Ilagan
S. Fernando
Mount Pulog 2930
Baguio
Bolinao
Lingayen G.
Dagupan
Bayombong
Luzon
S. Carlos
Tarlac
San Jose
Cabanatuan
S. Fernando
Olongapo
QUEZON CITY
Polillo Is.
MANILA
Sta. Cruz
Philippine Sea
Manila Bay
Cavite
Sta. Cruz
Lamon Bay
S. Pablo
Daet
Tagaytay City
Lucena
Naga
Catanduanes
Batangas
Boac
Virac
Calapan
Marinduque
Legazpi
Mindoro
Mount Halcon 2585
S. Jose
Burias
Sorsogon
Busuanga
Mindoro Strait
Tablas
Sibuyan
Bulan
Masbate
Laoang
Calamian Group
Ocoron
Kalibo
Samar
Culion
Panay
Masbate
Calbayog
Linapacan
S. Jose de Buenavista
Iloilo
Roxas
Catbalogan
Tacloban
Taytay
Cuyo Is.
Cadiz
Ormoc
Dumaran
Guimaras
Bacolod
San Carlos
Leyte
Palawan
1593
Negros
Toledo
Cebu
Baybay
Puerto Princesa
Cagayan Is.
Dumaguete
Bohol
Tagbilaran
Dinagat 10830
Siargao
Mount Mantalingajan 2054
Bayawan
Siquijor
Gingoog
Surigao
5575
Dipolog
Cagayan de Oro
Tandag
10400
Sulu Sea
Ozamis
Malaybalay
Butuan
Pagadian
Iligan
Balabac
Bugsuk
Balabac Strait
San Miguel Is.
Cotabato
Mount Apo 2954
Pulau Balambangan
Pulau Banggi
Cagayan Sulu
Zamboanga
Moro Gulf
DAVAO
Mati
Kudat
Pulau Jambongan
Pangutaran Group
Basilan City
Datu Piang (Dulawan)
Digos
Kota Kinabalu
Gunong Kinabalu 4101
Sandakan
Jolo Group
Basilan
General Santos
Malita
Sabah
Beaufort
Melalap
Lahad Datu
Tapul Group
Jolo
6220
Davao Gulf
Pulau Miangas
Weston
Samales Group
Tinaca Point
Sarangani Is.
Labuan
Bandar Seri Begawan
Tawitawi Group
Sulu Archipelago
Sitibu
Tawau
BRUNEI
2423 Gunong Murud
Pulau-Pulau Nanusa
Kepulauan Kawio
Kepulauan Talaud
Celebes Sea
1860
Pulau Karakelong
Pulau Kaburuang
Tarakan
Tanjungselor
Pulau Sangihe
3800
Pulau Makalehi
Tanjungredeb
Pulau Tahulandang
Selat Siau
Pulau Siau
Pulau Morotai
Pulau Maratua
Pulau Bangka
Galela
Sangkulirang
Tolitoli
Paleleh
Manado
Gunung Klabat 2022
Bukit Malino 2707
Bolliohertu 2070
Minahassa
Tondano
4970
1635
Pulau
Waigeo 0
Tomini
Gorontalo
4180
Ternate
Soasiu
Halmahera
Samarinda
Teluk Tomini
Kepulauan Togian
Pulau Makian
Pulau Kayoa
Donggala
Pulau Batudaka
Poh
Luwuk
Weda
Pulau Gebe
Balikpapan
Gunung Waikara 2355
Poso
Pulau Peleng
Kepulauan Banggai
Labuha
Laut Halmahera
Sorong
BORNEO
Tanjung
Tanah
Kepulauan Balabalangan
Sula
Pulau Bisa
Pulau Salawati
Klamono
(Kalimantan)
Kendari
Pulau Bacan
Pulau Kofiau
angkaraya
Kandan
Mamuju
Wotu
Malili
Saroako
Kepulauan Banggai
Sanana
Pulau Mangole
Obi
Pulau Misool
Kotabaru
Palopo
Danau Towuti
5800
Pulau Taliabu
Pulau Sanana
Cera
Ceram
marmasin
Martapura
Pulau Sebuku
Majene
Balu Bantaikombola
Mekongga 2799
3456
Kendari
Pulau Manui
Namlea
Pulau Boano
Piru
3010
Amahai
Buta
Geser
C. Selatan
Pulau Laut
Parepare
Singkang
Kolaka
Pulau Wowoni
Pulau Buru
Pulau Kelang
Ambon
Kepulauan Laut Kecil
Watampone (Bone)
Raha
Banda Sea
Pulau Ambelau
Bandanaira
Kepulauan Banda
Madura
UJUNG PANDANG (MAKASAR)
2871
Pulau Muna
Pulau Buton
Wangiwangi
Kepulauan Tayandu
Bantaeng
Pulau Kabaena
Kepulauan Tukangbesi
Kepulauan Lucipara
Kepulauan Penju
Pulau Manuk
Kepulauan Sapudi
Kepulauan Kangean
Pulau Sepanjang
Pulau Selajar
Baubau
Pulau Binongko
Pulau Serua
Selat Selajar
Benteng
Pulau Tanahjampea
Kepulauan Barat Daya
Pulau Damar
Pulau Teun
Pulau Nila
Bali Sea
Pulau Kalao
Pulau Kalaotoa
Pulau Romang
Pulau Serua
Pulau Babar
Singaraja
3142
Gunung Rinjani 3726
Pulau Moyo
Pulau Sangeang 2860
Komodo 6960
Larantuka
Pulau Adonara
Pulau Wetar
Pulau Kisar
Pulau Moa
Denpasar
Flores Sea
Ruteng
Pulau Flores
Pulau Lomblen
Pulau Atauro
Leti Is.
Pulau Bali
Sumbawa Besar
Ende
Maumere
Alor
Pulau Pantar 2960
Oti
3310
Mataram
Pulau Lombok
Pulau Sumbawa
Savu Sea
Okusi
Pulau Sumba
Waikabubak
Sumba Strait
1225
Waingapu
Pulau Timor
Pulau Sumba
Pulau Sawu
Kupang
Timor Sea
Pulau Raijua
Pulau Roti

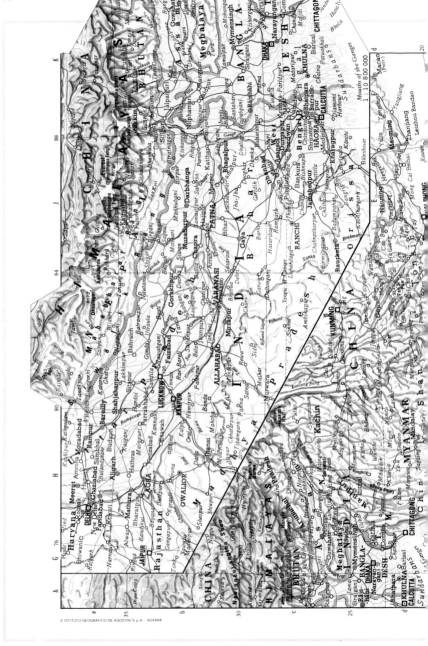

© ISTITUTO GEOGRAFICO DE AGOSTINI S p A - NOVARA

Scale 1 : 18 000 000

Modified conical projection

N. = Nagaland
T. = Tripura
M. = Mizoram

Long. East of Greenwich

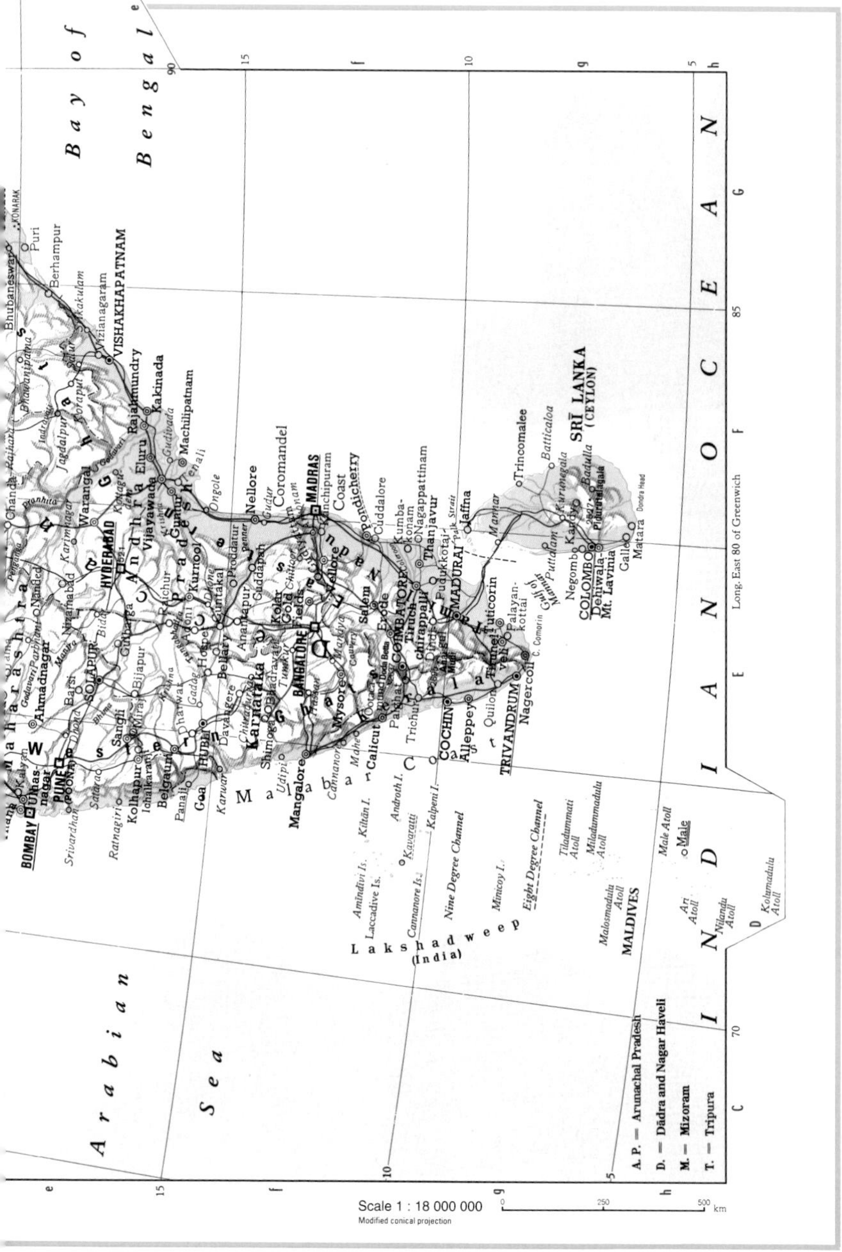

(BURMA)

(Akyab)

Bay of Bengal

Arabian Sea

INDIAN OCEAN

BOMBAY

Puri
Berhampur
Bhubaneswar
Jagdalpur
Vizianagaram
VISHAKHAPATNAM
Rajahmundry
Kakinada
Machilipatnam
Eluru
Vijayawada
HYDERABAD
Warangal
Nellore
Coromandel Coast
MADRAS
Pondicherry
Cuddalore
Nagappattinam
Thanjavur
Tiruchirappalli
MADURAI
Tuticorin
Jaffna
Trincomalee
Batticaloa
SRI LANKA (CEYLON)
Negombo
COLOMBO
Dehiwala
Mt. Lavinia
Galle
Matara
Anuradhapura

Maharashtra
Karnataka
Andhra Pradesh
BANGALORE
Mysore
Mangalore
Calicut
COIMBATORE
Salem
Erode
COCHIN
Alleppey
TRIVANDRUM
Nagercoil
C. Comorin
Quilon

KOLHAPUR
PUNE
Poona
Ulhasnagar
Ahmadnagar
Sangli
Kolhapur
Belgaum
Panaji
Goa
Hubli
Bijapur
Gulbarga
Raichur

Laccadive Is.
Amindivi Is.
Androth I.
Kiltan I.
Cannanore Is.
Kavaratti
Kalpeni I.
Minicoy I.
Nine Degree Channel
Eight Degree Channel

Lakshadweep (India)

MALDIVES
Male
Mal'e Atoll
Ari Atoll
Nilandu Atoll
Kolumadulu Atoll
Tiladummati Atoll
Miladummadulu Atoll
Malosmadulu Atoll

A. P. — Arunachal Pradesh
D. — Dādra and Nagar Haveli
M. — Mizoram
T. — Tripura

Long. East 80 of Greenwich

Scale 1 : 18 000 000
Modified conical projection

0   250   500 km

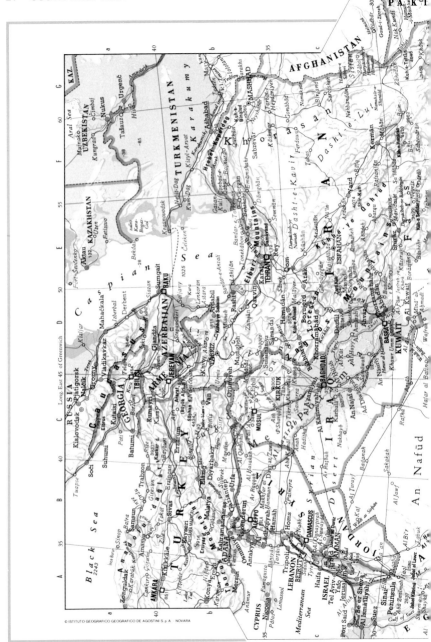

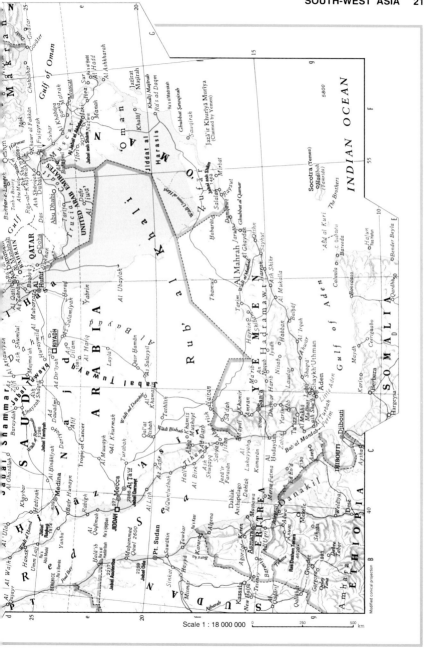

Scale 1 : 18 000 000

Modified conical projection

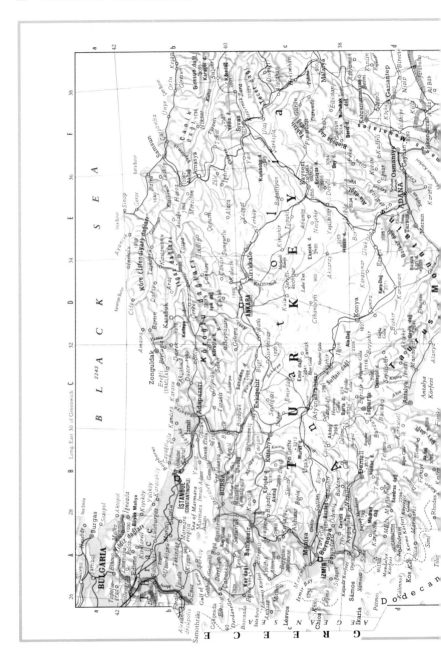

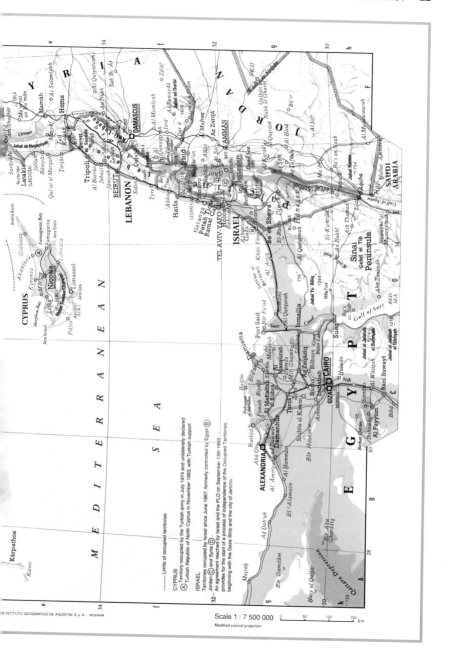

-------- Limits of occupied territories

CYPRUS
(A) Territory occupied by the Turkish army in July 1974 and unilaterally declared
(A) Turkish Republic of North Cyprus in November 1983, with Turkish support.

ISRAEL
Territories occupied by Israel since June 1967, formerly controlled by Egypt (B).
22- Jordan (C) and Syria (D)
An agreement reached by Israel and the PLO on September 13th 1993
provides for the start of a process of independence of the Occupied Territories,
beginning with the Gaza Strip and the city of Jericho.

Scale 1 : 7 500 000   0   50   100   150 km
Modified conical projection

© ISTITUTO GEOGRAFICO DE AGOSTINI S.p.A. - NOVARA

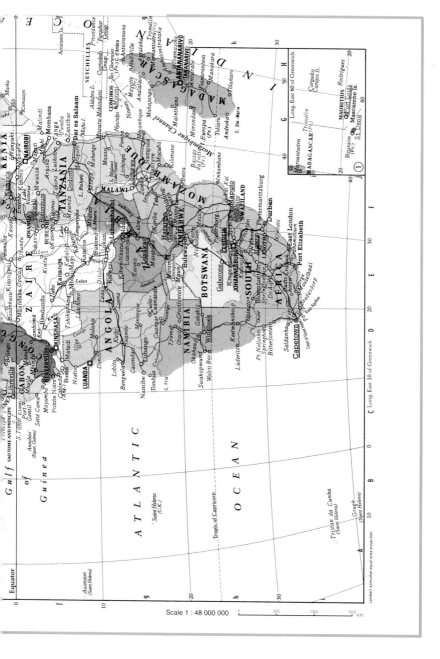

Scale 1 : 48 000 000

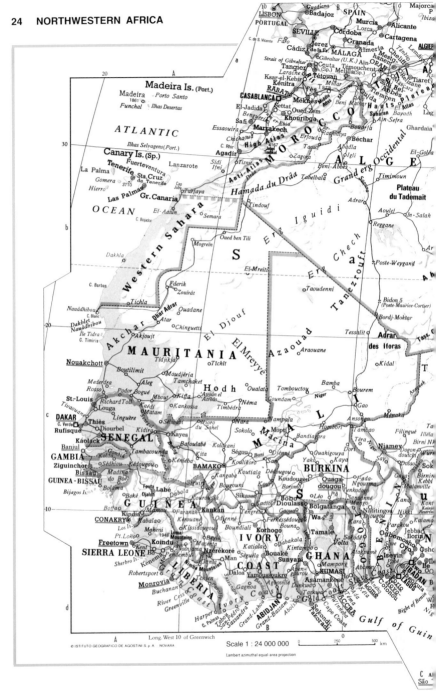

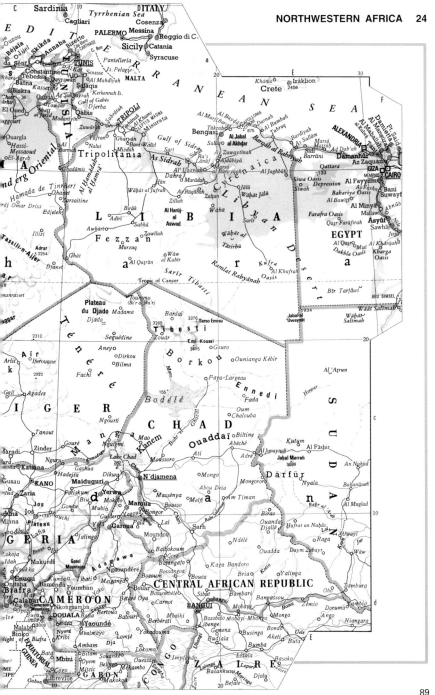

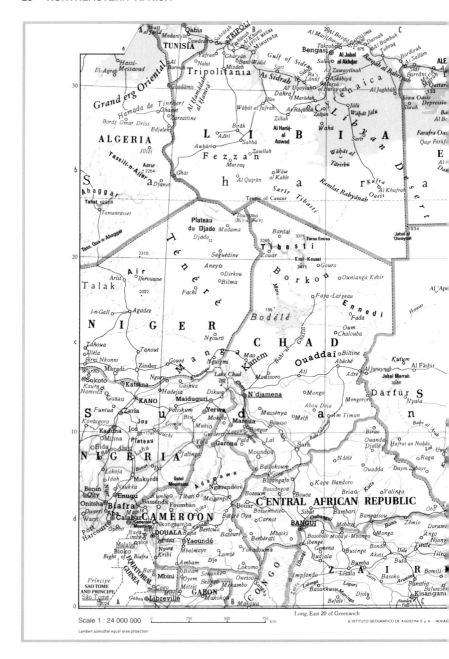

Scale 1 : 24 000 000

Lambert azimuthal equal-area projection

Long. East 20 of Greenwich

© ISTITUTO GEOGRAFICO DE AGOSTINI S.p.A. NOVARA

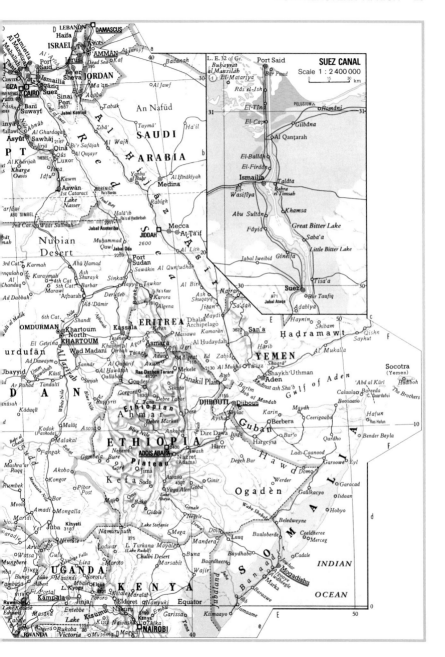

SUEZ CANAL
Scale 1 : 2 400 000

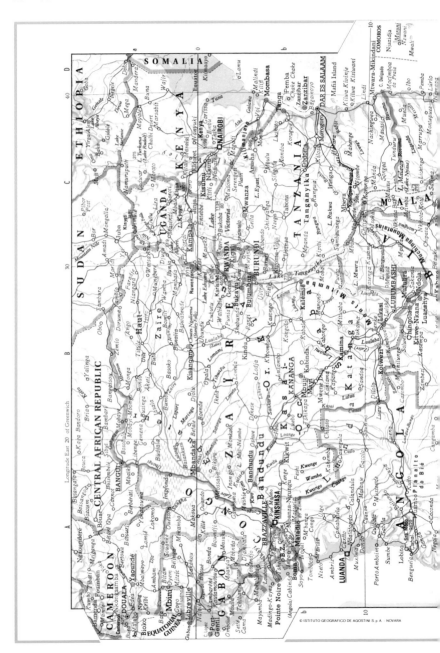

© ISTITUTO GEOGRAFICO DE AGOSTINI S.p.A. - NOVARA

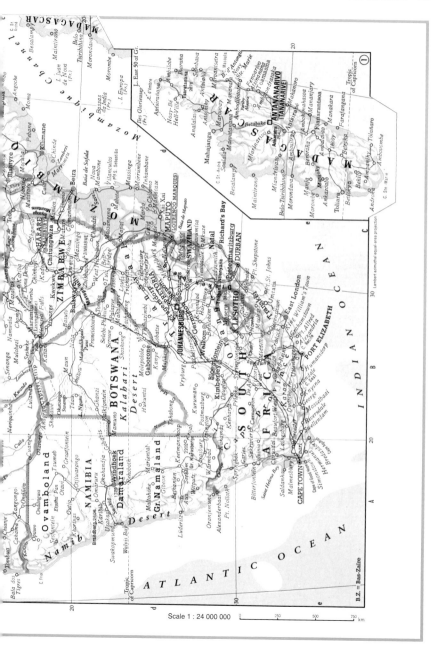

Scale 1 : 24 000 000

B.Z. = Bas-Zaïre

Lambert azimuthal equal-area projection

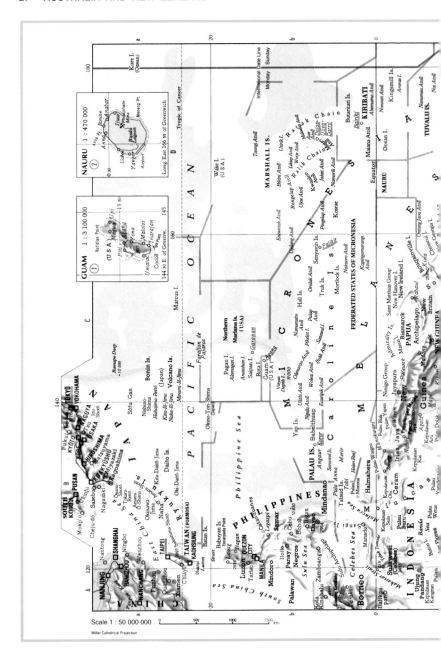

NAURU   1 : 470 000

GUAM   1 : 3 100 000   (USA)

Scale 1 : 50 000 000

Miller Cylindrical Projection

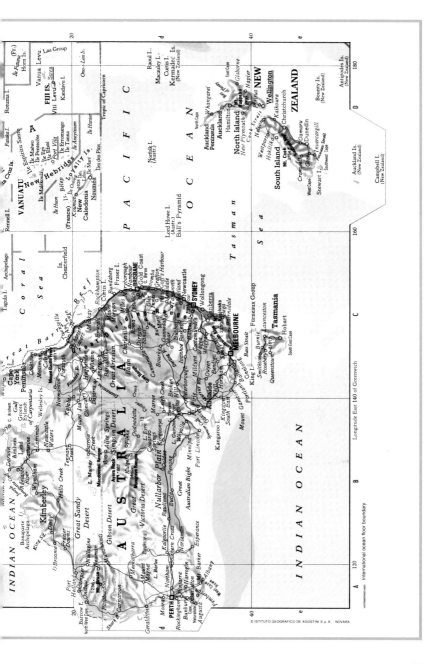

© ISTITUTO GEOGRAFICO DE AGOSTINI S.p.A. NOVARA

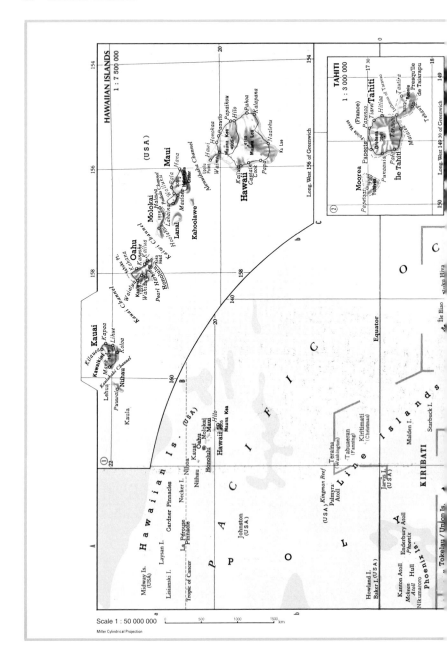

HAWAIIAN ISLANDS
1 : 7 500 000

(U S A)

Kauai
Kilauea Kapaa
Kawaikini Mana Lihue
Puuwai Koloa
Kauai Channel
Kaulakahi Channel
Niihau Channel
Lehua
Niihau
Kaula

Oahu
Waialua Kahana
Wahiawa Kaneohe
Waianae Honolulu
Pearl Harbor Koko Head
Kailua Kaena Pt.
Kaiwi Channel

Molokai
Hoolehua
Halawa
Kaunakakai
Kalaupapa
Pailolo Channel
Lanai
Lahaina
Maalaea Haiku
Kahoolawe
Alenuihaha Channel

Maui
Wailuku Hana
Haleakala
Crater 3055

Hawaii
Kailua Hilo
Kapaau Hawi
Waimea Honokaa Papaikou
Upolu Point Papaaloa Pahoa
Mauna Kea Mauna Loa 4169 Kalapana
4205
Capt. Cook Papa
Naalehu Ka Lae

Long. West 156 of Greenwich

TAHITI
1 : 3 000 000
(France)
Tahiti
Moorea
Teahupoo Tiarei
Papetoai Papenoo
Tohivea Orohena Taravao
2241 Hitiaa Presqu'île
Papeari Mahaena de Taiarapu
Pueu Taravao Tautira
Teavaro Taiarapu
Tiarei
Tekaraha Teahupoo Taravao
Maraa Vaitepiha Mataiea
Papeari
Tekauariki
Île Tahiti
Long. West 149 30 of Greenwich

P A C I F I C

O C

Hawaiian Is.
(U S A)
Necker I. Niihau Kauai Molokai Hilo
Gardner Pinnacles Kauai Oahu Maui
La Pérouse Niihau Honolulu Mauna Kea
Pinnacle Hawaii

Equator

Line Islands
Teraina
(Washington)
Tabuaeran
(Fanning)
Kiritimati
(Christmas)
Malden I.
Starbuck I.

Kingman Reef
(U S A)
Palmyra
Atoll
Jarvis I.
(U S A)

KIRIBATI

Midway Is.
(USA)
Lisianski I.
Laysan I.
Tropic of Cancer

Johnston
(USA)

Howland I.
Baker I.(USA)

Kanton Atoll
McKean Enderbury Atoll
Atoll Phoenix
Nikumaroro Hull

Phoenix Is.

Tokelau / Union Is.

Île Eiao
Nuku Hiva

Scale 1 : 50 000 000
0   500   1000   1500 km
Miller Cylindrical Projection

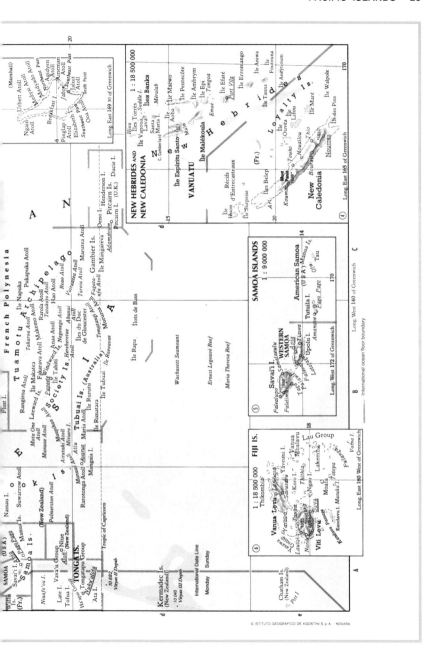

Arafura

130 E

10

Melville I.

Cobourg Penins

Dundas Str.

Bathurst I. Milikapiti

Van Diemen

Goulbu

Clarence Str.

Gulf

Manin

Rum Jungle

Darwin

Arnhe

Batchelor

Land

Adelaide
River

Pine Creek

Katherine

Port Keats

Deli R.

Larrim

Roper R.

Mataranka

Birdum

Daly
Waters

B   120   C   125   D

Cartier I.

INDIAN

Admiralty Gulf

C. Londonderry

Scott
Reel

Browse I.

Kalumburu

King Edward R.

Joseph
Bonaparte
Gulf

Kugunurra

Victoria Riv.
Downs

New
Wate

Adele I.

Kuri Bay

Mt. Hann

Wyndham

Victoria R.

a

15

Collier B.

776

Kimberley

Drysdale R.

Yampi Sd.

King
Sound

Mt. Ord

Kimberley
Plateau

Ord
River

900

Wave Hill

OCEAN

Lacepede Is.

C. Lévêque

King Leopold Ranges

936

Derby

Fitzroy
Crossing

Halls Creek

Nort

Rowley
Shoals

Broome

Fitzroy R.

Margaret River

Tanami
Desert

Tennant
Creek

Roebuck B.

Frazier
Downs

Lagrange

Tanami

The Granites

Barrow

b

Dampier Archipelago

Port
Hedland

Shay Gap

Eighty
Mile Beach

Gregory L.

Great   Sandy   Desert

Lander R.

Monte Bello Is.

Wickham

De Grey R.

Yuendumu

*Terri*t

Barrow I.

Dampier

Roebourne

Marble Bar

L. Waukarly-
carly

Percival
Lakes

Exmouth
Gulf

Pannawonica

Fortescue R.

Nullagine

L. Dora

L. Auld

L. Mackay

Macdonnell Ran

North West Cape

Onslow

Hamersley

Mt. Bruce

Wittenoom

Roy Hill

867
Mt.

Exmouth

Mt.
Brockman

1235

1510

Learmouth

Ashburton R.

Tom Price

Newman

L. Disappointment

L. Macdonald

Haasts Bluff

c

Uaroo

Paraburdoo

Mundiwindi

L. Hopkins

L. Neale

Erldunda

Tropic of Capricorn

Western

Gibson   Desert

L. Amadeus

Petermann Ranges

Mt.
Woodroffe

867

L. McLeod

Minilya

Mt. Augustus

1106

A U S T

R

Ayers Rock

Kulgera

Gascoyne R.

Carnegie

Warburton
Mission

Musgrave Ranges

1440

Abn

Carnarvon

Gascoyne
Junction

Peak Hill

L. Gregory

L. Carnegie

Mt.-Woodroffe

De Rose I

Naturaliste
Channel

Shark
Bay

Wooramel R.

Meekatharra

Wiluna

L. Wells

On

Cape
Inscription

Dirk
Hartog I.

Denham

Australia

L. Yeo

Great   Victoria   Desert

Serpentine
Lakes

d

Murchison R.

Cue

L. Austin

Sandstone

Agnew

Laverton

Coober

Northampton

Mount
Magnet

Yalgoo

Leonora

Rason L.

L. Carey

L. Minigwal

South

Geraldton

Mullewa

Morawa

Payne's Find

L. Barlee

L. Rebecca

Ooldea

Houtman
Abrolhos

Dongara

Three Springs

Menzie

L. Rebecca

Nullarbor   Plain

Yalata

Tarco

Walheroo

Kalgoorlie

Zanthus

Haig

Forrest

Penong

L

30

Milny

Moora

L. Moore

Dalwallinu

Kalannie

Coolgardie

Kambalda

Rawlinna

Fowler's
Bay

Nuyts

Ce

Lancelin

Mukinbudin

Bullfinch

Widgiemooltha

Cocklebiddy

Eucla

Archipelago

Streaky Bay

Merredin

Southern
Cross

L. Cowan

Balladonia

Investigator Gro

Kalamunda

PERTH

Norther

Kondinin

Norseman

L. Dandas

Rockingham

Beverley

Lake
Johnston

Great

Mandurah

Brookton

Narrogin

Wagin

Newdegate

Ravensthorpe

565

Australian   Bight

e

Geographe Bay

Pinj

Bunbury

Collie

Cape Naturaliste

Katanning

Gnowangerup

Hopetoun

C. Arid

Po

Busselton

Bridgetown

Archipelago of the Recherche

Augusta

Pemberton

Stirling Range

Denmark

Mount Barker

Albany

C. Leeuwin

Flinders B.

King George Sound

35

Pt. d'Entrecasteaux

West Cape Howe

115   B   120   C   125   D   Long. East 130 of Greenwich   E

0   250   500
km

Scale 1 : 18 000 000

© ISTITUTO GEOGRAFICO DE AGOSTINI S.p.A.   NOVA

Conical equal-area projection

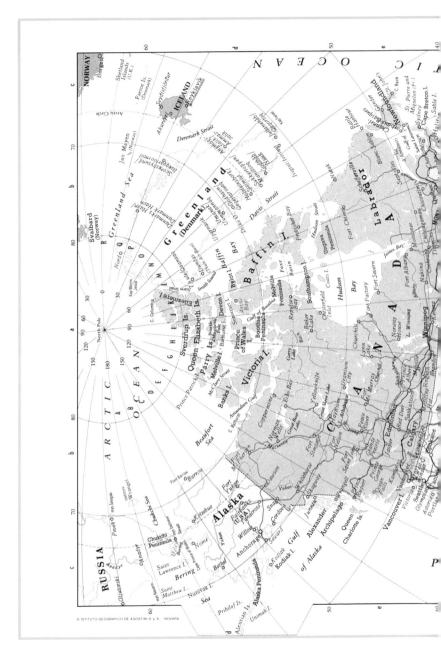

© ISTITUTO GEOGRAFICO DE AGOSTINI S.p.A   NOVARA

Scale 1 : 48 000 000

Lambert azimuthal equal-area projection

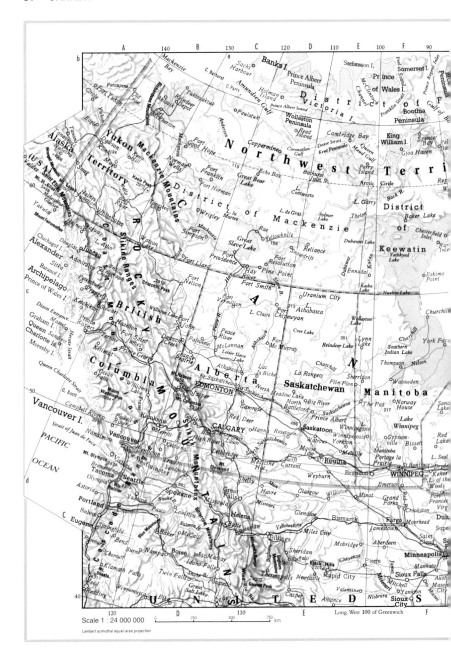

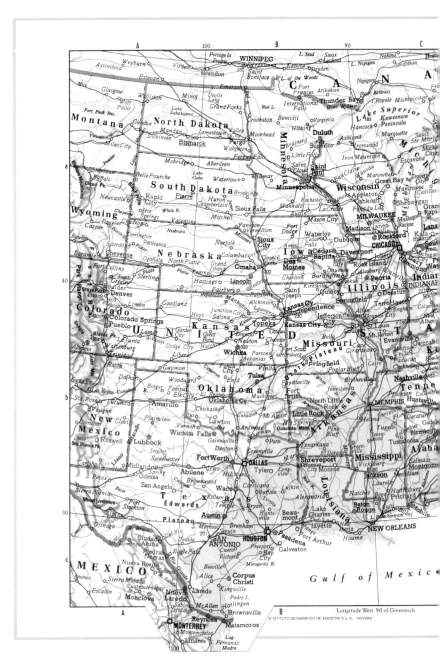

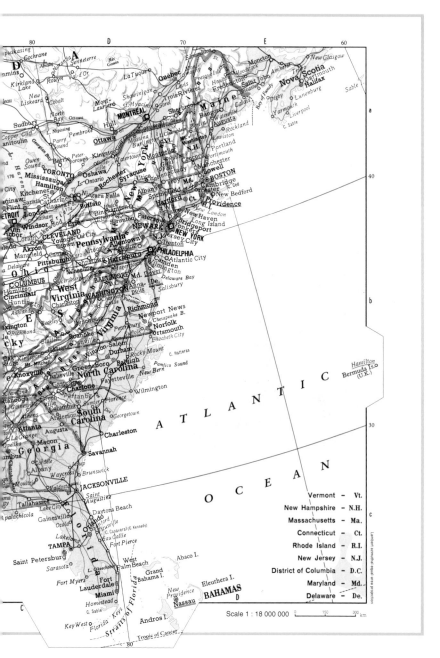

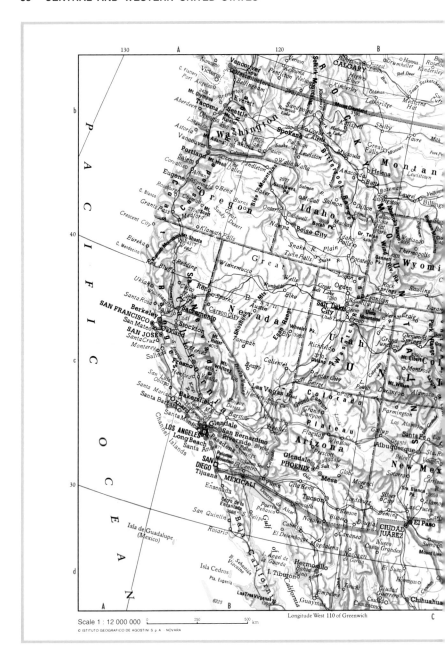

Scale 1 : 12 000 000

Longitude West 110 of Greenwich

© ISTITUTO GEOGRAFICO DE AGOSTINI S.p.A. NOVARA

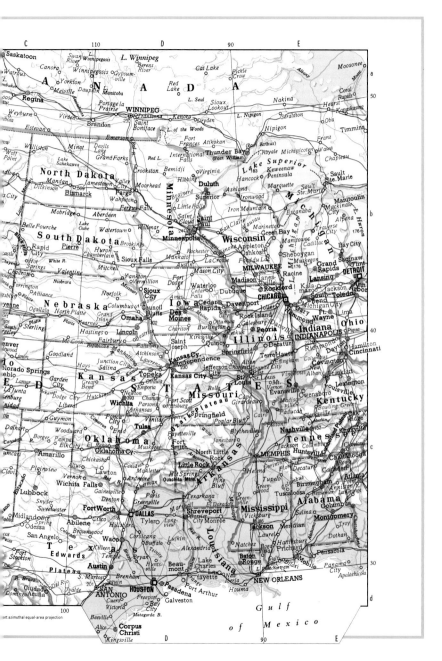

Scale 1 : 18 000 000

0   250   500 km

Lambert azimuthal equal-area projection

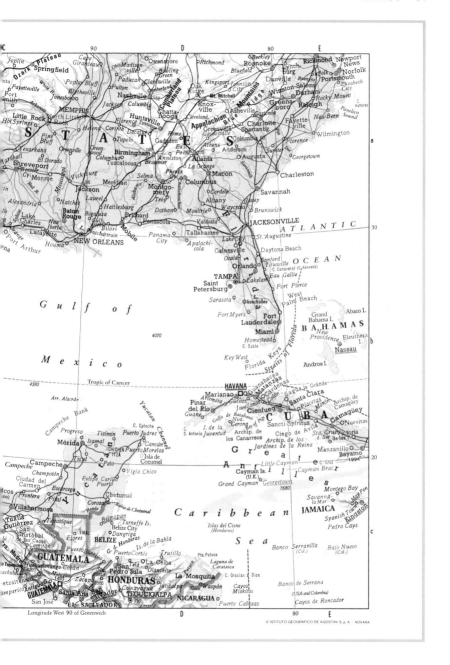

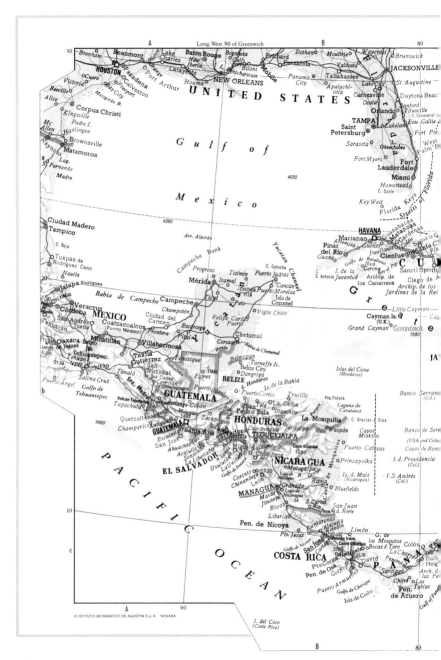

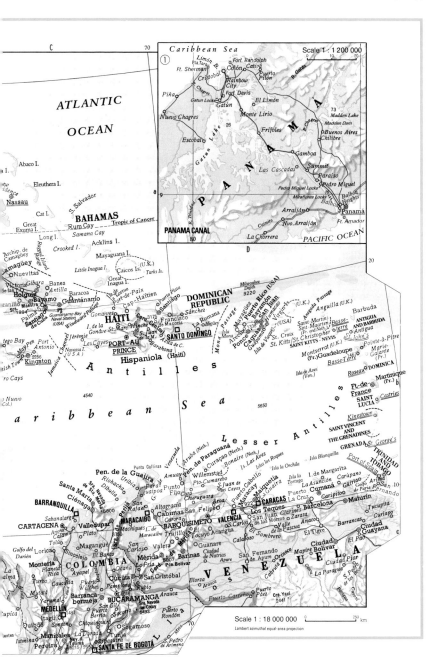

PANAMA CANAL

Scale 1 : 1 200 000

Scale 1 : 18 000 000

Lambert azimuthal equal-area projection

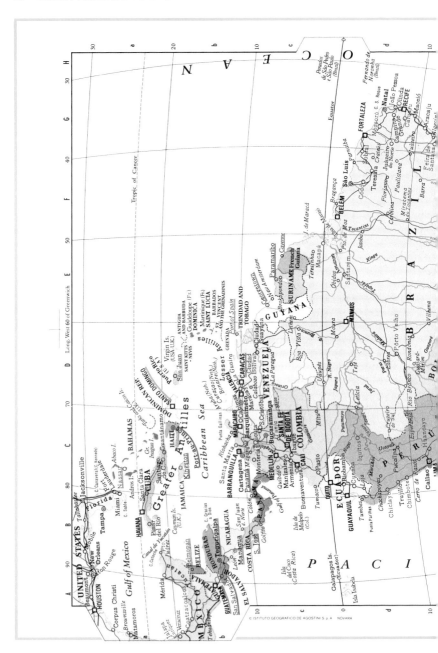

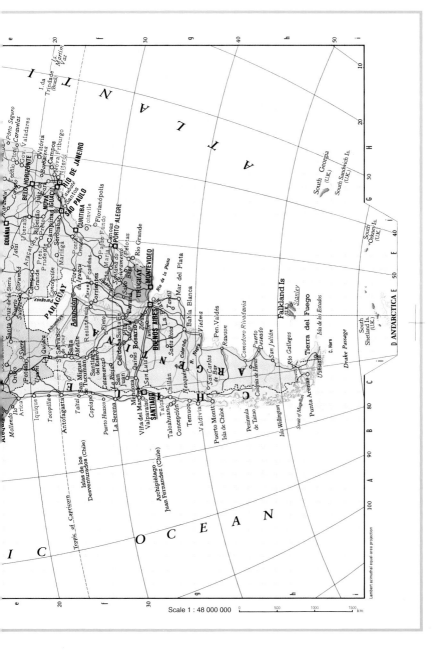

Scale 1 : 48 000 000

Lambert azimuthal equal-area projection

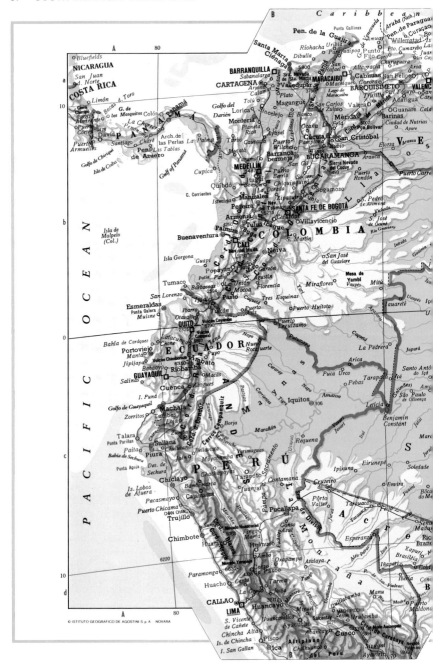

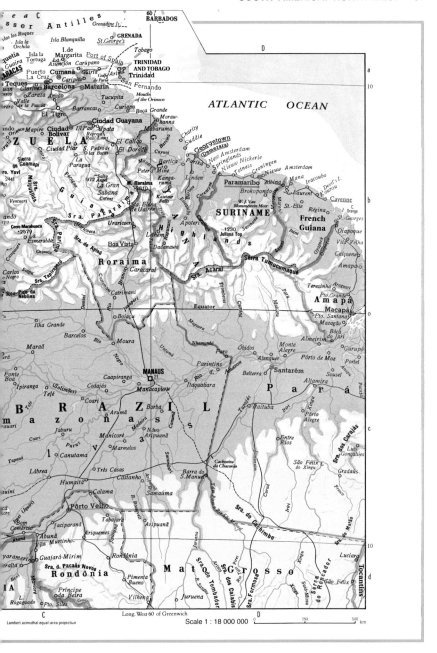

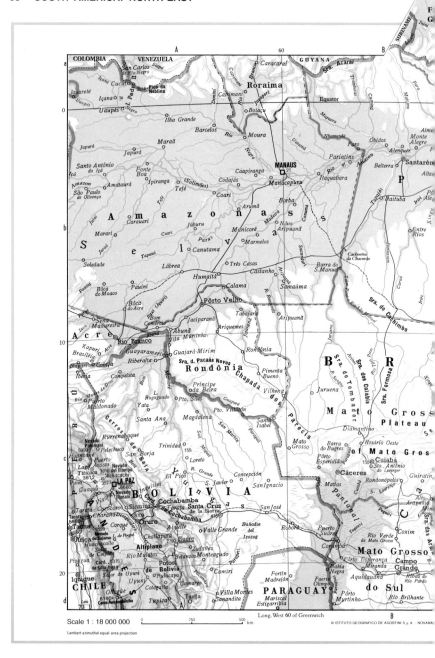

Scale 1 : 18 000 000

0   250   500 km

Lambert azimuthal equal-area projection

Long. West 60 of Greenwich

© ISTITUTO GEOGRAFICO DE AGOSTINI S.p.A.   NOVARA

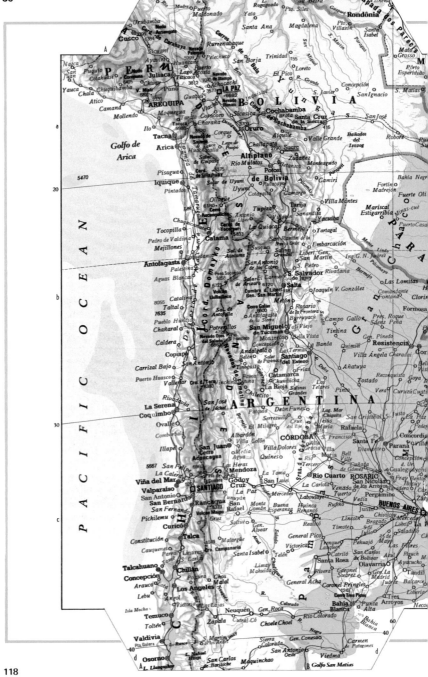

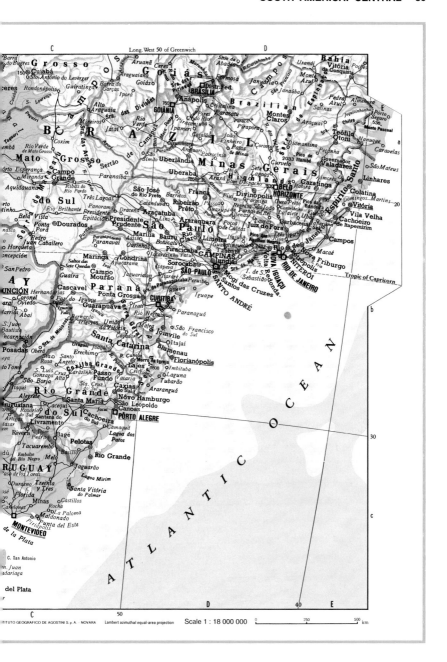

Long. West 50 of Greenwich

SOUTH AMERICA: CENTRAL

Barra do Bugres Grosso Aruanã João de Corinhanha Bahia
1500 Cuiabá Sítio da Abade Urandi Vitória da Conquista Poções
Stos. Antônio do Leverger Araguaiana Goiás Formosa Januário São Francisco Monte Azul
ceres Rondonópolis Barra do Garças Iporá Distr. Fed. Pedra Almenara Porto Seguro
Alto IBRASÍLIA São Januária Azul Jequitinhonha Monte Pascoal
Araguaia das Divisas Anápolis Brazilian Teófilo Caravelas
BRAZIL GOIÂNIA Paracatu Montes Claros de Araguari Otoni Nanuque
Rio Verde Pirapora Diamantina Teçanha Governador Valadares São Mateus
Coxim Simão Uberlândia Minas Gerais HORIZONTE Espírito Colatina
Mato Grosso Sertão Uberaba Araxá Bom Despacho BELO Itabira Vitória
do Sul Campo Grande Paranaíba São José do Rio Preto França Divinópolis Barbacena Vila Velha
Aquidauana Miranda Três Lagoas Barretos Passos Furnas Juiz de Fora Rio de Janeiro Campos
Rio Pardo Ribeirão Prêto São João Macaé
Presidente Araraquara Poços de Caldas NOVA Nova Friburgo
Dourados Prudente São Paulo Limeira IGUAÇU NITERÓI
Pôrto Marília Bauru Paulo Piracicaba CAMPINAS RIO DE JANEIRO
Paranavaí Assis Londrina Sorocaba SÃO PAULO I. de S. Tropic of Capricorn
Maringá Campo Mourão Paraná Santos Sebastião
Cascavel Ponta Grossa SANTO ANDRÉ
Guarapuava CURITIBA
Paranaguá
Guaíra
Santa Catarina São Francisco do Sul
Joinvile
Itajaí
Blumenau
Florianópolis
Lajes Imbituba
Laguna
Caxias Tubarão
Passo Fundo do Sul
Araranguá
Rio Grande Nôvo Hamburgo
Santa Maria São Leopoldo
do Sul Cachoeira PÔRTO ALEGRE
Bagé Pelotas Lagoa dos Patos
Tacuarembó Rio Grande
RUGUAY Melo Jaguarão
URUGUAY Lagoa Mirim
Treinta y Tres Santa Vitória do Palmar
Minas Rocha
MONTEVIDEO La Paloma
Maldonado
Punta del Este
de la Plata

ATLANTIC OCEAN

C. San Antonio

del Plata

ISTITUTO GEOGRAFICO DE AGOSTINI S.p.A. · NOVARA   Lambert azimuthal equal-area projection   Scale 1 : 18 000 000   0   250   500 km

Scale 1 : 18 000 000

0   250   500 km

Lambert azimuthal equal-area projection

C   50   D   40   E

URUGUAY
Florida
Minas
Santa Vitória do Palmar
Castillos
Rocha
La Paloma
Maldonado
Punta del Este
Piriápolis
MONTEVIDEO
de la Plata

C. San Antonio
n. Juan
adariaga

del Plata

a

A T L A N T I C

40

O C E A N

b

6100

50

Shag Rocks

c

Grytviken
South Georgia
(U.K.)
Mount Paget 2934

7750

C   Longitude West 50 of Greenwich   D   40   E   30

© ISTITUTO GEOGRAFICO DE AGOSTINI S.p.A. - NOVARA

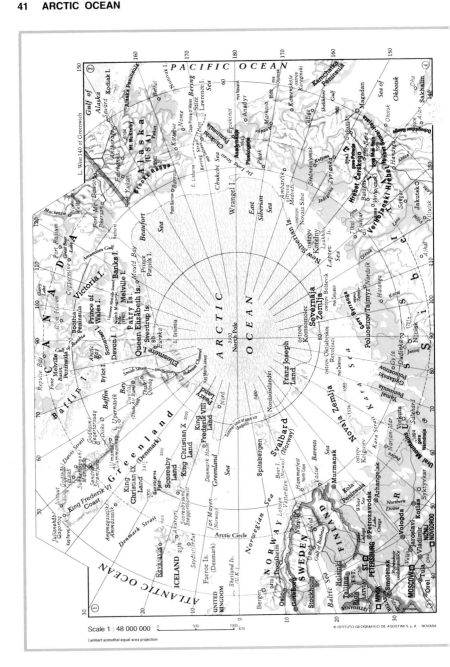

Scale 1 : 48 000 000

Lambert azimuthal equal-area projection

© ISTITUTO GEOGRAFICO DE AGOSTINI S.p.A. NOVARA

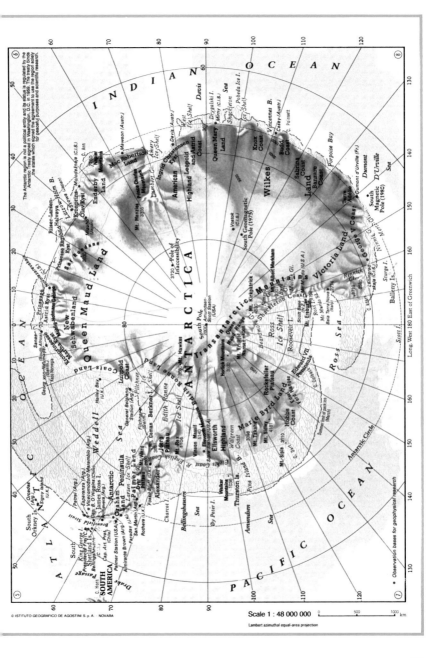

Scale 1 : 48 000 000

Lambert azimuthal equal-area projection

© ISTITUTO GEOGRAFICO DE AGOSTINI S.p.A. NOVARA

INDEX

Abbreviations used in the index

at.	atoll
Aut. Reg.	Autonomous Region
Aut. Rep.	Autonomous Republic
b.	bay
c.	cave
can.	canal
cap.	cape
co.	County
Dep.	Dependency, Colony
des.	desert
g.	gulf
gl.	glacier
hist. reg.	historical region
i.	island
Ind. St.	Independent State
is.	islands
l.	lake
lag.	lagoon
mt.	mountain
mts.	mountains
p.	pass
pen.	peninsula
phys. reg.	physical region
plat.	plateau, upland
prov.	Province
r.	ruins
reg.	Region
res.	reservoir
rf.	reef
riv.	river
riv. m.	river mouth
sal. l.	salt lake
sc. stat.	scientific station
s. m.	salt marsh
str.	strait
sw.	swamp, marsh
v.	valley
volc.	volcano
w.	wadi
wf.	waterfall

Ak.-U.S.	Alaska, U.S.	I.C.	Ivory Coast	Nor.	Norway
Al.-U.S.	Alabama, U.S.	Id.-U.S.	Idaho, U.S.	Nv.-U.S.	Nevada, U.S.
Alta.-Can.	Alberta, Canada	Il.-U.S.	Illinois, U.S.	N.Y.-U.S.	New York, U.S.
Ant.	Antarctica	In.-U.S.	Indiana, U.S.	N.Z.	New Zealand
Ar.-U.S.	Arkansas, U.S.	Indon.	Indonesia	Oh.-U.S.	Ohio, U.S.
Arg.	Argentina	Ire.	Ireland	Ont.-Can.	Ontario, Canada
Atg.	Antigua and	It.	Italy	Or.-U.S.	Oregon, U.S.
	Barbuda	Jam.	Jamaica	Pa.-U.S.	Pennsylvania, U.S.
Aus.	Austria	Jap.	Japan	Pak.	Pakistan
Austl.	Australia	Jor.	Jordan	Pan.	Panama
Az.-U.S.	Arizona, U.S.	Kaz.	Kazakhstan	Par.	Paraguay
Bah.	Bahamas	Ky.-U.S.	Kentucky, U.S.	Phil.	Philippines
Bel.	Belgium	Kyrg.	Kyrgyzstan	Pol.	Poland
Bela.	Belarus	La.-U.S.	Louisiana, U.S.	Port.	Portugal
Bngl.	Bangladesh	Lbr.	Liberia	Reu.	Reunion
Bol.	Bolivia	Leb.	Lebanon	Rom.	Romania
Braz.	Brazil	Lib.	Libya	S. Afr.	South Africa
Bul.	Bulgaria	Ma.-U.S.	Massachusetts, U.S.	S. Amer.	South America
Ca.-U.S.	California, U.S.	Mala.	Malaysia	S.C.-U.S.	South Carolina,
Can.	Canada	Me.-U.S.	Maine, U.S.		U.S.
C.A.R.	Central African	Mex.	Mexico	Scot.-U.K.	Scotland, U.K.
	Republic	Mi.-U.S.	Michigan, U.S.	S.D.-U.S.	South Dakota,
Cay. Is.	Cayman Islands	Mn.-U.S.	Minnesota, U.S.		U.S.
Co.-U.S.	Colorado, U.S.	Mo.-U.S.	Missouri, U.S.	Sp.	Spain
Col.	Colombia	Mold.	Moldova	Sud.	Sudan
C.R.	Costa Rica	Moz.	Mozambique	Sur.	Suriname
Cyp.	Cyprus	Ms.-U.S.	Mississippi, U.S.	Swe.	Sweden
Czech Rep.	Czech Republic	Mt.-U.S.	Montana, U.S.	Tn.-U.S.	Tennessee, U.S.
De.-U.S.	Delaware, U.S.	Mtna.	Mauritania	Trin.	Trinidad and
Dom. Rep.	Dominican	Mya.	Myanmar (Burma)		Tobago
	Republic	N. Amer.	North America	Tun.	Tunisia
Ec.	Ecuador	Nb.-U.S.	Nebraska, U.S.	Tur.	Turkey
Eg.	Egypt	N.B.-Can.	New Brunswick,	Tx.-U.S.	Texas, U.S.
El Sal.	El Salvador		Canada	U.K.	United Kingdom
Eng.-U.K.	England, U.K.	N.C.-U.S.	North Carolina,	Ukr.	Ukraine
Eth.	Ethiopia		U.S.	Ur.	Uruguay
Fl.-U.S.	Florida, U.S.	N.D.-U.S.	North Dakota, U.S.	U.S.	United States
Fr.	France	Nep.	Nepal	Va.-U.S.	Virginia, U.S.
Fr. Gui.	French Guiana	Neth.	Netherlands	Ven.	Venezuela
Fr. Poly.	French Polynesia	Newf.-Can.	Newfoundland,	Vt.-U.S.	Vermont, U.S.
Ga.-U.S.	Georgia, U.S.		Canada	Wa.-U.S.	Washington,
Ger.	Germany	N.H.-U.S.	New Hampshire,		U.S.
Grc.	Greece		U.S.	Wi.-U.S.	Wisconsin, U.S.
Guat.	Guatemala	Nic.	Nicaragua	W.V.-U.S.	West Virginia,
Hi.-U.S.	Hawaii, U.S.	Nig.	Nigeria		U.S.
H.K.	Hong Kong	N.Ire.-U.K.	Northern Ireland,	Wy.-U.S.	Wyoming, U.S.
Hond.	Honduras		U.K.	Yugo.	Yugoslavia
Ia.-U.S.	Iowa, U.S.	N.M.-U.S.	New Mexico, U.S.	Zimb.	Zimbabwe

A

Alakol, ozero– (l.) **13** He
Alakurtti **4** Gb
Alamagan Island **27** Cb
Alamein, El– **22** Bg
Alamogordo **33** Cc
Álamos **34** Bb
Alamos, Los– **33** Cc
Alamosa **33** Cc
Åland / Ahvenanmaa (is.) **4** DEc
Ålandshav (g.) **4** Dcd
Alanya **22** CDd
Alaotra, Farihy– **26** map no.1
Alapajevsk **13** Fd
Alaşehir **22** Bc
Alaska (State) **30** CDc
Alaska, Gulf of– **41** grid square no.2
Alaska Peninsula **41** grid square no.2
Alassio **10** Bbc
Alatri **10** Dd
Alatyr **13** Dd
Alavus **4** Ec
Alba **10** Bb
Albacete **9** DEc
Alba Iulia **6** Fcd
Albania (Ind. St.) **3** EFc
Albany (riv.) **31** Db
Albany [Austl.] **29** Bef
Albany [Ga.–U.S.] **32** Cb
Albany [N.Y.–U.S.] **32** Da
Albany [Or.–U.S.] **33** Ab
Albardón **39** Bc
Albarracin, Sierra de– (mts.) **9** Eb
Albatross Bay **29** Ga
Albenga **10** Bb
Alberche (riv.) **9** Cb
Albergaria–a–Velha **9** ABb
Albert, Lake– **25** Dd
Alberta (prov.) **31** Dc
Albert Markham, Mount– **42** grid square no.4
Albert Nile (riv.) **26** Ca
Albertville **8** FGe
Albi **8** Ef
Albina **37** Db
Albino **10** Bb
Ålborg **4** Bd
Albufeira **9** Ad
Albuquerque **33** Cc
Alburquerque **9** Bc
Albury **29** Hf
Alcalá de Chivert **9** EFb
Alcalá de Guadaira **9** Cd
Alcalá de Henares **9** Db
Alcalá la Real **9** Dd
Alcamo **10** Df
Alcañiz **9** EFb
Alcântara **38** Cb
Alcántara **9** Bc
Alcaraz, Sierra de– (mts.) **9** Dc
Alcarria, La– (hist. reg.) **9** Db
Alcázar de San Juan **9** Dc
Alčeusk **12** EFd
Alcira **9** Ec
Alcoy **9** Ec
Alcudia **9** Gc
Aldabra Islands **23** Gf
Aldan **14** Fd
Aldan (riv.) **14** Gc

Alderney (i.) **8** Bc
Aleg **24** Ac
Alegrete **39** Cb
Alejsk **13** Hd
Aleksandrov **12** EFb
Aleksandrov Gaj **13** DEde
Aleksandrovsk–Sahalinsk **14** Hd
Aleksandry, Zemlja– **13** CDa
Aleksin **12** Ec
Aleksinac **6** EFe
Alençon **8** Dc
Alenquer **38** Bb
Alentejo (phys. reg.) **9** ABcd
Alenuihaha Channel **28** map no.1
Aleppo **21** Bb
Aléria **8** map no.1
Alés **8** EFe
Alessandria **10** Bb
Ålesund **4** Ac
Aleutians Islands **30** Bd
Alexander Archipelago **31** Bc
Alexanderbaai **26** Ad
Alexander Island **42** grid square no.1
Alexandria [Austl.] **29** Fb
Alexandria [Eg.] **25** Ca
Alexandria [La.–U.S.] **32** Bb
Alexandria [Rom.] **6** Gde
Alexandria [S. Afr.] **26** Be
Alexandroúpolis **11** Fc
Alfambra **9** Eb
Alfenas **39** Db
Alföld (phys. reg.) **6** DEc
Alga **12** Id
Algarve (phys. reg.) **9** ABd
Algeciras **9** Cd
Algemesí **9** Ec
Algena **25** Dc
Algeria (Ind. St.) **23** Cbc
Alghero **10** Bd
Algiers **24** Ca
Al Harüj–al Aswad (mts.) **24** Db
Aliákmön (riv.) **11** DEcd
Alibunar **6** Ed
Alicante **9** EFc
Alice **32** Bc
Alice, Punta– (cap.) **10** Fe
Alice Springs **29** EFc
Alicudi (i.) **10** Ee
Aligarh **20** Ec
Aliwal North **26** Be
Aljustrel **9** Ad
Alkmaar **8** Fa
Al Kuwait **21** Dd
Allahabad **15** Cg
Allah–Jun **14** GHc
Allariz **9** ABa
Allegheny Mountains **32** CDab
Allen, Lake– **7** Bd
Allentown **32** Da
Alleppey **20** Eg
Aller (riv.) **5** BCb
Alliance **33** Cb
Allier (riv.) **8** Ee
Alloa **7** DEc
Alluitsup Paa / Sydprøven **31** Kb
Alma–Ata **13** Ge
Almada **9** Ac

Almadén **9** Cc
Almalyk **13** Fe
Almansa **9** Ec
Almanzor, Pico de– (mts.) **9** Cb
Almas, Rio das– (riv.) **39** Da
Almazán **9** Db
Almeirim **38** Bb
Almelo **8** Ga
Almenara **39** DEa
Almendralejo **9** BCc
Almería **9** Dd
Almería, Golfo de– **9** DEd
Almetjevsk **13** Fe
Älmhult **4** Cd
Almirante **35** Bc
Almirante Brown **42** grid square no.1
Almirós **11** Ed
Almorox **9** Cb
Almuñécar **9** Dd
Alofi **28** Ac
Alonnisos (i.) **11** EFd
Alor, Pulau– (i.) **18** FGf
Álora **9** Cd
Alor Setar **19** CDg
Alpena **32** Ca
Alpes Maritimes **10** Ab
Alpha **29** Hc
Alpi Carniche **10** Da
Alpi Cozie **10** Ab
Alpi Graie **10** Ab
Alpine **33** Cc
Alpi Retiche **10** BCa
Als (i.) **5** Ba
Alsace (hist. reg.) **8** Gcd
Alsasua **9** DEa
Alta **4** Ea
Altafjord (g.) **4** Ea
Alta Gracia **39** Bc
Altagracia **37** Ba
Altaj **14** Ce
Altaj (mts.) **13** Hde
Altamira **38** Bb
Altamura **10** Fd
Altata **34** Bb
Altay **13** He
Altdorf **10** Ba
Altenburg **5** Dc
Altinova **22** Ac
Alto Araguaia **38** Bc
Alton **32** BCb
Altoona **32** Da
Alto Parnaíba **38** Cb
Altos **38** Cb
Altun Shan (mts.) **20** FGb
Altus **33** CDc
Alvand, Kü– e– (mt.) **21** Dc
Alvdalen **4** Cc
Älvkarleby **4** Dc
Älvsbyn **4** Eb
Alwar **20** Ec
Alyangula **29** Fa
Alytus **4** EFe
Alzamaj **14** CDd
Amadeus, Lake– **29** Ecd
Amadi **25** Dd
Amadjuak Lake **31** Hlb
Amador, Fort– **35** map no.1
Amagasaki **16** Hlcd
Amahai **18** Ge
Amakusa–Nada **17** Ah
Amakusa–Shotō **17** Ah

Åmål **4** Cd
Amaliás **11** De
Amami–Shotō (is.) **16** GHe
Amanave **28** map no.5
Amanus Mountains **22** EFd
Amapá (State) **38** Ba
Amapá **38** Ba
'Amārah, Al– **21** Dc
Amarante **38** Cb
Amarillo **33** Cc
Amasra **22** CDb
Amasya **22** EFb
Amataurá **37** Cc
Amazon (riv.) **38** Bb
Amazon, Mouths of the– **38** Ca
Amazonas (State) **37** CDc
Ambala **15** Cf
Ambalavao **26** map no.1
Ambam **24** Dd
Ambarčik **14** Jc
Ambato **37** Bc
Ambatondrazaka **23** GHg
Ambelau, Pulau– (i.) **18** Ge
Amberg **5** CDd
Ambès **8** Ce
Ambikapur **20** Fd
Ambilobe **26** map no.1
Amble **7** Fd
Ambo **37** Bcd
Ambodifototra **26** map no.1
Ambohimahasoa **26** map no.1
Ambon **18** Ge
Ambositra **26** map no.1
Ambovombe **26** map no.1
Ambre, Cap d'– **23** GHg
Ambriz **26** Ab
Ambrym, Île– (i.) **28** map no.4
Amderma **13** Fbc
American Highland **42** grid square no.2
American Samoa (is.) **28** map no.5
Amersfoort **8** FGa
Amery Ice Shelf **42** grid square no.2
Ames **32** Cb
Amfilokhia **11** Dd
Ámfissa **11** DEd
Amga (riv.) **14** Fd
Amga **14** Gc
Amgu **17** Eb
Amgun (riv.) **14** Gd
Amherst **32** Da
Amiata, Monte– **10** Cc
Amiens **8** DEc
Amik Gölü **22** Fd
Amíndivi Islands **20** Df
Amirante Islands **15** Bj
'Āmiriyah, Al– **22** Bj
Amlekhganj **19** Ij
'Ammān **22** Fg
Ammassalik / Angmagssalik **30** Oc
Ammersee **5** Cde
Amnok–Kang (riv.) **16** FGb
Amorgós (i.) **11** FGe
Ampanihy **26** map no.1
Amposta **9** Fb
'Amran **21** Cf
Amrāvati **20** Ed
Amritsar **15** Cf

Arcos de la Frontera **9** BCd
Arctic Bay **31** Ga
Arda (riv.) **11** Fc
Ardabīl **21** Db
Ardakān **21** Ec
Ardatov **12** Gc
Arderin (mt.) **7** BCe
Ardestän **21** Ec
Ardmore **32** Bb
Ardrossan **7** Dd
Arecibo **35** Db
Areia Branca **38** Db
Arendal **4** Bd
Arequipa **39** Aa
Arévalo **9** Cb
Arezzo **10** Cc
Argens (riv.) **8** Gf
Argentan **8** CDc
Argentat **8** Ee
Argenteuil **8** Ec
Argentina (Ind. St.) **36** Dgh
Argentino, Lago– **40** Abc
Argenton–sur–Creuse **8** Dd
Argeş (riv.) **6** GHd
Arghandab (riv.) **20** Cb
Argolis, Gulf of– **11** Ee
Argonne (mts.) **8** Fc
Árgos **11** Ee
Argostólion **11** Dd
Argun (riv.) **16** Ea
Århus **4** Bd
Ariano Irpino **10** Ed
Arica [Chile] **39** Aa
Arica [Col.] **37** Bc
Arica, Golfo de– **39** Aa
Arid, Cape– **29** Ce
Ariège (riv.) **8** Df
Arima **37** Ca
Arinos (riv.) **38** Bc
Aripuanã (riv.) **37** CDc
Aripuanã **37** CDc
Ariquemes **37** Ccd
'Arîsh, Al– **25** Da
'Arish, Wâdî al– (riv.) **22** Dgh
Arizaro, Salar de– (s. m.) **39** Bb
Arizona (State) **33** Bc
Arjeplog **4** Db
Arjona **37** Bab
Arkadak **12** Fc
Arkalyk **13** Fde
Arkansas (riv.) **33** Cc
Arkansas (State) **32** Bb
Arkansas City **32** Bb
Arklow **7** CDe
Arkona, Kap– **5** Da
Arkonam **20** EFf
Arkticeskoga Instituta, ostrova– **13** GHb
Arlberg (p.) **5** Ce
Arles **8** Ff
Arlon **8** Fc
Armagh **7** Cd
Armagnac (hist. reg.) **8** Df
Armavir **13** De
Armenia **37** Bb
Armenia (Ind. St.) **13** Def
Armentières **8** Ec
Armidale **29** Ie
Armu (riv.) **17** DEab
Arnauti, Akra– **22** CDe

Arnedillo **9** DEa
Arnhem **8** FGb
Arnhem, Cape– **29** Fa
Arnhem Land **29** Ea
Arno (riv.) **10** Cc
Arnøy (i.) **4** DEa
Arnsberg **5** Bc
Arnstadt **5** Cc
Aroa **37** Ca
Aroab **26** ABd
Arorae Island **27** Dc
Är–Rachidiya **24** Ba
Arrah **20** Fc
Arraias **38** Cc
Arraiján **35** map no.1
Arran, Island of– **7** Dd
Arras **8** Eb
Arrée, Monts d'– (mts.) **8** ABc
Arsenjev **14** Ge
Arsenjevka (riv.) **17** Cbc
Arsuk **31** JKb
Art (i.) **28** map no.4
Árta **11** Dd
Artá **9** Gc
Artawiyah, Al– **21** Dd
Artem **14** Ge
Artemisa **35** Ba
Artemovsk [Russia] **14** Cd
Artemovsk [Ukr.] **12** Ed
Artemovski [Russia] **12** Jb
Artemovski [Russia] **14** Ed
Artic Ocean **41** grid square no.4
Artigas **39** Cc
Artois (hist. reg.) **8** DEb
Aru, Kepulauan– **27** Bc
Arua **26** Ca
Aruanã **39** CDa
Aruba (i.) **37** Ca
Arumã **37** Cc
Arunachal Pradesh (State) **19** BCc
Arusha **26** Cb
Aruwimi (riv.) **26** Ba
Arvida **31** Hd
Arvidsjaur **4** Db
Arvika **4** Cd
Arys **13** Fe
Arzamas **13** Dd
Arzgir **12** Fd
Aša **12** Ib
Asadābād **20** CDab
Asahikawa **16** Jb
Asamankese **24** Bd
Asansol **20** Gd
Asbest **13** Fd
Ascension (i.) **23** Af
Aschaffenburg **5** Bd
Ascó **9** Fb
Ascoli Piceno **10** Dc
Aseb **25** Ec
Åsele **4** Db
Asenovgrad **11** Fbc
Ašgabat (Ašhabad) **15** Bf
Ašhabad → Ašgabat **15** Bf
Ashburton River **29** Bc
Asheville **32** Cb
Ashibetsu **16** Jb
Ashikaga **16** Ic
Ashington **7** EFd
Ashizuri–Misaki **17** Ch
Ashkharah, Al– **21** FGe
Ashland [Ky.–U.S.] **32** Cb

Ashland [Wi.–U.S.] **32** BCa
Ashmün **22** Cg
Ashqelon **22** Eg
Ashuanipi **31** Ic
Asinara **10** Bd
Asinara, Golfo dell'– **10** Bd
Asino **13** Hd
'Asīr (hist. reg.) **21** Cef
Asker **4** Bd
Askersund **4** Cd
Askja (mt.) **4** map no.1
Asmara **25** Dc
Asnam, El– **24** BCa
Asosa **25** Dcd
Aso–San (mt.) **17** Bh
Asoteriba, Jabal– (mt.) **25** Db
Aspres–sur–Buëch **8** Fe
Aspromonte (mts.) **10** Ee
Assam (State) **19** BCc
Assen **8** Ga
Assens **5** BCa
Assiniboia **33** Cb
Assiniboine (riv.) **33** Cab
Assis **39** Cb
Assisi **10** Dc
Astakós **11** Dd
Astara **21** Db
Asti **10** Bb
Astipálata (i.) **11** Ge
Astorga **9** BCa
Astoria **33** Ab
Astrahan **13** De
Asturias (phys. reg.) **9** BCa
Asunción **39** Cb
Asunción, La– **37** Ca
Aswän **25** Db
Asyūt **25** CDb
Atacama, Desierto de– **39** ABb
Atacama, Salar de– (sal. l.) **39** Bb
Atafu Atoll **28** Ac
Ata Island **28** Ad
Atakpamé **24** Cd
Atalándi **11** Ed
Atalaya **37** Bd
Atami **17** Fg
Ataqa, Jabal– (mt.) **25** map no.1
Atar **24** Ac
Atasu **13** Ge
Atauat, Phou– (mt.) **19** Ee
Atauro, Pulau– (i.) **18** Gf
Atáviros (mt.) **11** GHe
'Aţbarah **25** Dc
'Aţbarah (riv.) **25** Dc
Atbasar **13** Fd
Atchinson **32** Bb
Aterau (Gurjev) **13** DEe
Atessa **10** Ec
Athabasca (riv.) **31** Dc
Athabasca **31** Dc
Athabasca, Lake– **31** Ec
Athenry **7** Be
Athens [Ga.–U.S.] **32** Cb
Athens [Grc.] **11** EFe
Atherton **29** GHb
Athi Galana **26** Cb
Athlone **7** BCe
Athos (mt.) **11** Fc
Ati **25** Bc
Atico **39** Aa
Atikokan **32** Ba

Atiu (i.) **28** Bcd
Atka **14** Ic
Atkarsk **12** FGc
Atlanta **32** Cb
Atlantic City **32** Db
Atlantic Ocean **2**
Atlin, Lake– **31** Bc
Atlixco **34** Cc
Atoyac, Río– (riv.) **34** Cc
Atoyac de Álvarez **34** Bc
Atrato (riv.) **37** Bb
Atrek (riv.) **21** Fb
'Aţrun, Al– **25** Cc
Atsumi **17** Fe
Attapu **19** Eef
Attawapiskat (riv.) **31** Db
Attica (hist. reg.) **11** Ed
Atuel (riv.) **39** Bc
Aubagne **8** FGf
Aube (riv.) **8** Fd
Aubenas **8** Fe
Aubrac, Monts d'– (mts.) **8** Ee
Aubusson **8** Ee
Aucanquilcha, Cerro– (mt.) **39** Bb
Auch **8** Df
Auckland **27** Dd
Auckland Islands **27** De
Auckland Peninsula **27** Dd
Aude (riv.) **8** Ef
Audincourt **8** Gd
Aue **5** Dc
Augathella **29** Hd
Augila **24** Eb
Augsburg **5** Cd
Augusta [Austl.] **29** ABe
Augusta [Ga.–U.S.] **32** Cb
Augusta [It.] **10** Ef
Augusta [Me.–U.S.] **32** Ea
Augustów **5** Ib
Augustus, Mount– **29** Bc
Auki **27** Dc
Auld, Lake– **29** Cc
Aumale **8** Dc
Aunis (hist. reg.) **8** Cd
Aurangabad **20** DEde
Aur Atoll **27** Db
Aurillac **8** Ee
Aus **26** Ad
Ausangate, Nudo– (mt.) **39** ABa
Austin [Mn.–U.S.] **32** Ba
Austin [Nv.–U.S.] **33** Bc
Austin [Tx.–U.S.] **32** Bb
Austin, Lake– **29** Bd
Australia (Ind. St.) **29** CGd
Australian Alps **29** Hf
Australian Capital Territory (State) **29** Hf
Australian Capital Territory → A.C.T. **29** Hf
Austria (Ind. St.) **3** Ec
Austvågøy (i.) **4** Ca
Autlán de Navarro **34** Bc
Autun **8** EFd
Auvergne (hist. reg.) **8** Ee
Auxerre **8** Ee
Avallon **8** EFd
Avalon Peninsula **31** JKd
Avanos **22** Ec
Avarua **28** Bd
Aveiro **9** Ab
Avellino **10** Ed

Bandiagara 24 Bc
Bandikui 19 Gi
Bandırma 22 ABb
Bandundu 26 Ab
Bandundu (reg.) 26 ABb
Bandung 15 Dj
Băneasa 6 Hd
Banes 35 Ca
Bañeza, La– 9 BCa
Banff [Can.] 31 Dc
Banff [U.K.] 7 Ec
Bangalore 15 Ch
Bangassou 25 Cd
Banggai (i.) 18 Fe
Banggai, Kepulauan– 18 Fe
Banggi, Pulau– (i.) 18 Ec
Bangil 18 Df
Bangka, Pulau– [Indon.] (i.)
  18 FGd
Bangka, Pulau– [Indon.] (i.)
  18 Ce
Bangkalan 18 Df
Bangkinang 18 ABd
Bangko 18 Be
Bangkok 15 Dh
Bangladesh (Ind. St.) 15 CDg
Bangor [N. Ire.–U.K.] 7 Dd
Bangor [U.S.] 32 DEa
Bangor [Wales–U.K.] 7 DEe
Bangriposi 19 Ik
Bangued 18 Fa
Bangui [C.A.R.] 25 Bd
Bangui [Phil.] 18 EFa
Bangweulu, Lake– 26 BCc
Banhã 22 Cg
Banī (riv.) 24 Bc
Banī Suwayf 25 Db
Banī Walīd 24 Da
Bāniyās 22 EFe
Banja Luka 6 Cd
Banjarmasin 18 De
Banjul 24 Ac
Banks, Îles– 28 map no.4
Banks Island 31 CDa
Banks Strait 29 map no.1
Bankura 20 Gd
Ban Mae Sariang 19 Ce
Bann (riv.) 7 Cd
Bannu 20 CDb
Banská Bystrica 5 GHd
Banská Stiavnica 5 Gd
Bansko 11 Ec
Bantaeng 18 Ef
Bantry 7 Bf
Bantry Bay 7 ABf
Banyak Islands 18 Ad
Banyuwangi 18 Df
Banzare Coast 42 grid square
  no.4
Bao'an 16 Df
Baoding 16 DEc
Baoji 15 Df
Baoshan 19 Ccd
Baotou 16 CDb
Baquedano 39 Bb
Bar [Ukr.] 6 Hb
Bar [Yugo.] 11 Cb
Baraawe 25 Ed
Barabinsk 13 GHd
Baracaldo 9 Da
Baracoa 35 Ca
Baradero 39 BCc
Bărăganului, Cîmpia– 6 Hd

Barahona 35 Cb
Baraka (riv.) 25 Dc
Baraki 20 Cb
Baramula 20 DEb
Baranof Island 31 Bc
Baranoviči 13 Bd
Barat Daya, Kepulauan– 18
  Gf
Barbacena 39 Db
Barbacoas 37 Bb
Barbados (i.) 35 Db
Barbados (Ind. St.) 30 Lh
Barbar 25 Dc
Barbas, Cabo– 24 Ab
Barbastro 9 Fa
Barbezieux 8 CDe
Barbuda (i.) 35 Db
Barcaldine 29 GHc
Barce → Al Marj 24 DEa
Barcellona 10 Ee
Barcelona [Sp.] 9 Gb
Barcelona [Ven.] 37 Cab
Barcelonnette 8 FGe
Barcelos [Braz.] 37 Cc
Barcelos [Port.] 9 Ab
Barcoo River 29 Gcd
Barcs 6 Ccd
Bardaï 25 Bb
Bardawîl, Sabkhet el– (l.) 22
  Dg
Bardejov 5 Hd
Bardīyah 24 Ea
Bareeda 25 Fc
Bareilly 20 EFc
Barentsburg 13 Ab
Barents Sea 41 grid square
  no.3
Barentu 21 Bfg
Barfleur, Pointe de– (cap.) 8
  Cc
Barga 20 Fb
Barhi 20 Gd
Bari 10 Fd
Barīm 25 Ec
Barima (riv.) 37 Db
Baripada 19 Ik
Barisal 20 GHd
Barisan, Pegunungan– 18 Be
Barito (riv.) 18 Df
Barka 21 Fe
Barkam 16 Bd
Barkly Tableland 29 Fb
Barkol 14 Cf
Barla dağı (mt.) 22 Ccd
Bar–le–Duc 8 Fc
Barlee, Lake– 29 Bd
Barletta 10 Fd
Barmer 20 Dc
Barnaul 13 Hd
Barnstaple 7 Df
Baro 24 Cd
Barqah al Bahriyah (phys.
  reg.) 24 Ea
Barquisimeto 37 BCab
Barra 38 Cc
Barra (is.) 7 BCc
Barrackpur 19 Jk
Barra de Navidad 34 Bc
Barra do Bugres 39 Ca
Barra do Garças 39 Ca
Barra do São Manuel 38 Bb
Barra Head 7 BCc

Barrancabermeja 37 Bb
Barrancas 37 Cb
Barranquilla 36 Cb
Barreiras 38 Cc
Barreiro 9 Ac
Barreiros 38 Db
Barretos 39 Db
Barrie 31 GHd
Barrington Tops (mt.) 29 Ie
Barrow 30 CDb
Barrow (riv.) 7 Ce
Barrow, Point– 41 grid square
  no.2
Barrow Creek 29 Ec
Barrow–in–Furness 7 Ed
Barrow Island 29 ABc
Barruecopardo 9 Bb
Barry 7 Ef
Barsi 20 Ee
Barstow 33 Bc
Bar–sur–Aube 8 Fc
Barth 5 Da
Bartica 37 Db
Bartin 22 Db
Bartle Frere, Mount– 29 Hb
Bartoszyce 5 Ha
Barun–Urt 14 Ee
Barwon River 29 Hde
Baryš 12 Gc
Basankusu 25 BCd
Basel 5 Ae
Bashi Haixia (str.) 16 Ff
Bashkir (Aut. Rep.) 13 Ed
Basilan (i.) 18 Fc
Basilan City 18 Fc
Basilicata (reg.) 10 EFde
Basilio 39 Cc
Basoko 25 Cd
Basque Provinces (phys.
  reg.) 9 Da
Basra 21 Dc
Bass, Îlots de– 28 BCd
Bassano del Grappa 10 Cb
Bassein 15 Dh
Basseterre 35 Db
Bass Strait 29 map no.1
Bastak 21 EFd
Basti 19 Hj
Bastia 8 map no.1
Bastogne 8 FGbc
Basuto 26 Bc
Bas Zaïre (reg.) 26 Ab
Bata 24 CDd
Batabanó, Golfo de– 35 Ba
Batagaj 14 Gc
Batajsk 12 EFd
Batak 11 Fc
Batala 20 Eb
Batan (i.) 18 Fa
Batang 15 Df
Batanga 24 Ce
Batangafo 25 Bd
Batangas 18 EFb
Batanghari (riv.) 18 Be
Batan Islands 15 Eg
Batanta, Pulau– (i.) 18 GHe
Batchelor 29 Ea
Bătdâmbâng 19 Df
Bath 7 Ef
Bathinda 20 DEb
Bathurst [Austl.] 29 He
Bathurst [Can.] 31 Id
Bathurst, Cape– 31 BCa

Bathurst Inlet 31 DEb
Bathurst Island [Austl.] 29 Da
Bathurst Island [Can.] 30 Hlb
Bātin, Wādī al– 21 Dd
Batna 24 Ca
Baton Rouge 32 BCb
Batopilas 34 Bb
Batouri 24 Dd
Batrūn, Al– 22 Ee
Batticaloa 20 Fg
Battle Harbour 30 Md
Battonya 6 Ec
Batu, Kepulauan– 18 Ade
Batudaka, Pulau– (i.) 18 Fe
Batumi 21 Ca
Baturaja 18 BCe
Baturité 38 Db
Bau 18 Dd
Baubau 18 Ff
Bauchi 24 CDcd
Baudh 16 Cf
Bauld, Cape– 31 Jc
Baule–Escoublac, La– 8 Bd
Bauru 39 Db
Bautzen 5 Ec
Bavaria (State) 5 CDd
Bawean, Pulau– (i.) 18 Df
Bawiṭi, Al– 25 CDb
Bayamo 35 Ca
Bayamón 35 Db
Bayana 19 Gj
Bayan Har Shan (mts.) 16
  ABd
Bayan Obo 16 CDb
Bayawan 18 Fc
Baybay 18 FGb
Bayburt 21 Ca
Bay City [Mi.–U.S.] 32 Ca
Bay City [Tx.–U.S.] 32 Bc
Bayḍā', Al– 24 DEa
Bayerischer Wald (mts.) 5 Dd
Bayeux 8 Cc
Bayındır 22 Ac
Bayombong 18 Fa
Bayonne 8 Cf
Bayreuth 5 Ccd
Baza 9 Dd
Beagle, Canal– 40 Ac
Beal Range 29 Gcd
Ḟ ardmore Glacier 42 grid
  ,quare no.4
ear Island 41 grid square
  no.3
Béarn (hist. reg.) 8 Cf
Beas (riv.) 20 DEb
Beatrice 32 Ba
Beatty 33 Bc
Beauce (phys. reg.) 8 DEc
Beaudesert 29 Id
Beaufort 18 Ec
Beaufort Sea 41 grid square
  no.2
Beaufort West 26 Be
Beaujolais, Monts du– (mts.)
  8 Fde
Beaumont 32 Bb
Beaune 8 Fd
Beauvais 8 Ec
Beawar 20 Dc
Bečej 6 DEd
Béchar 24 Ba
Beckley 32 Cb
Bedford 7 FGe

Bed - Big

Bedourie **29** Fc
Be'er Sheva **22** Eg
Beeville **32** Bc
Befale **26** Ba
Bega **29** Hlf
Bègles **8** Ce
Behbahän **21** Ec
Behshahr **21** Eb
Beihai **16** Cf
Beijing (Peking) **16** Ebc
Beira (hist. reg.) **9** ABb
Beira **26** Cc
Beirut **22** Ef
Bei Shan (mts.) **16** Ab
Beitbridge **26** Cd
Beiuş **6** EFc
Beja **9** Bcd
Béjaïa **24** Ca
Béjar **9** Cb
Bejneu **13** Ee
Békés **6** Ec
Békéscsaba **6** Ec
Bekily **26** map no.1
Bela [India] **20** Fc
Bela [Pak.] **20** Cc
Bela Crkva **6** Ed
Belaja (riv.) **13** Ed
Bela Cerkov **6** IJb
Bel'an **16** Ga
Belarus (Ind. St.) **13** BCd
Bela Vista **39** Cb
Bel'c' **13** Be
Belcher Islands **31** GHc
Belebej **12** Hc
Beledweyne **25** Ed
Belém **38** Cb
Belen **33** Cc
Belén **39** Bb
Belene **11** Fb
Bélep, Iles– **27** Dc
Belev **12** Ec
Belfast **7** Dd
Belfort **8** Gd
Belgaum **20** De
Belgium (Ind. St.) **3** Db
Belgorod **13** Cd
Belgorod–Dnestrovski **6** IJc
Belgrade **6** Ed
Belgrade–Zemun **6** Ed
Bélinga **26** Aa
Belitung, Pulau– (i.) **15** Dj
Belize (Ind. St.) **30** Jh
Belize City **35** Bb
Belkovski, ostrov– **14** Gb
Bellac **8** Dd
Bellary **20** Eef
Bellavista **37** Bc
Bella Vista [Arg.] **39** Cb
Bella Vista [Arg.] **39** Bb
Belle Fourche **33** Cb
Bellegarde–sur–Valserine **8** FGde
Belle–Ile (i.) **8** Bd
Belle Isle (i.) **31** Jc
Belle Isle, Strait of– **31** IJcd
Belleville **31** Hd
Bellin (Payne Bay) **31** Hlbc
Bellingham **33** Ab
Bellingshausen **42** grid square no.1
Bellingshausen Sea **42** grid square no.1
Bellinzona **10** Ba

Belluno **10** Da
Bell Ville **39** Bc
Belmonte **38** Dc
Belmopan **35** Bb
Belo **26** map no.1
Belogorsk **14** FGd
Belo Horizonte **39** Dab
Beloje ozero **12** Ea
Belomorsk **13** Cc
Belopolje **12** DEc
Beloreck **13** EFd
Belovo **13** Hd
Belozersk **12** Eab
Belterra **38** Bb
Beluha, gora– (mt.) **13** Hde
Bely, ostrov– **13** FGb
Belyando River **29** Hc
Bely Jar **13** Hd
Bemidji **32** Ba
Benalla **29** Hf
Benares → Varanasi **20** Fcd
Benavente **9** BCab
Benbecula (i.) **7** BCc
Bend **33** Ab
Bender (Bendery) **6** Ic
Bender Beyla **25** Fd
Bendery → Bender **6** Ic
Bendigo **29** GHf
Benešov **5** Ed
Benevento **10** Ed
Bengal (phys. reg.) **20** Gd
Bengal, Bay of– **20** Gef
Bengasi **24** DEa
Bengbu **16** Ed
Bengkulu **18** Be
Benguela **23** Dg
Benguerir **24** Ba
Ben Hope (mt.) **7** Db
Beni (riv.) **37** Cd
Beni–Abbès **24** Bab
Benicarló **9** Fb
Benidorm **9** Fc
Benin (Ind. St.) **23** Cde
Benin, Bight of– **24** Cd
Benin City **24** Cd
Benjamin Constant **37** BCc
Ben Macdhui (mt.) **7** DEc
Ben More Assynt (mt.) **7** Db
Bennet, ostrov– **14** Hb
Ben Nevis (mt.) **7** Dc
Benoni **26** Bd
Bensheim **5** Bd
Benson **33** BCc
Bent **21** Fd
Benteng **18** Ff
Bentinck (i.) **19** Cf
Bentinck Island **29** FGb
Benue (riv.) **24** Cd
Benxi **16** Fb
Beppu **17** Bh
Berati **11** CDc
Berbera **25** Ec
Berberati **25** Bd
Berbice (riv.) **37** Db
Berchtesgaden **5** De
Berck–Plage **8** Db
Berčogur **12** Id
Berdičev **12** Ccd
Berdjansk **12** Ed
Beregomet **6** Gb
Beregovo **5** Id
Berenice (r.) **25** Db
Bereza **5** Jb

Berežany **6** Gb
Berezina (riv.) **12** Cc
Berezniki **13** Ed
Berezovka **12** Dd
Berezovo **13** Fc
Berga **9** Fa
Bergama (Pergamum) **22** Ac
Bergamo **10** Bb
Bergen **4** Ac
Bergen (Rügen) **5** Da
Bergerac **8** De
Berhampur **20** FGe
Beringa, ostrov– **14** Jd
Beringovski **14** Kc
Bering Sea **41** grid square no.2
Bering Strait **41** grid square no.2
Berit daği (mt.) **22** Fcd
Berja **9** Dd
Berkeley **33** Ac
Berkner Island **42** grid square no.1
Berkovica **11** Eb
Berlengas, Ilhas– **9** Ac
Berlin [Ger.] **5** DEb
Berlin [U.S.] **32** Da
Bermejo **39** Bb
Bermejo, Rio– [Arg.] (riv.) **39** Bbc
Bermejo, Rio– [Bol.] (riv.) **39** Bb
Bermeo **9** Da
Bermuda Islands **30** Lf
Bern **5** Ae
Bernalda **10** Fd
Bernardo de Irigoyen **39** Cb
Bernay **8** Dc
Bernburg **5** CDc
Berner Alpen **10** ABa
Bernina (mt.) **10** Ba
Beroroha **26** map no.1
Beroun **5** Ed
Berounka (riv.) **5** Dcd
Berre, Étang de– (sw.) **8** Ff
Berre–l'Étang **8** Ff
Berrouaghia **9** Gd
Berry (hist. reg.) **8** DEd
Berry, Canal de– **8** Ed
Bertolinia **38** Cb
Bertoua **24** Dd
Berwick–upon–Tweed **7** EFd
Besalampy **26** map no.1
Besançon **8** Gd
Beskidy Zachodnie (mts.) **5** GHd
Besna Kobila (mt.) **11** Eb
Besni **22** Fd
Bessarabia (phys. reg.) **6** Hlbc
Bessarabka **6** Ic
Bessemer **32** Cb
Betanzos [Bol.] **39** Ba
Betanzos [Sp.] **9** ABa
Bétaré Oya **24** Dd
Bethanien **26** Ad
Bethel **30** Bc
Bethlehem [Jor.] **22** Eg
Bethlehem [S. Afr.] **26** Bd
Béthune **8** Eb
Béticos, Sistema– (mts.) **9** CEcd
Betioky **26** map no.1

Betpak–Dala **13** FGe
Betroka **26** map no.1
Bet She'an **22** Ef
Betsiboka (riv.) **26** map no.1
Bettiah **19** Hlj
Bettyhill **7** Fe
Betul **20** Ed
Betwa (riv.) **20** Ec
Beverley [Austl.] **29** Be
Beverley [U.K.] **7** FGe
Beycuma **22** CDb
Bey daği (mt.) **22** EFc
Bey dağları (mts.) **22** BCd
Beyla **24** Bd
Beyoneisu–Retsugan **17** Fi
Beypazarı **22** CDb
Beyşehir **22** CDd
Beyşehir Gölü **22** Cd
Bežeck **12** Eb
Béziers **8** Ef
Bhabua **19** Hj
Bhadgaon **20** Gc
Bhadrak **20** Gd
Bhadravati **20** Ef
Bhagalpur **15** CDg
Bhamo **19** Cd
Bharatpur **20** Ec
Bharuch **20** Dd
Bhatpara **20** Gd
Bhavnagar **20** Dd
Bhawanipatna **20** Fe
Bheri (riv.) **19** Hi
Bhilai **20** Fd
Bhima (riv.) **20** DEe
Bhind **20** Ec
Bhiwani **19** Gi
Bhola (i.) **19** Jk
Bhopal **20** Ed
Bhubaneswar **20** FGde
Bhuj **20** Cd
Bhusawal **20** Ed
Bhutan (Ind. St.) **15** Dg
Biafra (phys. reg.) **24** Cd
Biafra, Bight of– **24** Ccd
Biak, Pulau– **27** Bc
Biała Podlaska **5** Ibc
Białobrzegi **5** Hc
Białogard **5** Fab
Białystok **5** Ib
Biarritz **8** Cf
Bibä **22** Ch
Bibai **17** Gc
Biberach an der Riss **5** BCde
Bicaz **6** GHc
Biçer **22** Cc
Bickerton Island **29** Fa
Bida **24** Cd
Bidar **20** Ee
Bideford **7** Df
Bidon 5 → Poste–Maurice–Cortier **24** Cb
Bié, Planalto do– **26** Ac
Biel **5** Ae
Bielawa **5** Fc
Bielefeld **5** Bbc
Biella **10** Bb
Bielsko–Biała **5** Gd
Bielsk Podlaski **5** Ib
Bien Hoa **19** Ef
Biga **22** Ab
Biğadiç **22** Bc
Biggar **33** Ca
Bighorn (riv.) **33** Cb

Bighorn Mountains **33** Cb
Big Island **31** Hb
Big River **31** Ec
Big Spring **33** Cc
Bihać **6** Bd
Bihar (State) **20** FGc
Bihar **20** Gcd
Biharamulo **26** Cb
Bihoro **17** Ic
Bija (riv.) **13** Hd
Bijagos Islands **24** Ac
Bijapur **20** Ee
Bijauri **19** Hi
Bijeljina **6** Dd
Bijie **16** Ce
Bijsk **13** Hd
Bikaner **20** Dc
Bikin (riv.) **16** HIa
Bikin **14** Ge
Bikini Atoll **27** Db
Bikljan **12** Hb
Bikoro **26** Ab
Bilaspur **20** Fd
Bilauktaung Range **19** Cf
Bilbao **9** Da
Bilbays **22** Cg
Bileća **11** Cb
Bilecik **22** BCb
Bilė Karpaty (mts.) **5** FGd
Bilin **19** Ce
Billings **33** Cb
Bill of Portland **7** EFf
Bilma **24** Dc
Biloela **29** HIc
Bilo gora (mts.) **6** Ccd
Biloxi **32** Cb
Biltine **25** Cc
Bina **20** Ed
Binalud, Kuh– e– (mt.) **21** Fb
Binboğa dağ (mts.) **22** Fcd
Bingen **5** ABcd
Binghamton **32** Da
Bingöl **21** Cb
Binhai **16** EFd
Binjai **18** Ad
Binongko, Pulau– (i.) **18** Ff
Bintuhan **18** Bc
Bintulu **18** Dd
Bio Bio, Rio– (riv.) **39** Ac
Biograd na Moru **6** Bde
Bioko **24** Cd
Biqā', Al– (phys. reg.) **22** EFef
Bi'r, Al– **21** Bd
Birāk **24** Db
Bi'r al Wa'r **24** Db
Birao **25** Ccd
Biratnagar **19** Ij
Bīr Damdūm **22** Ag
Birdsville **29** FGd
Birdum **29** Eb
Birecik **22** Gd
Bireuen **18** Ac
Birganj **20** FGc
Birjand **21** FGc
Birjusa (riv.) **14** Cd
Birk, Al– **21** Cf
Birkenhead **7** Ee
Bîrlad **6** HIc
Bîrlad (riv.) **6** Hcd
Birmingham [U.K.] **7** Fe
Birmingham [U.S.] **32** Cb
Birmitrapur **19** Ik

Birnin Kebbi **24** Cc
Birni Nkonni **24** Cc
Birobidžan **14** Ge
Birpur **19** Ij
Birr **7** BCe
Bi'r Safājah **25** Db
Birsk **13** Ed
Bīr Tarfāwi **25** Cb
Biržai **4** Fd
Bisa, Pulau– (i.) **18** Ge
Bisbee **33** BCc
Biscay, Bay of– **8** BCef
Bisceglie **10** Fd
Bischofshofen **5** De
Bishah, Wādī– **21** Cf
Bishnupur **19** Ik
Biškek (Frunze) **13** Ge
Biskra **24** Ca
Bismarck **33** CDb
Bismarck Archipelago **27** Cc
Bissau **24** Ac
Bissett **31** Fc
Bistrita **6** Gc
Bistrita (riv.) **6** Gc
Bitam **24** Dd
Bitlis **21** Cb
Bitola **11** Dc
Bitonto **10** Fd
Bitterfontein **23** Di
Bitterroot Range **33** Bb
Biu **24** Dc
Biwa–Ko **16** Ic
Biyad, Al– (phys. reg.) **21** De
Biyalā **22** Cg
Bizerte **24** CDa
Bjala Slatina **11** Eb
Bjargtangar (cap.) **4** map no.1
Bjelovar **6** Ccd
Bjerkreim **4** Ad
Bjuröklubb (cap.) **4** Eb
Blackall **29** Hc
Blackburn **7** Ee
Black Forest (mts.) **5** ABde
Black Hills **33** Cb
Blackpool **7** Ee
Black River **19** Dd
Black Sea **13** Ce
Black Volta (riv.) **24** Bcd
Blackwater (riv.) **7** Be
Blackwood River **29** Be
Blagodarny **12** Fd
Blagojevgrad **11** Ebc
Blagoveščensk [Russia] **14** FGd
Blagoveščensk [Russia] **12** HIb
Blair Athol **29** Hc
Blaj **6** FGc
Blanc, Cap– [Mtna.] **24** Ab
Blanc, Cap– [Tun.] **24** CDa
Blanc, Le– **8** Dd
Blanc, Mont– **10** Ab
Blanca, Bahía– (b.) **39** BCcd
Blanca, Cordillera– (mts.) **37** Bc
Blanca, Costa– **9** Ec
Blanca Peak **33** Cc
Blanche, Lake– **29** FGd
Blanco, Cape– **33** Ab
Blanc–Sablon **31** IJc
Blanquilla, Isla– (i.) **35** Db
Blantyre **26** Cc
Blåvands Huk (cap.) **5** ABa

Blaye **8** Ce
Bloemfontein **23** Eh
Blois **8** Dd
Błonie **5** Hb
Bluefield **32** Cb
Bluefields **35** Bb
Blue Mountains **33** Bb
Blue Nile **25** Dc
Blue Ridge **32** Cb
Blumenau **39** Db
Blyth **7** Fd
Blythe **33** Bc
Blytheville **32** BCb
Bo **24** Ad
Boac **18** Fb
Bo'ai **16** Dc
Boano, Pulau– (i.) **18** Ge
Boa Vista **37** Cb
Bobbio **10** Bb
Bobo Dioulasso **24** Bc
Bóbr (riv.) **5** Ec
Bobriki (Novomoskovsk) **13** CDd
Bobrka **6** Gb
Bobrujsk **13** BCd
Bôca do Acre **37** Cc
Bôca do Jari **38** Bb
Bôca do Moaco **37** Cc
Boca Grande (riv. m.) **37** CDb
Bocas del Toro **35** Bc
Bochnia **5** Hd
Bocholt **5** Ac
Bochum **5** Ac
Bocşa **6** Ed
Böda **4** Dd
Bodajbo **14** Ed
Bodélé (phys. reg.) **25** Ac
Boden **4** Ed
Bodmin **7** Df
Bodø **4** Cb
Bodrum **22** ABd
Boende **25** Cde
Boffa **24** Acd
Bogalusa **32** BCb
Bogan River **29** He
Bogatynia **5** Ec
Boğazlıyan **22** Ec
Bogdanovič **12** Jb
Bogor **18** Cf
Bogorodick **12** Fc
Bogorodsk **12** Fb
Bogra **19** Jj
Bogué **24** Ac
Bo Hai (b.) **16** EFc
Bohemia (phys. reg.) **5** DEcd
Bohemian Forest (mts.) **5** DEd
Bohol (i.) **18** Fbc
Boiaçu **37** Cc
Bois (riv.) **39** CDa
Boise **33** Bb
Bojador, Cabo– **24** Ab
Bojnurd **21** Fb
Boké **24** Ac
Boknafjorden (b.) **4** Ad
Bokspits **26** Bd
Bolama **24** Ac
Bolbec **8** Dc
Bolehov **6** FGb
Bolesławiec **5** Ec
Bolgatanga **24** Bcd
Bolgrad **6** Id
Boli **15** Ha

Boliden **4** DEb
Bolinao **18** Ea
Boliohertu (mt.) **18** Fd
Bolívar, Pico– (mt.) **37** Bb
Bolivia (Ind. St.) **36** De
Bolivia, Altiplano de– **38** Acd
Bolkar dağlari (mts.) **22** Ed
Bollnäs **4** Dc
Bollon **29** Hd
Boločanka **14** Cb
Bologna **10** Cb
Bologne **8** Fc
Bologoje **12** Db
Bol'šaja Ussurka (riv.) **16** HIa
Bolsena, Lago di– **10** Cc
Bol'ševik, ostrov– **41** grid square no.4
Bol'šôj Anjuj (riv.) **14** Jc
Bol'šoj Begičev, ostrov– **14** Eb
Bol'soj Jenisej (riv.) **14** Cd
Bolsoj Ljahovski, ostrov– (i.) **14** HIb
Bol'šôj Uzen (riv.) **12** Gd
Bolton **7** Ee
Bolu **22** Cb
Bolzano **10** Ca
Boma **26** Ab
Bombala **29** HIf
Bombay **15** Ch
Bom Comércio **37** Cc
Bom Despacho **39** Da
Bomili **26** Ba
Bom Jesus **38** Cb
Bom Jesus da Lapa **38** Cc
Bon, Cape– **24** Da
Bonaire (i.) **35** Db
Bonaparte Archipelago **29** CDa
Bonavista **31** Jd
Bonda **26** Ab
Bondo **25** Cd
Bondowoso **18** Df
Bone → Watampone **18** EFe
Bone, Teluk– **18** Fef
Bongor **25** Bcd
Bonifacio **8** map no.1
Bonifacio, Strait of– **10** Bd
Bonin Islands **27** Ca
Bonn **5** Ac
Bontoc **18** Fa
Bonyhád **6** Dc
Boosaaso **25** EFc
Boothia Gulf **31** FGab
Boothia Peninsula **31** Fa
Booué **26** Ab
Bophuthatswana (hist. reg.) **26** Bd
Bor [Russia] **12** Fb
Bor [Sud.] **25** Dd
Bor [Tur.] **22** Ed
Bor [Yugo.] **6** Fd
Borah Peak **33** Bb
Borås **4** Cd
Borāzjān **21** DEd
Borba **37** CDc
Borcea, Bratul– (riv.) **6** Hd
Bordeaux **8** Ce
Borden Peninsula **31** Ga
Bordertown **29** FGf
Bordj Omar Driss **24** Cb
Borgá **4** Fc
Borgarnes **4** map no.1
Børgefjell (mt.) **4** Cb

Bor - Bun

Borger **33** Cc
Borgholm **4** Dd
Borgomanero **10** Bb
Borislav **5** Id
Borisoglebsk **13** Dd
Borisov **5** Ka
Borispol **12** Dc
Borja **37** Bc
Borkou (phys. reg.) **25** BCc
Borlänge **4** Cc
Borlu **22** Bc
Borneo (Kalimantan) (i.) **18** DEd
Bornholm (i.) **4** CDe
Bornholmsgatten (str.) **4** Ce
Bornova **22** Ac
Boromo **24** Bc
Borovići **12** Db
Borroloola **29** EFb
Borşa **6** Gc
Borščovočny, Hrebet– **14** DEde
Borujerd **21** Dc
Borzja **14** Ed
Bosa **10** Bd
Bosanska Gradiška **6** Cd
Bosanska Krupa **6** Cd
Bosanski Novi **6** Cd
Bosanski Petrovac **6** Cd
Bosansko Grahovo **6** Cd
Bose **16** Cf
Boshan **16** Ec
Bosna (riv.) **6** CDd
Bosnia (phys. reg.) **6** CDd
Bosnia–Herzegovina (Ind. St.) **6** CDde
Bosobolo **26** ABa
Bösö–Hantō **17** Gg
Bosphorus (str.) **22** Bb
Bossangoa **25** Bd
Bossembélé **25** Bd
Bossier City **32** Bb
Bostan **20** Cb
Boston [U.K.] **7** FGe
Boston [U.S.] **32** DEa
Botev (mt.) **11** Fb
Bothnia, Gulf of– **4** DEbc
Botletle (riv.) **26** Bd
Botoşani **6** Hc
Botswana (Ind. St.) **23** Eh
Botucatu **39** Db
Bouaké **24** Bd
Bouar **25** Bd
Bouârfa **24** Ba
Bouca **25** Bd
Boudouaou **24** Ca
Boufarik **9** Gd
Bougainville Island **27** Cc
Bougouni **24** Bc
Bouguenais **8** Cd
Boulder **33** Cbc
Boulia **29** FGc
Boulogne–sur–Mer **8** Db
Bouna **24** Bd
Boundiali **24** Bd
Boundji **24** De
Bountiful **33** Bb
Bounty Islands **27** DEe
Bourail **28** map no.4
Bourem **24** BCc
Bourbonnais (hist. reg.) **8** Ed
Bourg–en–Bresse **8** Fd
Bourges **8** Ed

Bourg–lès–Valence **8** Fe
Bourgogne, Canal de– **8** Fd
Bourg–Saint–Maurice **8** Ge
Bourke **29** GHde
Bournemouth **7** Ff
Bou–Saada **24** Ca
Bousso **25** Bc
Boutilimit **24** Ac
Bow (riv.) **31** Ba
Bowen **29** Hbc
Bowling Green **32** Cb
Bowmore **7** Cd
Boxian **16** Ed
Bozburun **11** He
Bozcaada (i.) **22** Ac
Bozdağ (mt.) **22** Bc
Bozeman **33** BCb
Bozhen **16** Ec
Bozkır **22** Dd
Bozoum **25** Bd
Bozüyük **22** Cbc
Bra **10** Ab
Brač (i.) **11** Bb
Bracciano, Lago di– **10** Dc
Bräcke **4** CDc
Brad **6** Fc
Bradford **7** EFe
Braga **9** Ab
Bragado **39** Bc
Bragança [Braz.] **38** Cb
Bragança [Port.] **9** Bb
Brahmani (riv.) **20** FGd
Brahmaputra (Maquan He) (riv.) **20** GHc
Brahmaputra (Yarlung Zangbo Jiang) **20** GHc
Bräila **6** Hd
Brainerd **32** Ba
Brake **5** Bb
Branco, Rio– (riv.) **37** Cbc
Brandberg (mt.) **26** Ad
Brandenburg **5** Db
Brandenburg (hist. reg.) **5** Db
Brandon **31** EFcd
Braniewo **5** GHa
Bransfield Strait **42** grid square no.1
Brasiléia **37** Cd
Brasilia **39** Da
Braşov **6** GHd
Bratislava **5** Fd
Bratsk **14** CDd
Bratskoje vodohranilišče **14** Dd
Braunau am Inn **5** Dd
Braunschweig **5** BCb
Brava, Costa– **9** Cd
Bravo, Rio– (riv.) **34** Bb
Bray (hist. reg.) **8** DEc
Brazil (Ind. St.) **36** DFde
Brazilian Highlands **39** Da
Brazos (riv.) **32** Bb
Brazzaville **26** Ab
Brčko **6** Dd
Brdy (mt.) **5** Dd
Breakfast Island **28** map no.3
Breaza **6** Gd
Břeclav **5** Fd
Brecon **7** Ef
Breda **8** Fb
Bredasdorp **23** Ei
Bredy **12** Jc
Bregalnica (riv.) **11** Ec

Bregenz **5** BCe
Breidafjördur (g.) **4** map no.1
Bremen **5** Bb
Bremerhaven **5** Bb
Bremerton **33** Ab
Brenham **32** Bbc
Brenne (phys. reg.) **8** Dd
Brennero (p.) **10** Ca
Breno **10** Cb
Brenta (riv.) **10** Cab
Brescia **10** Cb
Breslav **5** Fc
Bressanone / Brixen **10** Ca
Bressuire **8** CDd
Brest [Bela.] **5** IJb
Brest [Fr.] **8** Ac
Breton, Pertuis– (str.) **8** Cd
Breueh, Pulau– (i.) **18** Ac
Breves **38** BCb
Brewarrina **29** Hde
Bria **25** Cd
Briançon **8** Ge
Briare **8** Ed
Bričany **6** Hb
Bridgeport **32** Da
Bridgetown **29** Be
Bridgwater **7** Ef
Bridlington **7** FGd
Brie (phys. reg.) **8** Ec
Brig **10** ABa
Brighton **7** FGf
Brijuni **6** Ad
Brilon **5** Cc
Brindisi **10** Fd
Brisbane **29** Id
Bristol **7** Ef
Bristol Channel **7** DEf
British Columbia (prov.) **31** Cc
Brittany (phys. reg.) **8** BCcd
Brive–la–Gaillarde **8** De
Briviesca **9** Ca
Brixen / Bressanone **10** Ca
Brixlegg **5** CDe
Brjansk **13** Cd
Brno **5** Fd
Broad Sound **29** HIc
Brocken (mt.) **5** Cc
Brockman, Mount– **29** Bc
Brodeur Peninsula **31** Ga
Brodnica **5** Gb
Brody **12** BCcd
Broken Hill **29** Ge
Broken Hill → Kabwe **26** Bc
Brokopondo **37** Db
Bron **8** Fe
Brønnøysund **4** Cb
Bronte **10** Ef
Brookings **32** Ba
Brooks Range **41** grid square no.2
Brookton **29** Be
Broome **29** Cb
Brothers, The– (i.) **21** Eg
Brownsville **32** Bc
Brownwood **32** Bb
Browse Island **29** Ca
Bruay–en–Artois **8** Eb
Bruce, Mount– **29** Bc
Bruck an der Leitha **5** Fde
Bruck an der Mur **5** Ee
Brugge **8** Eb
Brumado **39** Da
Brunei (Ind. St.) **15** Di

Brunsbüttel **5** Ba
Brunswick **32** CDb
Brunswick, Peninsula de– **40** Ac
Bruny Island **29** map no.1
Brussel / Bruxelles **8** Fb
Bruxelles / Brussel **8** Fb
Bryan **32** Bb
Brza Palanka **6** Fd
Brzeg **5** Fc
Buada Lagoon **27** map no.2
Buala **27** Cc
Bučač **6** Gb
Bucak **22** Cd
Bucaramanga **36** CDc
Buchanan **24** ABd
Buchans **31** Jd
Bucharest **6** Hd
Buckingham Bay **29** Fa
Budapest **6** Dc
Budardalur **4** map no.1
Budaun **20** EFc
Budd Coast **42** grid square no.4
Bude **7** Df
Budennovsk **3** Hc
Búdir **4** map no.1
Budjala **25** Bd
Budogošč **12** Db
Budva **11** Cb
Buea **24** Cd
Buena Esperanza **39** Bc
Buenaventura **36** BCc
Buenos Aires [Arg.] **39** Bc
Buenos Aires [Pan.] **35** map no.1
Buenos Aires, Lago– **40** ABb
Buffalo [N.Y.–U.S.] **32** Da
Buffalo [Tx.–U.S.] **32** Bb
Buffalo [Wy.–U.S.] **33** Cb
Bug (riv.) **5** Jc
Buga **37** Bb
Bugsuk (i.) **18** Ec
Bugulma **12** Hc
Buguruslan **12** Hc
Buhara **13** Ff
Buhayrat al–Assad (l.) **22** Fde
Builth Wells **7** Ee
Buinsk **12** Gbc
Buir–Nur (l.) **16** Ea
Buj **13** Dd
Bujalance **9** CDd
Bujumbura **26** Bb
Bukačača **14** Ed
Bukama **26** Bb
Bukavu **26** Bb
Bukit Mertajam **19** Dgh
Bukittinggi **18** ABde
Bükk **6** Ebc
Bukoba **25** De
Bukovina (hist. reg.) **6** GHbc
Bula **18** He
Bulan **18** Fb
Bulandshahr **19** Gi
Bulawayo **23** Egh
Buldan **22** Bc
Bulgan **14** De
Bulgaria (Ind. St.) **3** Fc
Bullfinch **29** Be
Bulloo River **29** Gd
Bumba **25** Cd
Bumbah, Al– **24** Ea
Buna **26** CDa

© ISTITUTO GEOGRAFICO DE AGOSTINI · Novara

134

Bunbury 29 ABe
Bundaberg 29 Icd
Bundoran 7 Bd
Bungo−Suidō 17 BCh
Bunguran (i.) 18 Cd
Bunja 25 CDd
Buon Me Thuot 19 Ef
Buqayq 21 DEd
Buraydah 21 Cd
Buraymī, Al− 21 Fe
Burdekin River 29 Hbc
Burdur 22 BCd
Burdur Gölü 22 BCd
Burdwan 20 Gd
Bure 25 Dd
Bureinski Hrebet 14 Gde
Bureja (riv.) 14 Gd
Bureja 14 FGe
Bür Fuad 25 map no.1
Burgas 11 Gb
Burgas, Gulf of− 11 GHb
Burgenland (phys. reg.) 5 Fe
Burghausen 5 Dd
Burgio 10 Df
Burgos 9 Da
Burgsvik 4 Dd
Burgundy (phys. reg.) 8 EFd
Burias (i.) 18 Fb
Burjasot 9 EFc
Burketown 29 Fb
Burkina (Ind. St.) 23 BCd
Burlington [Ia.−U.S.] 32 Ba
Burlington [Vt.−U.S.] 32 Da
Burmah, Al− 24 CDa
Burnie 29 map no.1
Burnley 7 Ee
Burns 33 Bb
Bur'o 25 Ed
Burra 29 Fe
Burravoe 7 Fa
Burriana 9 EFc
Burruyacú 39 Bb
Bursa 22 Bb
Bür Taufiq 25 map no.1
Burton−upon−Trent 7 Fe
Buru, Pulau− (i.) 18 Ge
Burullus, Buḥayrat al− 22 Cg
Burundi (Ind. St.) 26 BCb
Bururi 26 BCb
Buryat (Aut. Rep.) 14 Dd
Bury Saint Edmunds 7 Ge
Büshehr 21 Ed
Businga 26 Ba
Busko Zdrój 5 Hc
Buşrá ash Shām 22 Ff
Busselton 29 ABe
Busto Arsizio 10 Bb
Busuanga (i.) 18 Eb
Buta 25 Cd
Butarirari Islands 27 Db
Butha Qi 16 Fa
Butte 33 Bb
Butuan 18 Gc
Butung (i.) 18 Fef
Buuloberde 25 Ed
Büyük Ağrı dağı → Ararat
  (mt.) 21 Cb
Büyük Egri dağ (mt.) 22 Dd
Büyük Mahya (mt.) 22 ABb
Büyük Menderes (riv.) 22 ABd
Buzançais 8 Dd
Buzău 6 Hd
Buzuluk 13 Ed

Bydgoszcz 5 FGb
Bygdeå 4 DEb
Byhov 12 Dc
Bylot Island 30 Kb
Byrd Glacier 42 grid square
  no.4
Byron, Cape− 29 Id
Byrranga Gory 14 CDb
Bytom 5 Gc
Bytów 5 Fa
Bzura (riv.) 5 Gb

C

Ca (riv.) 19 DEe
Caanood, Laas− 25 Ed
Caapiranga 37 Cc
Caatinga 38 Cbc
Cabanatuan 18 Fa
Cabedelo 38 Db
Cabeza del Buey 9 Cc
Cabezón de la Sal 9 Ca
Cabimas 37 Ba
Cabinda 26 Ab
Caborca 34 Aa
Cabot Strait 31 IJd
Cabra 9 Cd
Cabras 10 Be
Cabrera, Isla− (i.) 9 Gc
Cabrera, Sierra de la− (mts.)
  9 Ba
Cábriel (riv.) 9 Ec
Cabruta 37 Cb
Caçador 39 Cb
Čačak 6 Ede
Caccia, Capo− 10 Bd
Cacequí 39 Cbc
Cáceres [Braz.] 39 Ca
Cáceres [Sp.] 9 Bc
Cachimbo, Serra do− (mts.)
  38 Bb
Cachoeira 38 Dc
Cachoeira do Sul 39 Cbc
Cachoeiro de Itapemirim 39
  DEb
Cacolo 26 Abc
Caconda 26 Ac
Cadale 25 Ed
Čadan 14 BCd
Cadillac 32 Ca
Cádiz 9 Bd
Cadiz 18 Fb
Cádiz, Golfo de− 9 Bd
Čadyr−Lunga 6 Ic
Caen 8 CDc
Caernarvon 7 De
Caetité 38 Cc
Cagan−Aman 12 Gd
Cagayan (riv.) 18 Fa
Cagayan de Oro 18 Fc
Cagayan Islands 18 Fc
Cagayan Sulu (i.) 18 Ec
Čagda 14 Gd
Cagliari 10 Be
Cagliari, Golfo di− 10 Be
Caguas 35 Db
Cahama 26 Ac
Cahersiveen 7 Af
Cahora Bassa, Lago de− 26
  Cc
Cahors 8 De

Caia 26 Cc
Caiabis, Serra dos− (mts.) 38
  Bc
Caicó 38 Db
Caicos Islands 32 Dc
Caimito (riv.) 35 map no.1
Cairns 29 Hb
Cairo [Eg.] 25 Dab
Cairo [Il.−U.S.] 32 Cb
Cajamarca 37 Bc
Cajàzeiras 38 Db
Čajkovski 12 Hlb
Çal 22 Bcd
Calabar 24 Cd
Calabozo 36 Cc
Calabria (reg.) 10 EFef
Calafat 6 Fde
Calafate 40 Ac
Calahorra 9 Ea
Calais [Fr.] 8 Db
Calais [U.S.] 32 Ea
Calama [Braz.] 37 Cc
Calama [Chile] 39 Bb
Calamar 37 Bab
Calamian Group 18 EFb
Calamocha 9 Eb
Cãlan 6 Fd
Calandula 26 Ab
Calapan 18 Fb
Cãlãraşi 6 Hd
Calatayud 9 Eb
Calatrava (r.) 9 CDc
Calayan (i.) 18 Fa
Calbayog 18 FGb
Calçoene 38 BCa
Calcutta 15 Cg
Caldas da Rainha 9 Ac
Caldera 39 Ab
Caldwell 33 Bb
Caledon (riv.) 26 Bde
Caledonian Canal 7 Dc
Calera, La− 39 Ac
Caletta 10 Bd
Calgary 30 Gde
Cali 36 Cc
Calicut 20 DEf
Caliente 33 Bc
California (State) 33 ABc
California, Gulf of− 33 Bcd
Cãliman, Munţii− 6 Gc
Cãlimãneşti 6 Gd
Callabonna, Lake− 29 Gde
Callao 36 Ce
Callao, El− 37 Cb
Caloundra 29 Id
Calpe 9 Fc
Caltagirone 10 Ef
Caltanissetta 10 Ef
Caluire−et−Cuire 8 Fe
Caluula 25 EFc
Calvi 8 map no.1
Calvinia 26 ABe
Calw 5 Bd
Camabatela 26 Ab
Camacupa 26 Ac
Camagüey 35 Ca
Camagüey, Archipiélago de−
  (is.) 35 Ca
Camaná 39 Aa
Camapuã, Sertão de−
  (steppe) 39 Ca
Camaquã 39 Cc
Camargo 39 Bb

Camargue (phys. reg.) 8 Ff
Camarones 40 Bb
Ca Mau Point 19 Dg
Cambodia (Ind. St.) 15 Dh
Cambrai 8 Eb
Cambrian Mountains 7 DEef
Cambridge [U.K.] 7 FGe
Cambridge [U.S.] 32 DEa
Cambridge Bay 31 Eb
Çam Burun 22 FGb
Camden 32 Db
Cameroon (Ind. St.) 23 CDe
Cameroon Mountains 24 CDd
Cametá 38 BCb
Camiguin (i.) 18 Fa
Camiri 39 Bb
Camocim 38 CDb
Camooweal 29 Fbc
Camorta (i.) 19 Bg
Campagna 10 Ed
Campana, Isla− (i.) 40 Ab
Campanario, Cerro− (mt.) 39
  ABc
Campania (reg.) 10 DEd
Campanquiz, Cerros− (mt.)
  37 Bc
Campbell Island 27 De
Campbell River 31 Cc
Campbellton 31 Id
Campbell Town 29 map no.1
Campbeltown 7 Dd
Campeche 34 Cc
Campeche, Bahía de− 34 Cc
Campeche Bank 34 CDb
Camperdown 29 Gf
Campina Grande 38 Db
Campinas 39 Db
Campobasso 10 Ed
Campo Formoso 38 Cc
Campo Gallo 39 Bb
Campo Grande 39 Cab
Campo Maior 38 Cb
Campo Mourão 39 Cb
Campos 39 Db
Campos [Braz.] (phys. reg.)
  38 Cc
Campos [Braz.] (phys. reg.)
  38 Bc
Campos, Tierra de− (phys.
  reg.) 9 Cab
Cam Ranh 19 Ef
Camrose 31 Ab
Çan 11 Gc
Canada (Ind. St.) 30 GKcd
Cañada de Gómez 39 Bc
Canadian River 32 Bb
Çanakkale 22 Ab
Canal du Centre (can.) 8 Fd
Cananea 33 BCc
Canarreos, Archipiélago de
  los− (is.) 35 Bb
Canary Islands 24 Aab
Canaveral, Cape− (Kennedy,
  Cape−) 32 CDc
Canavieiras 38 Dc
Canberra 29 HIf
Cancún 34 Db
Çandır 22 Db
Canelones 39 Cc
Cangamba 26 ABc
Cangas de Narcea 9 Ba
Cangzhou 16 Ec
Caniapiscau (riv.) 31 Ic

Canicatti **10** Df
Canik dağları (mts.) **22** Fb
Çankırı **22** Db
Cannanore **20** DEf
Cannanore Islands **20** Df
Cannes **8** Gf
Cann River **29** Hf
Canoas **39** CDbc
Canoas, Rio– (riv.) **39** Cb
Canora **33** Ca
Canta **37** Bd
Cantabria (phys. reg.) **9** CDa
Cantal, Plomb du– (mts.) **8** Ee
Canterbury **7** Gf
Can Tho **19** Efg
Canton **32** CDa
Canton (Guangzhou) **15** Dg
Canumã (riv.) **37** Dc
Canutama **37** Cc
Cao Bang **19** Ed
Cap, El– **25** map no.1
Čapajev **12** Hc
Čapajevsk **13** DEd
Capanema **38** Cb
Capbreton **8** Cf
Cape Barren Island **29** map no.1
Cape Breton Island **31** IJd
Cape Coast **24** BCd
Cape Dorset **31** Hb
Cape Dyer **31** IJb
Cape Girardeau **32** BCb
Capelongo **26** Ac
Cape Province (prov.) **26** ABde
Cape Town **26** Ae
Cape Verde (Ind. St.) **2**
Cape York Peninsula **29** Ga
Cap–Haïtien **35** Cab
Capim (riv.) **38** Cb
Capitano Arturo Prat (sc. stat.) **42** grid square no.1
Čaplygin **12** EFc
Capraia **10** Bc
Caprara, Punta– (cap.) **10** Bd
Caprera **10** Bd
Capri **10** Ed
Capricorn Channel **29** Ic
Caprivi Strip (phys. reg.) **26** Bc
Captain Cook **28** map no.1
Captain's Flat **29** HIf
Caquetá (riv.) **37** Bb
Čara (riv.) **14** Ed
Carabaya, Cordillera de– (mts.) **39** ABa
Caracal **6** Gd
Caracaraí **37** CDb
Caracas **37** Ca
Carajás, Serra dos– (mts.) **38** Bb
Caransebeş **6** Fd
Caratasca, Laguna de– **35** Bb
Caratinga **39** Da
Carauari **37** Cc
Caravaca **9** DEc
Caravelas **39** Ea
Caràzinho **39** Cb
Carballo **9** Aa
Carbonia **10** Be
Carcassonne **8** Ef

Cárdenas [Cuba] **35** Ba
Cárdenas [Mex.] **34** Cb
Cardiff **7** Ef
Cardigan **7** De
Cardigan Bay **7** De
Cardona **9** Fb
Čardžev (Čardžou) **13** Ff
Čardžou → Čardžev **13** Ff
Carei **6** Fc
Carentan **8** Cc
Carey, Lake– **29** Cd
Cargados Carajos Islands **23** map no.1
Carhaix–Plouguer **8** Bc
Cariñena **9** Eb
Carinhanha **38** Cc
Carinhanha, Rio– (riv.) **39** Da
Carinthia (reg.) **5** DEe
Caripito **37** Ca
Carlisle **7** Ed
Carlota, La– **39** Bc
Carlow **7** Ce
Carlsbad **33** Cc
Carmarthen **7** Df
Carmaux **8** Ee
Carmelo **39** Cc
Carmen, El– **39** Bb
Carmen de Patagones **40** Bb
Carmona **9** BCd
Carnac **8** Bd
Carnarvon [Austl.] **29** Acd
Carnarvon [S. Afr.] **26** Be
Carnegie **29** Cd
Carnegie, Lake– **29** Cd
Carn Eige (mt.) **7** Dc
Car Nicobar (i.) **19** Bg
Carnot **25** Bd
Carnsore Point **7** CDe
Carolina **38** Cb
Carolina, La– **9** Dc
Caroline Atoll **28** Bc
Caroline Islands **27** BDb
Caroní (riv.) **37** Cb
Carora **37** Ba
Carpentaria, Gulf of– **29** FGa
Carpentras **8** Fe
Carrantuohill **7** Bef
Carrara **10** Cb
Carribean Sea **35** CDb
Carrión (riv.) **9** Ca
Carrizal Bajo **39** Ab
Carrizozo **33** Cc
Çarşamba **22** Fb
Čarsk **13** GHe
Carson City **33** Bc
Cartagena [Col.] **36** Cb
Cartagena [Sp.] **9** Ed
Cartago **35** Bc
Carthage (r.) **24** Da
Cartier Island **29** Ca
Cartwright **31** Jc
Caruaru **38** Db
Carúpano **37** Ca
Carvoeiro, Cabo– **9** Ac
Casablanca **24** ABa
Casale Monferrato **10** Bb
Casarea Mazaca → Kayseri **22** EFc
Cascadas, Las– **35** map no.1
Cascade Range **33** Ab
Cascais **9** Ac
Cascavel [Braz.] **38** Db
Cascavel [Braz.] **39** Cb

Caserta **10** Ed
Casey **42** grid square no.4
Casino **29** Id
Casiquiare (riv.) **37** Cb
Caspe **9** EFb
Casper **33** Cb
Caspian Depression **12** GHd
Caspian Sea **13** DEef
Cassai (riv.) **26** Bb
Cassino **10** Dd
Castanho **37** Cc
Castelfranco Veneto **10** Cb
Castellammare, Golfo di– **10** De
Castellammare del Golfo **10** De
Castellammare di Stabia **10** Ed
Castellana Grotte **10** Fd
Castellane **10** Ac
Castellón de la Plana **9** EFbc
Castelnaudary **8** DEf
Castelo Branco **9** Bc
Castelo do Piaui **38** Cb
Castelsarrasin **8** De
Castelvetrano **10** Df
Castilla–La Mancha (phys. reg.) **9** CDbc
Castilla–León (phys. reg.) **9** Cab
Castillos **39** Cc
Castlebar **7** Be
Castres **8** Ef
Castries **35** Db
Castro **40** Ab
Castro del Río **9** Cd
Castro Urdiales **9** Da
Castrovillari **10** Fe
Castuera **9** Cc
Catalão **39** Da
Catalina **39** Ab
Catalonia (phys. reg.) **9** Fb
Catamarca **39** Bb
Catanduanes **18** FGb
Catanduva **39** CDb
Catania **10** Ef
Catania, Golfo di– **10** Ef
Catanzaro **10** Fe
Catarroja **9** EFc
Catastrophe, Cape– **29** EFef
Catbalogan **18** FGb
Cat Island **32** Dc
Cativa **35** map no.1
Catoche, Cabo– **34** Db
Cato Island **29** Jc
Catrilό **39** Bc
Catrimani **37** Cb
Catrimani (riv.) **37** Cb
Catwick, Îles– **19** Eg
Cauca (riv.) **37** Bb
Caucaia **38** Db
Caucasia **37** Bb
Caucasus (mts.) **13** De
Caungula **26** ABb
Cauquenes **39** Ac
Caura (riv.) **37** Cb
Causses (mts.) **8** Ee
Cauvery (riv.) **20** Ef
Cava, La– **9** Fb
Cavaillon **8** Ff
Cavally (riv.) **24** Bd
Cavan **7** Ce
Caviana, Ilha– **38** BCa

Cavite **18** Fb
Caxias **38** Cb
Caxias do Sul **39** CDb
Caxito **26** Ab
Cayağzi (Riva) **22** Bb
Cayambe, Volcán– (mt.) **37** Bbc
Cayenne **37** Db
Cayes, Les– **35** Cb
Cayman Brac (is.) **35** Cb
Cayman Islands **35** Bab
Cayo, El– **35** Bb
Čazma **6** Cd
Cazombo **26** Bc
Cazorla **9** Dd
Cea (riv.) **9** Ca
Ceará (State) **38** CDb
Ceará Mirim **38** Db
Čeboksary **13** Dd
Cebu **18** Fbc
Cebu (i.) **15** Ehi
Cecerleg **14** De
Cecina **10** Cc
Cedar City **33** Bc
Cedar Falls **32** Ba
Cedar Rapids **32** Ba
Cedros, Isla– (i.) **34** Ab
Ceduna **29** Ee
Ceeldheree **25** Ed
Ceerigaabo **25** Ec
Cefalù **10** Ee
Čegdomyn **14** Gd
Ceglέd **6** Dc
Čehov **14** He
Ceiba, La– **35** Bb
Çekerek (riv.) **22** Fbc
Cela **26** Ac
Celaya **34** BCb
Celebes → Sulawesi (i.) **18** EFe
Celebes Sea **18** Fd
Čeleken **21** Eb
Celinograd **13** Gd
Čeljabinsk **13** Fd
Celje **6** Bc
Čelkar **13** EFe
Celle **5** Cb
Celtic Sea **7** BCf
Čelyuskin, mys– **41** grid square no.4
Cenis, Mont– (p.) **10** Ab
Central, Sistema– (mts.) **9** BDb
Central African Republic (Ind. St.) **23** DEe
Central Balkans (mts.) **11** EFb
Central Siberian Uplands **14** CDc
Centro, El– **33** Bc
Cephalonia (i.) **11** CDd
Ceram (i.) **18** GHe
Ceram Sea **18** GHe
Cerbère **8** Ef
Čerdyn **12** Ia
Čeremhovo **14** CDd
Čerepovec **3** Gb
Ceres **38** BCc
Cergy–Pontoise **8** Ec
Cerignola **10** Ed
Čerkassy **13** BCe
Çerkeş **22** Db
Čerkessk **13** De

Chorzów 5 Gc
Chōshi 16 Jc
Chos Malal 39 ABc
Choszczno 5 EFb
Christchurch 27 De
Christmas → Kiritimati 28 Bb
Christmas Island 18 Cg
Chrudim 5 EFd
Chubut (riv.) 40 Bb
Chūgoku–Sanchi 17 BDg
Chukchi Peninsula 14 Lc
Chukchi Sea 14 Lc
Chulucanas 37 ABc
Chumbicha 39 Bb
Chumphon 19 CDf
Ch'unchŏn 16 Gc
Ch'ungmu 17 Ag
Chuŏr Phnum Krăvanah 19 Df
Chuquibamba 39 Aa
Chuquicamata 39 ABb
Chur 5 Db
Churchill 31 Fc
Churchill [Alta.–Can.] (riv.) 31 Ec
Churchill [Newf.–Can.] (riv.) 31 Ic
Churchill Peak 31 Cc
Churk 19 Hj
Churu 20 Dc
Churuguara 37 BCa
Chuvash (Aut. Rep.) 13 Dd
Chuxiong 16 Bef
Cianjur 18 Cf
Cide 22 Db
Ciechanów 5 Hb
Ciechanowiec 5 Hlb
Ciego de Ávila 35 BCa
Ciénaga 37 Ba
Cienfuegos 35 Ba
Cieszyn 5 Gd
Cieza 9 Ec
Čiganak 13 Ge
Ciguela (riv.) 9 Dc
Cihanbeyli 22 Dc
Cilacap 18 Cf
Cilician Gates (p.) 22 Ed
Cimarron (riv.) 32 Bb
Čimbaj 13 EFe
Čimkent → Šimkent 13 FGe
Cimljansk 12 Fd
Cimljanskoje vodohranilišče 12 Fd
Cimone, Monte– 10 Cb
Cimpia Turzii 6 Fc
Cimpina 6 GHd
Cimpulung 6 Gd
Cimpulung Moldovenesc 6 Gc
Cinca (riv.) 9 Fb
Cincinnati 32 Cb
Cindrelu, Vîrful– (mt.) 6 Fd
Çine 11 GHe
Čingirlau 12 Hc
Cinto, Monte– 8 map no.1
Ciotat, La– 8 Ff
Circeo, Monte– 10 Dd
Čirčik 13 FGe
Circle 31 Ab
Cirebon 18 Cf
Ciró Marina 10 Fe
Čirpan 11 Fb
C.I.S. → Commonwealth of Independent States 15 BDd
Cisa, Passo della– 10 Bb

Cisco 32 Bb
Ciskei (hist. reg.) 26 Be
Cisnădie 6 Gd
Cisne, Islas del– 35 Bb
Čistopol 13 Ed
Čita 14 Ed
Citlaltépetl (mt.) 34 Cc
Citrusdal 26 ABe
Cittanova 10 Fe
Ciucaşu, Vîrful– (mt.) 6 GHd
Ciudad Acuña 34 Bb
Ciudad Altamirano 34 Bc
Ciudad Bolívar 37 Cb
Ciudad Camargo 34 Bb
Ciudad Cuauhtémoc 34 Bb
Ciudad del Carmen 34 Cc
Ciudad Delicias 34 Bb
Ciudad de Rio Grande 34 Bb
Ciudadela 9 GHbc
Ciudad Guayana 37 Cb
Ciudad Guerrero 34 Bb
Ciudad Juárez 34 Ba
Ciudad Madero 34 Cb
Ciudad Mante 34 Cb
Ciudad Obregón 34 ABb
Ciudad Piar 37 Cb
Ciudad Real 9 CDc
Ciudad Rodrigo 9 Bb
Ciudad Valles 34 Cb
Ciudad Victoria 34 Cb
Civita Castellana 10 Dc
Civitanova Marche 10 Dc
Civitavecchia 10 Cc
Civray 8 Dd
Çivril 22 Bc
Cizre 21 Cb
Clacton–on–Sea 7 GHf
Claire, Lake– 31 Dc
Clamecy 8 Ed
Claremorris 7 Be
Clarence Strait 29 DEa
Clarines 37 Cb
Clarión (i.) 30 Gh
Clark Fork (riv.) 33 Bb
Clarksville 32 Cb
Clearwater, Lake– 31 Hc
Clermont 29 Hc
Clermont–Ferrand 8 Ee
Cleveland [Oh.–U.S.] 32 CDa
Cleveland [Tn.–U.S.] 32 Cb
Cleveland, Mount– 33 Bb
Cleveland Hills 7 Fd
Clifden 7 ABe
Clipperton, Île– (i.) 30 Hhi
Clisham (mt.) 7 Cb
Clonakilty 7 Bf
Cloncurry 29 FGc
Clonmel 7 Ce
Cloppenburg 5 Bb
Clorinda 39 Cb
Cloud Peak 33 Cb
Clovis 33 Cc
Cluj Napoca 6 Fc
Cluny 8 Ef
Clyde 31 Ia
Clyde (riv.) 7 Ed
Clyde, Firth of– (b.) 7 Dd
Cna (riv.) 12 Fc
Cnossus (r.) 11 Ff
Côa (riv.) 9 Bb
Coari (riv.) 37 Cc
Coari 37 Cc
Coast Mountains 31 BCab

Coast Ranges 33 Abc
Coats Island 30 Jc
Coats Land 42 grid square no.1
Coatzacoalcos (Puerto México) 34 Cc
Cobalt 31 GHd
Cobán 35 ABb
Cobar 29 He
Cobh 7 Bf
Cobija 37 Cd
Cobourg Peninsula 29 Ea
Coburg 5 Cc
Cochabamba (mts.) 39 Ba
Cochabamba, Cordillera de– 39 Ba
Cochem 5 Ac
Cochin 20 DEfg
Cochin China (phys. reg.) 19 Efg
Cochrane 31 GHd
Cocklebiddy 29 De
Coco (riv.) 35 Bb
Coco, Isla del– (i.) 30 Ji
Cocos (i.) 27 map no.1
Cocos Islands [Austl.] 2
Cocos Islands [Mya.] 19 Bf
Cod, Cape– 32 DEa
Codajás 37 Cc
Codlea 6 Gd
Codó 38 Cb
Coen 29 Ga
Coesfeld 5 Abc
Coetivy (i.) 15 Bj
Cœur d'Alene 33 Bb
Coff's Harbour 29 IJe
Cognac 8 Ce
Cogo 26 Aa
Coiba, Isla de– (i.) 35 Bc
Coihaique 40 Ab
Coimbatore 20 Ef
Coímbra 9 Ab
Coín 9 Cd
Coipasa, Salar de– (s. m.) 39 Ba
Čojbalsan 14 Ee
Čokurdah 14 Hlb
Colac 29 Gf
Colatina 39 DEab
Colbeck, Cape– 42 grid square no.3
Colchester 7 Gf
Coleraine 7 Cd
Coleroon (riv.) 20 Ef
Colima 34 Bc
Colima, Nevado de– (mt.) 34 Bbc
Colinas 38 Cb
Coll (i.) 7 Cc
Collie 29 Be
Collier Bay 29 Cb
Collinsville 29 Hc
Colmar 8 Gc
Colmenar 9 CDd
Colmenar Viejo 9 Db
Colômbia 39 Dab
Colombia (Ind. St.) 36 CDc
Colombo 15 Ci
Colón [Cuba] 35 Ba
Colón [Pan.] 35 BCc
Colonia del Sacramento 39 Cc
Colonia las Heras 40 Bb
Colonsay (i.) 7 Cc

Coast Ranges 33 Abc
Colorado (State) 33 Cc
Colorado [Co.–U.S.] (riv.) 33 Bc
Colorado [Tx.–U.S.] (riv.) 33 CDc
Colorado, Rio– [Arg.] (riv.) 39 Bb
Colorado, Rio– [Arg.] (riv.) 39 Bc
Colorado Plateau 33 BCc
Colorado Springs 33 Cc
Columbia (riv.) 33 ABb
Columbia [S.C.–U.S.] 32 Cb
Columbia [Tn.–U.S.] 32 Cb
Columbia, Cape– 41 grid square no.2
Columbia, District of– (State) 32 Db
Columbretes, Islas– 9 Fbc
Columbus [Ga.–U.S.] 32 Cb
Columbus [In.–U.S.] 32 Cb
Columbus [Nb.–U.S.] 32 Ba
Columbus [Oh.–U.S.] 32 Cb
Colwyn Bay 7 Ee
Comacchio 10 Db
Comacchio, Valli di– (lag.) 10 Db
Coman, Mount– 42 grid square no.1
Comandante Fontana 39 BCb
Comăneşti 6 GHc
Comayagua 35 Bb
Combarbalá 39 Ac
Comilla 20 Hd
Cómiso 10 Ef
Comitán de Dominguez 34 Cc
Commentry 8 Ed
Commercy 8 Fc
Commonwealth of Independent States (C.I.S.) 15 BDd
Como 10 Bb
Como, Lago di– 10 Bab
Comodoro Rivadavia 36 DEh
Comorin, Cape– 20 Eg
Comoros (Ind. St.) 23 Gg
Compiègne 8 Ec
Čona (riv.) 14 Ec
Conakry 24 Ad
Concarneau 8 ABd
Conceição do Araguaia 38 BCb
Concepción [Arg.] 39 Bb
Concepción [Bol.] 39 Ba
Concepción [Chile] 39 Ac
Concepción [Par.] 39 Cb
Concepción del Oro 34 Bb
Concepción del Uruguay 39 BCc
Conchos (riv.) 34 Bb
Concord 32 Da
Concordia 39 Cc
Condamine River 29 Hld
Conde 38 Dc
Condobolin 29 He
Condom 8 Df
Condor, Cordillera del– (mts.) 37 Bc
Congo (Ind. St.) 23 Def
Congo (riv.) 26 Ab
Cong Tum → Kontum 19 Ef
Conn, Lake– 7 Bde
Connaught (prov.) 7 Be

Dab - Dew

Dabola **24** Ac
Dąbrowa Górnicza **5** GHc
Däbuleni **6** FGe
Dachau **5** Cd
Dachstein (mt.) **5** De
Dadanawa **37** Db
Daday **22** Db
Dädra and Nagar Haveli **20** Dd
Dadu **20** Cc
Dadu He (riv.) **16** Be
Daet **18** Fb
Dafir **21** Ee
Dagestan (Aut. Rep.) **13** De
Dagupan **18** Fa
Dahlak (i.) **21** Cf
Dahna', Ad– (phys. reg.) **21** CDde
Dahra **24** Db
Dahra (phys. reg.) **9** Fd
Daimiel **9** Dc
Dai–Sen **17** Cg
Daitō Islands **16** He
Dajarra **29** FGc
Dakar **24** Ac
Dakhla **24** Ab
Dakhla Oasis **25** Cb
Đakovica **11** Db
Dalai Nur (l.) **16** Eb
Dalälven (riv.) **4** Dc
Dalaman (riv.) **22** Bd
Dalan–Dzadagad **14** De
Dalan–Džargalan **16** CDa
Dalap–Uliga–Darrit **27** Db
Da Lat **19** Ef
Dalbandin **20** Bc
Dalby **29** Id
Dale **4** Ac
Dalhart **33** Cc
Dali [China] **19** CDc
Dali [China] **16** CDcd
Dalian (Lüda) **16** Fc
Dalías **9** Dd
Dallas **32** Bb
Dalles, The– **33** Ab
Dalmatia (phys. reg.) **6** BDde
Dalmatovo **12** Jb
Dalnegorsk **14** Ge
Dalnerečensk **14** Ge
Daloa **24** Bd
Dalrymple, Mount– **29** Hc
Daltonganj **20** Fd
Dalupiri (i.) **18** Fa
Dalwallinu **29** Be
Daly River **29** Ea
Daly Waters **29** Eb
Daman **20** Dd
Damanhûr **25** CDa
Damar, Pulau– (i.) **18** Gf
Damaraland (hist. reg.) **26** Ad
Damâs **22** Cg
Damascus **22** Ff
Damāvand (mt.) **21** Eb
Dämghän **21** EFb
Damietta **25** Da
Daming **16** DEc
'Dämir, Ad– **25** Dc
Dammäm, Ad– **21** Ed
Damme **5** ABb
Damodar (riv.) **19** Ik
Damoh **20** EFd
Dampier **29** Bc
Dampier Archipelago **29** ABbc

Dampier Strait **18** He
Damqawt **21** Ef
Danakil Plain (phys. reg.) **25** DEc
Da Nang **19** Ee
Dandong **16** Fbc
Daneborg **31** Ma
Dangjin Shankou **16** Ec
Dangriga **35** Bb
Danilov **12** Fb
Dankov **12** Ec
Danmark Havn **30** PQb
Danube (riv.) **6** Fd
Danube, Mouths of the– **6** Id
Danville [Il.–U.S.] **32** Ca
Danville [Va.–U.S.] **32** CDb
Danxian **16** Cg
Danzig → Gdańsk **5** Ga
Dar' ä **22** Ff
Däräb **21** EFd
Darabani **6** Hb
Đaravica (mt.) **11** Db
Darb, Ad– **21** Cf
Darbhanga **20** Gc
Dardanelles (str.) **11** Gcd
Darende **22** Fc
Dar es Salaam **23** FGf
Därfür (State) **25** Cc
Darhan **15** De
Darién, Golfo de– **37** Bb
Dariyah **21** Ce
Darjeeling **20** Gc
Darlag **16** Ad
Darling Range **29** Be
Darling River **29** Ge
Darlington **7** EFd
Darłowo **5** EFa
Darmstadt **5** Bd
Darnah **24** Ea
Daroca **9** Eb
Dart, Cape– **42** grid square no.3
Dartmoor (mt.) **7** DEf
Dartmouth [Can.] **31** Id
Dartmouth [U.K.] **7** Ef
Daru **27** Cc
Daruvar **6** Cd
Darwin **29** Ea
Das (i.) **21** Ede
Dašhovuz (Tašauz) **13** Ee
Dasht (riv.) **20** Bc
Dasht–e–Kavir (des.) **21** EFc
Dasht–e–Lut (des.) **21** Fc
Datca **22** Ad
Date **17** Gc
Datia **19** Gj
Datong **16** Dbc
Datu Piang (Dulawan) **18** Fc
Daugavpils **13** Bd
Dauphin **33** CDa
Dauphine (hist. reg.) **8** FGe
Davangere **20** DEf
Davao **15** Ei
Davao Gulf **18** Gc
Davenport **32** BCa
David **35** Bc
Davis, Fort– **35** map no.1
Davis Sea **42** grid square no.2
Davis Strait **31** Jb
Davlekanovo **12** Hlc
Davos **5** BCe

Dawadmi, Ad– **21** Ce
Dawäsir, Wädï ad– **21** Ce
Dawei **18** Ab
Dawson **30** Ec
Dawson, Isla– (i.) **40** ABc
Dawson Creek **31** Cc
Dawson River **29** Hlcd
Dawu **16** Bd
Dax **8** Cf
Daxian **16** Cd
Daxinggou **17** ABc
Daym Zubayr **25** Cd
Dayr az Zawr **21** BCb
Dayton **32** Cb
Daytona Beach **32** CDc
Dayu **16** De
De Aar **23** Ef
Dead Sea **22** EFg
Deán Funes **39** Bc
Dease Strait **31** Eb
Death Valley **33** Bc
Deauville **8** CDc
Debao **16** Cf
Debar **11** Dc
Debica **5** Hc
Dębno **5** Hb
Debrecen **6** EFc
Debre Markos **25** Dcd
Debre Tabor **25** Dc
Decatur [Il.–U.S.] **32** Cab
Decatur [U.S.] **32** Cb
Decazeville **8** Ee
Deccan **20** Eef
Déčin **5** Hc
Decize **8** Ed
Deda **6** Gc
Dedegül daği (mt.) **22** Cd
Dédougou **24** Bc
Dee [Scot.–U.K.] (riv.) **7** Ec
Dee [Wales–U.K.] (riv.) **7** Ee
Deer Lake **31** Jd
Degeh Bur **25** Ed
Deggendorf **5** Dd
De Grey River **29** BCc
Dehiwala–Mount Lavinia **20** Eg
Dehra Dun **20** Ebc
Dehri **19** Hlj
Dej **6** Fc
Dekese **26** Bb
Delano Peak **33** Bc
Delaware **32** Ca
Delaware Bay **32** Db
Delft **8** Fab
Delfzijl **8** Ga
Delgado, Cape– **26** Dc
Delhi **20** Ec
Delice (riv.) **22** Ec
Delingha **16** Ac
Deljatin **12** Bd
Delmenhorst **5** ABb
Delmiro Gouveia **38** Db
De Long Islands **14** Hlb
De Long Strait **41** grid square no.4
Delphi (r.) **11** Ed
Del Rio **33** CDd
Delvina **11** CDd
Demanda, Sierra de la– (mts.) **9** Da
Demerara → Georgetown **37** Db

Deming **33** Cc
Demini (riv.) **37** Cbc
Demirci **11** Hd
Demirköy **11** GHc
Demjanskoje **13** FGd
Demmin **5** Db
Dempo, Gunung– (mt.) **18** Be
Denain **8** Eb
Dengkou **16** Cb
Denham **29** Ad
Den Helder **8** EFa
Denia **9** Fc
Deniliquin **29** GHf
Denizli **22** Bd
Denmark (Ind. St.) **3** DEb
Denmark **29** Bef
Denmark Strait **30** OPc
Denpasar **18** Ef
Denton **32** Bb
D'Entrecasteaux Islands **27** Cc
Denver **33** Cc
Deoghar **19** Ij
Deo Mu Gia (p.) **19** Ee
Deoria **19** Hj
Deputatski **14** GHc
Dera Ghazi Khan **20** CDbc
Dera Ismail Khan **20** CDb
Derażnja **6** Hb
Derbent **13** De
Derby [Austl.] **29** Cb
Derby [U.K.] **7** Fe
Derecske **6** Fc
Dereköy **22** Ab
Derg, Lake– **7** Bd
Dermatás, Ákra– **11** Ed
De Rose Hill **29** Ed
Derudeb **25** Dc
Derventa **6** CDd
Derwent (riv.) **7** Fde
Desaguadero [Arg.] (riv.) **39** Bc
Desaguadero [Bol.] (riv.) **39** Ba
Dese **25** DEc
Deseado (riv.) **40** Bb
Desemboque, El– **34** Aa
Desenzano del Garda **10** Cb
Desertas, Ilhas– (is.) **24** Aa
Des Moines (riv.) **32** Ba
Des Moines **32** Ba
Desna (riv.) **12** Dc
Desolación, Isla– (i.) **40** Ac
Desroches (i.) **15** Bi
Dessau **5** Dc
Detroit **32** Ca
Deutsche Bucht (b.) **5** Aa
Deva **6** Fd
Develi **22** Ec
Deventer **8** Fga
Devil's Island **37** Db
Devils Lake **32** Ba
Devin **11** Fc
Devolli (riv.) **11** Dc
Devoluy (mt.) **8** Fe
Devon (co.) **7** DEf
Devon Island **41** grid square no.1
Devonport **29** map no.1
Devrek **22** CDb
Devrez (riv.) **22** Db
Dewa (riv.) **25** Dd
Dewas **20** Ed

Dewa–Sanchi (mts.) **17** Gde
Dez (riv.) **21** Dc
Dezful **21** Dc
Dezhou **16** Ec
Dežneva, mys– **14** LMc
Dhaka **15** CDg
Dhalak Archipelago **25** DEc
Dhalli Rajhara **20** Fde
Dhamar **21** Cg
Dhamtari **20** Fd
Dhanbad **20** Gd
Dhangarhi **19** Hi
Dharwar **20** DEe
Dhaulagiri (mt.) **20** Fc
Dhidhimótikhon **11** FGc
Dhikti Óros (mt.) **11** Ff
Dhílos (i.) **11** Fe
Dhirfis Óros (mt.) **11** Ed
Dholpur **19** Gj
Dhond **20** DEe
Dhone **20** Ee
Dhonoúsa (i.) **11** FGe
Dhoraji **20** Dd
Dhubri **19** ABc
Dhule **20** DEd
Dhulian **19** IJj
Dhuri **20** Eb
Día (i.) **11** Ff
Diala (riv.) **21** Dbc
Diamante **39** Bc
Diamantina **39** Da
Diamantina, Chapada– (plat.) **38** Cc
Diamantina River **29** Gc
Diamantino **38** Bc
Diamond Harbour **19** Jk
Dianópolis **38** Cc
Dibrugarh **19** BCc
Dibulla **37** Ba
Dickinson **33** Cb
Diefenbaker, Lake– **33** Ca
Diego Garcia (i.) **15** Cj
Diego Ramirez, Islas– **40** ABc
Dien Bien Phu **19** Dd
Diepholz **5** Bb
Dieppe **8** Dc
Digby **31** Id
Digne **8** Ge
Digoin **8** Ed
Digos **18** Gc
Dijon **8** Fd
Dikson **13** Hb
Dikwa **24** Dc
Dilam, Ad– **21** De
Dili **15** Ej
Dillon **33** Bb
Dilolo **23** Efg
Dimboola **29** Gf
Dîmbovița (riv.) **6** Gd
Dimitrovgrad [Bul.] **11** FGb
Dimitrovgrad [Russia] **13** DEd
Dimitrovgrad [Yugo.] **11** Eb
Dimona **22** Eg
Dinagat (i.) **18** Gbc
Dinajpur **19** Jj
Dinan **8** BCc
Dinant **8** Fb
Dinapur **19** Ij
Dinar **22** BCc
Dinard **8** Bc
Dinaric Alps **6** Cde
Dindigul **20** Efg

Dingbian **16** Cc
Dingle Bay **7** Aef
Dingwall **7** Dc
Diourbel **24** Ac
Dipolog **18** Fc
Dir **20** Da
Dire Dawa **25** Ecd
Dirk Hartog Island **29** Ad
Dirkou **24** Dc
Dirranbandi **29** Hd
Disappointment, Lake– **29** Cc
Disko Bugt **31** Jb
Disko Ø (i.) **41** grid square no.1
Dispur **19** Bc
Distrito Federal **39** Da
Diu **20** Dd
Divinópolis **39** Db
Divisões, Serra das– (mts.) **39** Ca
Divisor, Sierra de– (mts.) **37** Bc
Divnoje **12** Fd
Divriği **22** FGc
Diwaniyah, Ad– **21** CDc
Dixon Entrance **31** Bc
Diyarbakır **21** BCb
Diz (i.) **20** Bc
Dja (riv.) **26** Aa
Djado **24** Db
Djado, Plateau du– (plat.) **24** Db
Djambala **26** Ab
Djanet **24** CDb
Djedeïda **10** Bf
Djelfa **24** Ca
Djénné **24** Bc
Djerba (i.) **24** Da
Djibouti (Ind. St.) **25** Ec
Djibouti **23** Gd
Djolu **26** Ba
Djougou **24** Ccd
Djugu **26** BCa
Dmitrijev–Lgovski **12** DEc
Dmitri Laptev Strait **14** GHb
Dmitrov **12** Eb
Dnepr (riv.) **13** Ce
Dneprodzeržinsk →
    Kamenskoje **12** Dd
Dnepropetrovsk →
    Jekaterinoslav **13** Ce
Dnestr (riv.) **13** Be
Dno **12** CDb
Dobbiaco / Toblach **10** Da
Doboj **6** CDd
Dobrič (Tolbuhin) **11** GHb
Dobrjanka **12** HIb
Dobruja (phys. reg.) **6** HIde
Doce, Rio– (riv.) **39** Da
Doda Betta (mt.) **20** Ef
Dodecanese (is.) **11** Gde
Dodge City **33** CDc
Dodoma **23** Ff
Dogai Coring **19** Ab
Döger **22** Cc
Dōgo (i.) **17** Cf
Dogondoutchi **24** Cc
Doha **21** Ed
Dohad **20** Dd
Dokšicy **4** Fe
Dolak, Pulau– **27** Bc
Dolbeau **31** Hd
Dole **8** Fd
Dolgellau **7** DEe

Dolina **6** FGb
Dolinsk **14** He
Dolinskaja **12** Dd
Dolinskoje **6** Ic
Dolo **25** Ed
Dolomites (mts.) **10** CDa
Dolores **39** Cc
Domaniç **22** BCc
Domažlice **5** Dd
Dombarovski **13** Ed
Dombas **4** Bc
Dombóvár **6** CDc
Domeyko, Cordillera– (mts.) **39** Bb
Domfront **8** Cc
Domingos Martins **39** DEab
Dominica (Ind. St.) **36** DEb
Dominican Republic (Ind. St.) **30** KLgh
Domo **25** Ed
Domodossola **10** Ba
Dom Pedrito **39** Cc
Don [Russia] (riv.) **13** De
Don [U.K.] (riv.) **7** Ec
Donaueschingen **5** Bde
Donauwörth **5** Cd
Don Benito **9** Cd
Doncaster **7** Fe
Dondo **26** Abc
Dondra Head **20** Fg
Donec (riv.) **12** Ed
Doneck → Juzovka **13** Ce
Donegal **7** BCd
Donegal Bay **7** Bd
Dongara **29** ABd
Dong Hoi **19** Ef
Dongliao He (riv.) **16** Fb
Dongning **17** Bb
Dong Rak, Phanom– **19** Df
Dongsha Dao (i.) **16** Ef
Dongting Hu (l.) **16** De
Dora, Lake– **29** Cc
Dora Baltea (riv.) **10** Ab
Dorada, La– **37** Bb
Dorado, El– [U.S.] **32** Bb
Dorado, El– [Ven.] **37** Cb
Dorchester **7** Ef
Dordogne (riv.) **8** De
Dordrecht **8** EFb
Dore, Monts– (mts.) **8** Ee
Dorgali **10** Bd
Dori **24** BCc
Dornbirn **5** BCe
Dornoch **7** DEc
Dorohoi **6** Hc
Dorotea **4** Db
Dorset (co.) **7** Ef
Dortmund **5** ABc
Doruma **26** Ba
Dosatuj **16** Ea
Dos Hermanas **9** BCd
Dosso **24** Cc
Dossor **13** Ee
Dothan **32** Cb
Douai **8** Eb
Douala **24** CDd
Douarnenez **8** ABc
Douglas [Ak.–U.S.] **31** Bc
Douglas [Az.–U.S.] **33** Cc
Douglas [S. Afr.] **26** Bd
Douglas [U.K.] **7** Dd
Douglas [Wy.–U.S.] **33** Cb

Dourada, Serra– (mts.) **38** BCc
Dourados **39** Cb
Douro (riv.) **9** Bb
Dovbyš **6** Ha
Dover [U.K.] **7** Gf
Dover [U.S.] **32** Db
Dover, Strait of– **8** Db
Dovrefjell (mts.) **4** Bc
Downpatrick **7** Dd
Dozen (i.) **17** Cf
Drâa **34** Bab
Drâa, Hamada du– (des.) **24** Bb
Dracena **39** Cb
Drăgășani **6** Gd
Draguignan **8** FGf
Drakensberg **26** BCde
Drake Passage **40** ABc
Dráma **11** Fc
Drammen **4** Bd
Drancy **8** Ec
Drangajökull (mt.) **4** map no.1
Dravograd **6** Bc
Drawsko Pomorskie **5** Eb
Dresden **5** DEc
Dreux **8** Dc
Drevsjø **4** BCc
Drina (riv.) **6** Dd
Drin Gulf **11** Cc
Drini (riv.) **11** Db
Drogheda **7** Ce
Drogobyč **5** Id
Drôme (riv.) **8** Fe
Dronne (riv.) **8** De
Drontes (riv.) **22** Fe
Drumheller **33** Ba
Drummond Range **29** Hc
Drumochter, Pass of– **7** DEc
Druskininkai **5** IJab
Družba (i.) **12** Dc
Družba **13** He
Družina **14** Hc
Drvar **6** Cd
Dryden **31** Fd
Drygalski Island **42** grid square no.4
Drysdale River **29** Dab
Dubai **21** EFde
Dubawnt (riv.) **31** Eb
Dubawnt Lake **31** Eb
Dubbo **29** He
Dubesar **6** Ic
Dublin (Baile Átha Cliath) **7** CDe
Dubna **12** Eb
Dubno **12** Cc
Dubovka **12** FGd
Dubrovnik **11** BCb
Dubuque **32** Ba
Duc de Gloucester, Îles du– **28** Bd
Ducie Island **28** Cd
Dudinka **13** Hc
Dudley **7** Ee
Duero (riv.) **9** Cb
Dugi Otok **6** Bd
Dugo Selo **6** BCd
Duisburg **5** CDc
Dukhan **21** Ede
Dukielska, Przełęcz– **5** HId
Dulawan → Datu Piang **18** Fc
Dulce, Rio– (riv.) **39** Bb

Dulovo **11** Gb
Duluth **32** Ba
Dümä **22** Ff
Dumaguete **18** Fc
Dumaran (i.) **18** EFb
Dumbarton **7** Dcd
Dumfries **7** Ed
Dumka **19** Ij
Dumond d'Urville **42** grid square no.4
Dumont D'Urville Sea **42** grid square no.4
Dunaföldvár **6** Dc
Dunaharaszti **6** Dc
Dunajevcy **6** Hb
Dunántúl (phys. reg.) **6** CDc
Dunaújváros **6** Dc
Duncansby Head **7** Eb
Dundalk **7** Cde
Dundalk Bay **7** CDe
Dundas, Lake– **29** Ce
Dundas Strait **29** Ea
Dundee **7** Ec
Dunedin **27** De
Dunfermline **7** DEc
Dungarpur **20** Dd
Dungarvan **7** Cef
Dungenèss (cap.) **7** Gf
Dunhua **16** Gb
Dunkerque **8** Eb
Dunkwa **24** Bd
Dún Laoghaire / Dunleary **7** CDe
Dunleary / Dún Laoghaire **7** CDe
Dunqulah **25** CDc
Duns **7** Ed
Duolun **16** Eb
Durance (riv.) **8** Ge
Durango **33** Cc
Durazno **39** Cc
Durazzo **11** Cc
Durban **23** Fhi
Durg **20** Fd
Durgapur **19** IJk
Durham [U.K.] **7** EFd
Durham [U.S.] **32** Db
Durmitor (mt.) **11** Cb
Durness **7** Db
Dursunbey **11** Hd
Durüz, Jabal al– (mt.) **22** Ff
Dušanbe **13** Ff
Dushan **16** Ce
Düsseldorf **5** CDc
Dutch Harbor **31** Bc
Duwaym, Ad– **25** Dc
Duyun **16** Ce
Düzce **22** Cb
Dyer Plateau (plat.) **42** grid square no.1
Dymer **6** IJa
Dyrhólaey (cap.) **4** map no.1
Dżalal–Abad **13** Ge
Dżalinda **14** Fd
Dżambul **13** Ge
Dzamyn–Ud **16** Db
Dżankoj **12** Dd
Dżardżan **14** Fc
Dżargalant, Ar– **16** DEa
Dzerżinsk **12** Fb
Dżetygara **13** Fd
Džezkazgan → Žezkazgan **13** Fe

Dzhugdzhur Range **14** Gd
Dżiałdowo **5** Hb
Dzierżoniów **5** Fc
Dzun–Bajan **16** CDb
Dzungarian Basin (phys. reg.) **14** Be
Džungarski Alatau, Hrebet– (mts.) **13** GHe
Dzun–Mod **14** De
Džusaly **13** Fe

E

Eagle **31** Ab
Eagle Pass **33** CDd
Eastbourne **7** Gf
East Cape **27** Dd
East China Sea **16** FGde
Easter Island **2**
Eastern Carpathians (mts.) **6** FHbc
Eastern Ghats (mts.) **20** EFef
Eastern Malaysia **18** DEcd
Eastern Prussia (hist. reg.) **5** Glab
East Falkland (i.) **40** Cc
East London **26** Be
Eastmain (riv.) **31** Eb
Eastmain **31** Hc
East Point **32** Cb
East Saint Louis **32** BCb
East Sea / Japan, Sea of– **16** HIbc
East Siberian Sea **41** grid square no.4
Eau Claire **32** BCa
Eau Gallie **32** CDc
Eauripik Atoll **27** Cb
Ebensee **5** DEe
Eber Gölü **22** Cc
Eberswalde **5** Db
Ebla (r.) **21** Bb
Eboli **10** Ed
Ebro (riv.) **9** Da
Eceabat **22** Ab
Echigo–Sanmyaku (mts.) **17** FGef
Echo Bay **30** GHc
Echuca **29** GHf
Écija **9** Cd
Ecuador (Ind. St.) **36** BCd
Ed **25** Ec
Edéa **24** CDd
Edefors **4** Eb
Eden **29** Hlf
Edgeøya **13** Bb
Edhessa **11** DEc
Edinburgh **7** Ed
Edirne **11** Gc
Edith Ronne Ice Shelf **42** grid square no.1
Edith Ronne Land **42** grid square no.1
Edjeleh **24** Cb
Edmonton **30** Gd
Edmundston **31** Id
Edremit **22** Ac
Edremit Körfezi **22** Ac
Edsel Ford Ranges **42** grid square no.3
Edward, Lake– **25** Ce

Edwards Creek **29** Ee
Edwards Plateau **33** CDcd
Edward VII Peninsula **42** grid square no.3
Efaté, Île– (i.) **28** map no.4
Effingham **32** Cb
Eforie **6** Id
Egadi, Isole– **10** Df
Egan Range **33** Bbc
Egedesminde / Aasiaat **31** JKb
Eger **6** Ec
Egersund **4** Ad
Eğnar **22** Ed
Eğridir **22** Cd
Eğridir Gölü **22** Ccd
Eğriğöz dağı (mt.) **22** Bc
Egvekinot **14** KLc
Egypt (Ind. St.) **23** EFc
Ehingen **5** Bd
Eiao, Île– (i.) **28** Bc
Eibar **9** Da
Eichstätt **5** Cd
Eifel (mt.) **5** Ac
Eigg (i.) **7** Cc
Eight Degree Channel **20** Dg
Eights **42** grid square no.1
Eights Coast **42** grid square no.1
Eighty Mile Beach **29** Cb
Eindhoven **8** Fb
Eiriksjökull (gl.) **4** map no.1
Eirunepé **37** BCc
Eisenach **5** BCc
Eisenerz **5** Ee
Eisenhüttenstadt **5** Eb
Eisenstadt **5** Fe
Eisleben **5** Cc
Ejin Qi **16** Bb
Ekecek dağı (mt.) **22** DEc
Ekenäs **4** EFcd
Ekibastuz **13** Gd
Ekonda **14** Dc
El Affroun **9** Gd
Elafonísou, Stenón– (str.) **11** Ee
Elassón **11** Ed
Elat **22** Eh
Elâzığ **21** BCb
Elba (i.) **10** Cc
Elbasani **11** CDc
El–Bayadh **24** Ca
Elbe (riv.) **5** Cb
Elbert, Mount– **33** Cc
Elbeuf **8** Dc
Elbistan **22** Fc
Elblag **5** Ha
El Boulaïda **24** Ca
Elbrus (mt.) **21** Ca
Elburz Mountains **21** DEb
Elche **9** Ec
Elda **9** Ec
Eldoret **25** Dde
Elektrostal **12** EFb
Eleusís **11** Ed
Eleuthera Island **32** Dc
Elgin **7** Ec
Elgon (mt.) **25** Dd
Elhovo **11** Gb
Elista **12** Fb
Elizabeth City **32** Db
Elizabeth Island **28** map no.3
Elk **5** Ib

Elk City **33** CDc
Elko **33** Bb
Ellesmere Island **41** grid square no.1
Elliston **29** EFe
Ellora (r.) **20** Id
Ellsworth Highland **42** grid square no.3
Ellsworth Mountains **42** grid square no.1
Elmalı **22** BCd
Elmira **32** Da
Elmshorn **5** BCb
Elne **8** Ef
Elorza **37** BCb
El Salvador (Ind. St.) **30** IJh
Eluru **20** Fe
Elvas **9** Bc
Elverum **4** BCc
Ely **33** Bc
Emaé (i.) **28** map no.4
Emämshahr **21** Fb
Emba **13** Ee
Emba (riv.) **13** Ee
Embarcación **39** Bb
Embetsu **17** Gb
Embu **26** Db
Emden **5** Ab
Emerald **29** Hd
Emerson **31** Fd
Emet **22** Bc
Emi Koussi (mt.) **25** Bbc
Emilia–Romagna (reg.) **10** BCb
Emine, Nos– **22** ABa
Emirdağ **22** Cc
Emir dağları (mts.) **22** Cc
Emmen **8** Ga
Emmendingen **5** ABd
Emmet **29** Gc
Empalme **34** ABb
Émpoli **10** Cc
Emporia **32** Bb
Ems (riv.) **5** Ab
Encantada, Cerro de la– (mt.) **34** Aa
Encarnación **39** Cb
Ende **18** Ff
Endeavour Strait **29** Ga
Enderbury Atoll **28** Ac
Enderby Land **42** grid square no.2
Enewetak Atoll **27** Db
Enez **11** Gc
Enez Körfezi **11** Fc
Engaru **17** Hb
Engels **13** Dd
Enggano, Pulau– (i.) **18** Bf
England (reg.) **7** EFde
Englewood **33** Cc
English Channel **8** ACbc
Enid **32** Bb
Enkhuizen **8** Fa
Enköping **4** Dd
Enna **10** Ef
Ennadai **31** Eb
Ennedi (plat.) **25** Cc
Ennis **7** Be
Enniscorthy **7** CDe
Enniskillen **7** Cd
Enns (riv.) **5** DEe
Enontekiö **4** EFa
Enschede **8** Ga

Ensenada **34** Aa
Enshi **16** Cde
Entebbe **25** Dde
Entinas, Punta– (cap.) **9** Dd
Entrecasteaux, Point d'– **29** ABef
Entrecasteux, Récifs d'– **28** map no.4
Entre Rios **38** Bb
Entroncamento **9** Ac
Enugu **24** Cd
Envira **37** BCc
Eolie o Lipari, Isole– **10** Ee
Épernay **8** EFc
Ephesus (r.) **22** Ad
Épi, Île– (i.) **27** Dc
Épinal **8** Gc
Équateur (reg.) **26** ABab
Equatorial Guinea (Ind. St.) **23** CDe
Eraclea → Ereğli **22** Cb
Erbîl **21** CDb
Erciyas dağ (mt.) **22** EFc
Érd **6** Dc
Erdek **11** Gc
Erebus, Mount– **42** grid square no.4
Ereğli **22** DEd
Ereğli (Eraclea) **22** Cb
Erenhot **16** Db
Erexim **39** Cb
Erfoud **24** Ba
Erfurt **5** Cc
Erg Chech (des.) **24** Bb
Ergene (riv.) **11** Gc
Erg Iguidi (des.) **24** Bb
Erice **10** De
Erie **32** CDa
Erie, Lake– **32** CDa
Erimo–Misaki **17** Hd
Eritrea (Ind. St.) **25** DEc
Erlangen **5** Cd
Erldunda **29** Ed
Ermenek **22** Dd
Ermesinde **9** Ab
Ermoúpolis **11** Fe
Ernest Legouvé Reef **28** Bd
Erode **20** Ef
Eromanga **29** Gd
Errigal Mountain **7** Bd
Erris Head **7** ABd
Erromango, Île– (i.) **28** map no.6
Erseka **11** Dc
Ertix He (riv.) **13** He
Erzincan **21** Bab
Erzurum **21** Cb
Esan–Misaki **17** Gd
Esashi [Jap.] **17** Hb
Esashi [Jap.] **17** FGd
Esbjerg **4** ABe
Escada **38** Db
Escalón **34** Bb
Escanaba **32** Ca
Escárcega **34** CDc
Escarpada Point **18** Fa
Escatròn **9** Eb
Esch–sur–Alzette **8** FGc
Eschwege **5** Cc
Escobal **35** map no.1
Escuintla **35** Ab
Esfahān **21** Ec
Eskifjörður **4** map no.1

Eskilstuna **4** Dd
Eskimo Point **31** Fb
Eskişehir **22** Cc
Esla (riv.) **9** Ca
Eslöv **5** Da
Eşme **22** Bc
Esmeralda, La– **37** Cb
Esmeraldas **37** ABb
Esperance **29** Ce
Esperanza [Ant.] **42** grid square no.1
Esperanza [Peru] **37** Bc
Espichel, Cabo– (cap.) **9** Ac
Espinhaço, Serra do– (mts.) **39** Da
Espinho **9** Ab
Espírito Santo (State) **39** Dab
Espíritu Santo, Île– (i.) **28** map no.4
Espoo **4** EFc
Esquel **40** Ab
Essaouira **24** ABa
Essen **5** Ac
Essequibo (riv.) **37** Db
Essex (co.) **7** FGf
Esslingen am Neckar **5** Bd
Estaca de Bares, Punta de la– (cap.) **9** Ba
Estados, Isla de los– **40** Bc
Estância **38** Dc
Estella **9** Da
Estepona **9** Cd
Estevan **33** Cb
Estonia (Ind. St.) **4** Fd
Estoril **9** Ac
Estrada, La– **9** Aa
Estrela, Serra da– (mts.) **9** Bb
Estremoz **9** Bc
Estrondo, Serra do– (mts.) **38** Cb
Esztergom **6** Dc
Étampes **8** DEc
Etawah **20** EFc
Ethiopia (Ind. St.) **23** FGe
Ethiopian Plateau **25** Ccd
Etna, Monte– (Mongibello) **10** Ef
Etorofu Tō / Iturup, ostrov– (i.) **14** He
Etosha Pan (sw.) **26** Ac
Eu **8** Dbc
Euboea (i.) **11** EFd
Eucla **29** De
Eugene **33** Ab
Eugenia, Punta– (cap.) **34** Ab
Euphrates (riv.) **22** FGd
Eure (riv.) **8** Dc
Eureka [Can.] **41** grid square no.1
Eureka [U.S.] **33** Ab
Europa, Ile– **26** Dd
Europa, Picos de– (mts.) **9** Ca
Europa, Punta de– (cap.) **9** Cd
Evans, Lake– **32** Da
Evanston **33** BCb
Evansville **32** Cb
Everard, Lake– **29** Ee
Everest (Qomolangma Feng) (mt.) **20** Gc
Everett **33** Ab
Evje **4** Ad

Évora **9** Bc
Evreux **8** Dc
Exe (riv.) **7** Ef
Exeter **7** Ef
Exmouth [Austl.] **29** Ac
Exmouth [U.K.] **7** Ef
Exmouth Gulf **29** Ac
Extremadura (phys. reg.) **9** Ac
Eyasi, Lake– **26** Cb
Eyjafjallajökull (gl.) **4** map no.1
Eyl **25** EFd
Eymoutiers **8** DEe
Eyre, Lake– **29** Fd
Eyre Creek **29** Fd
Eyre Peninsula **29** Fe
Ezcaray **9** Da
Ezine **22** Ac
Ezraa **22** Ff

F

Fabriano **10** Dc
Fachi **24** Dc
Fada **25** Cc
Fada–Ngourma **24** Cc
Faddejevski, ostrov– (i.) **14** Hb
Faenza **10** Cb
Faeroe Island **3** BCa
Fafe **9** ABb
Făgăraş **6** Gd
Făgăraşului, Munţii– **6** Gd
Fagataufa Atoll **28** Cd
Fagernes **4** Bc
Fagersta **4** CDcd
Fairbanks **30** CDc
Fairbury **32** Bab
Fair Island **7** Fb
Fairview **31** Dc
Fairweather Mount **31** ABc
Faisalabad **20** Db
Faistós (r.) **11** Ff
Faizabad **20** Fc
Fakaofo Atoll **28** Ac
Fakarava Atoll **28** Bc
Falaise **8** CDc
Falakrón Óros (mts.) **11** EFc
Falam **19** Bd
Fălciu **6** HIc
Falealupo **28** map no.5
Falelima **28** map no.5
Falémé (riv.) **24** Ac
Falešty **6** Hc
Falevai **28** map no.5
Falkensee **5** Db
Falkland Islands **36** DFi
Falkland Sound **40** BCc
Falköping **4** Cd
Falls City **32** Bab
Falmouth **7** Df
Falso, Cabo– **34** Ab
Falster **5** Da
Falterona, Monte– **10** Cc
Fálticeni **6** Hc
Falun **4** Dc
Famagusta **22** DEe
Famagusta Bay **22** DEe
Famatina **39** Bb
Famatina, Nevados de– **39** Bb

Fang **19** Ce
Fangak **25** Dd
Fangxian **16** Dd
Fangzheng **17** Ab
Fangzi **16** Ec
Fanning (i.) **28** Bb
Fanning → Tabuaeran **28** Bb
Fano **10** Dc
Fanø (i.) **5** ABa
Fan Si Pan (mt.) **19** Dd
Faradje **26** Ba
Farafangana **26** map no.1
Farafra Oasis **25** Cb
Farah **20** Bb
Farah rud (riv.) **20** Bb
Faranah **24** ABcd
Farasān, Jazā'ir– **21** Cd
Fargo **32** Ba
Faridabad **20** Ec
Faridpur **19** Jk
Farmington **33** Cc
Fårö (i.) **4** Dd
Faro [Braz.] **38** Bb
Faro [Port.] **9** ABd
Faro, Punta del– → Peloro, Capo– **10** Ee
Farquhar Group **23** GHg
Farrukhabad **20** EFc
Färs (phys. reg.) **21** Ed
Fársala **11** Ed
Farsund **4** Ad
Farvel, Kap– **31** Kc
Fasā **21** Ed
Fasano **10** Fd
Fāshir, Al– **25** Cc
Fashn, Al– **25** CDb
Fashoda → Kodok **25** Dcd
Fastov **6** Ia
Fataka Island **27** Dc
Fatehpur **19** Hj
Fátima **9** Ac
Fatu Hiva, Île– (i.) **28** Cc
Fáurei **6** Hd
Fauske **4** CDb
Favignana (i.) **10** Df
Fāw, Al– **21** Dcd
Faxaflói **4** map no.1
Faya–Largeau **25** BCc
Faydzābād **20** Da
Fayetteville [Ak.–U.S.] **32** Bb
Fayetteville [N.C.–U.S.] **32** Db
Fâyid **25** map no.1
Fayyūm, Al– **25** CDb
Fderick **24** Ab
Fécamp **8** CDc
Federal **39** Cc
Federated States of Micronesia (Ind. St.) **27** CDb
Fehmarn (i.) **5** Ca
Feijó **37** Dc
Feira de Santana **38** CDc
Feke **22** EFcd
Felanitx **9** Gc
Feldberg (mt.) **5** Be
Feldkirch **5** Be
Felipe Carillo Puerto **34** Dc
Feltre **10** Ca
Femund (l.) **4** Bc
Fengcheng **16** DEe
Fengtai **16** Dc
Fenoarivo Atsinanana **26** map no.1

Frýdek–Místek **5** FGd
Fuente de Cantos **9** BCc
Fuente de San Esteban, La– **9** Bb
Fuenteguinaldo **9** Bb
Fuerte (riv.) **34** Bb
Fuerte Olimpo **39** Cb
Fuerteventura (i.) **24** Ab
Fugu **16** Dc
Fujayrah, Al– **21** Fde
Fujian (prov.) **16** Ee
Fujin **16** Ha
Fuji–San (mt.) **16** Ic
Fujisawa **17** Fg
Fukagawa **17** GHc
Fukuchiyama **17** Dg
Fukue **17** Ah
Fukue–Jima (i.) **17** Ah
Fukui **16** Ic
Fukuoka **16** GHd
Fukushima **16** Jc
Fukuyama **16** Hcd
Fulanga (i.) **28** map no.6
Fulda **5** Bc
Fulda (riv.) **5** Bc
Fuling **16** Ce
Fulton **32** Cb
Funabashi **17** FGg
Funafuti (i.) **27** DEc
Funchal **24** Aa
Fundão **9** Bb
Fundy, Bay of– **31** Id
Funtua **24** Cc
Furancungo **26** Cc
Furano **17** Hc
Furmanov **12** EFb
Furnas, Reprêsa de– (l.) **39** Db
Furneaux Group **29** map no.1
Fürstenfeld **5** EFe
Fürstenfeldbruck **5** Cd
Fürstenwalde **5** Eb
Fürth **5** Cd
Furukawa **17** Ge
Fushun **14** Fe
Füssen **5** Ce
Futuna, Île– (i.) **27** DEc
Fuwah **22** Cg
Fu Xian **16** Fc
Fuxin **16** Fb
Fuyang **16** DEd
Fuyu **16** FGa
Fuyuan **16** Ha
Fuzhou [China] **16** EFe
Fuzhou [China] **16** Ee
Fyn (i.) **4** Be

G

Gaalkacyo **25** Ed
Gabela **26** Ac
Gabès, Gulf of– **24** Da
Gabon (riv.) **24** Cde
Gabon (Ind. St.) **23** CDef
Gaborone **26** Bd
Gabrovo **11** Fb
Gacko **11** Cb
Gadag **20** Ee
Gäddede **4** Cb
Gadjač **12** Dc
Gádor **9** Dd

Gadsden **32** Cb
Gǎeşti **6** Gd
Gaeta **10** Dd
Gaeta, Golfo di– **10** Dd
Gagarin **12** DEb
Gagnoa **24** Bd
Gagnon **31** Ic
Gaïdouronésion → Chrysé (i.) **11** Ff
Gainesville [Fl.–U.S.] **32** Cc
Gainesville [Ga.–U.S.] **32** Cb
Gainesville [Tx.–U.S.] **32** Bb
Gairdner, Lake– **29** Fe
Gairloch **7** CDc
Gaj **12** Ic
Gajny **12** Ha
Gajsin **6** Ib
Gajvoron **6** Ib
Galán, Cerro– **39** Bb
Galapagos Islands **36** ABcd
Galaţi **6** Hld
Galatina **10** Gd
Galela **18** Gb
Galera, Punta– [Chile] (cap.) **39** Ac
Galera, Punta– [Ec.] (cap.) **37** Ab
Galesburg **32** BCa
Galič [Russia] **12** Fb
Galič [Ukr.] **6** Gb
Galicia [Pol.] (phys. reg.) **5** Hld
Galicia [Sp.] (phys. reg.) **9** ABa
Galilee, Sea of– → Tiberias, Lake– **22** EFf
Galite, La– (i.) **10** Bf
Galle **15** Ci
Gállego (riv.) **9** Ea
Gallinas, Punta– (cap.) **37** Ba
Gallipoli **10** Gd
Gallipoli → Gelibolu **22** Ab
Galloway, Mull of– (cap.) **7** Dd
Gallup **33** Cc
Gallur **9** Eb
Galveston **30** Ig
Galway **7** Be
Galway Bay **7** Be
Gambela **25** Dd
Gambia (Ind. St.) **23** Ad
Gambia (riv.) **24** Ac
Gambier Islands **28** Cd
Gamboa **35** map no.1
Gamboma **26** Ab
Gambos **26** Ac
Gammelstad **4** Eb
Gamova, mys– **17** Bc
Ganda **26** Ac
Gandak (riv.) **19** Hlj
Gander **31** Jd
Gandhinagar **20** Dd
Gandía **9** EFc
Ganganagar **20** Dc
Gangapur **19** Gj
Gangdisê Shan **20** FGbc
Ganges (riv.) **20** Fc
Ganges, Mouths of the– **20** GHd
Gangtok **15** Cg
Gangu **16** Cd
Gan Jiang (riv.) **16** DEe

Gannat **8** Ed
Gannett Peak **33** BCb
Ganso Azul **37** Bc
Gansu (prov.) **16** Bc
Ganzhou **16** DEe
Gao **24** Cc
Gaoua **24** Bcd
Gaoyou **16** Ed
Gap **8** FGe
Garacad **25** EFd
Garanhuns **38** Db
Garapan **27** Cb
Garda **10** Cb
Garda, Lago di– (l.) **10** Cb
Gardanne **8** FGf
Gardelegen **5** Cb
Garden City **32** Bb
Gardez **20** Cb
Gardner Pinnacles (i.) **28** Aa
Gargaliánoi **11** De
Gargano, Monte– **10** Ed
Garies **26** Ae
Garissa **26** Cb
Garmisch–Partenkirchen **5** Ce
Garonne (riv.) **8** CDe
Garoowe **25** Ed
Garoua **24** Dd
Garrovillas **9** Bc
Garrucha **9** Ed
Garry, Lake– **31** EFb
Garut **18** Cf
Garwa **19** Hj
Gary **32** Ca
Garyarsa **20** Fb
Garzê **16** ABd
Garzón **37** Bb
Gasan–Kuli **21** Eb
Gascony (hist. reg.) **8** CDf
Gascoyne Junction **29** Bd
Gascoyne River **29** ABcd
Gashua **24** Dc
Gaspé **31** Id
Gaspé, Péninsule de– **31** Id
Gastonia **32** Cb
Gastre **40** Bb
Gata, Akra– **22** De
Gata, Cabo de– (cap.) **9** DEd
Gata, Sierra de– (mts.) **9** Bb
Gatčina **4** Ec
Gateshead **7** EFd
Gâtine, Hauteurs de la– (mts.) **8** Cd
Gatton **29** Id
Gatún **35** map no.1
Gatún, Rio– (riv.) **35** map no.1
Gatun Lake **35** map no.1
Gatun Locks **35** map no.1
Gaucín **9** Cd
Gaud–i–Zirreh (l.) **21** Gd
Gauja (riv.) **4** Fd
Gavdhopoúla (i.) **11** Ef
Gávdhos (i.) **11** EFf
Gave de Pau (riv.) **8** Cf
Gävle **4** Dc
Gawahati **19** Bc
Gawler **29** Fe
Gawler Ranges **29** EFe
Gaxnun Nur (l.) **16** ABb
Gaya [India] **20** FGcd
Gaya [Niger] **24** Cc
Gayndah **29** Id

Gaza **22** Eg
Gaziantep **21** Bb
Gazipaşa **22** CDd
Gdańsk (Danzig) **5** Ga
Gdańsk, Gulf of– **5** Ga
Gdov **4** FGd
Gdynia **5** FGa
Gebe, Pulau– (i.) **18** Gde
Gebze **11** Hc
Gediz (riv.) **22** ABc
Gediz **22** Bc
Gedser **4** BCe
Geelong **29** Gf
Geelvink Channel **29** Ad
Geesthacht **5** Cb
Geita **26** Cb
Gejiu **16** Bf
Gela **10** Ef
Gelegra **22** CDbc
Gelibolu (Gallipoli) **22** Ab
Gelsenkirchen **5** Ac
Gemena **26** ABa
Gemlik **22** Bb
Genale (riv.) **25** DEd
General Acha **39** Bc
General Alvear **39** Bc
General Belgrano Station **42** grid square no.1
General Bernardo O'Higgins **42** grid square no.1
General Carrera, Lago– **40** Ab
General Conesa **40** Bab
General Juan Madariaga **39** Cc
General La Madrid **39** Bc
General Paz **39** Cb
General Pico **39** Bc
General Pinedo **39** Bb
General Roca **39** Bc
General Santos **18** FGc
General Toševo **11** GHb
Geneva **5** Ae
Geneva, Lake– (Leman, Lac–) **10** Aa
Genicek **12** DEd
Gennargentu (mts.) **10** Bde
Genoa **10** Bb
Genoa, Gulf of– **10** Bb
Genrietty, ostrov– **14** IJb
Gent **8** Eb
Genthin **5** CDb
Geographe Bay **29** ABe
Geographe Channel **29** Acd
Georga, Zemlja– **13** DEab
George **26** Be
George Town **29** map no.1
Georgetown [Cay. Is.] **35** BCb
Georgetown [Mala.] **19** CDgh
Georgetown [U.S.] **32** Db
Georgetown (Demerara) **37** Db
George V Coast **42** grid square no.4
Georgia (State) **32** Cb
Georgia (Ind. St.) **13** De
Georgian Bay **31** GHd
Georgina River **29** Fc
Georg von Neumayer **42** grid square no.1
Gera **5** CDc
Geral, Serra– (mts.) **39** CDb
Geral de Goiás, Serra– (mts.) **38** Cc

Geraldton [Austl.] **29** Ad
Geraldton [Can.] **31** Gd
Gereshk **20** Bb
Gerlachovský štit (mt.) **5** Hd
Germany (Ind. St.) **3** DEbc
Germiston **26** Bd
Gerona **9** Gab
Gers (riv.) **8** Df
Gerze **22** Eb
Geser **18** He
Getafe **9** CDb
Geteina, El– **25** Dc
Gevgelija **11** Ec
Geyik dağ (mt.) **22** Dd
Geysir **4** map no.1
Ghadāmis **24** CDab
Ghaghara (riv.) **20** Fc
Ghana (Ind. St.) **23** BCe
Ghanzi **26** Bd
Ghardaïa **24** Ca
Ghardimaou **10** Bf
Gharyān **24** Da
Ghāt **24** CDb
Ghatsila **19** Ik
Ghaydah, Al– **21** Ef
Ghazāl, Baḥr al– (riv.) **25** CDd
Ghazālah, Al– **21** Cd
Ghaziabad **19** Gi
Ghazipur **19** Hj
Ghazni **20** Cb
Gheorghe Gheorghiu–Dej **6** Hc
Gheorghieni **6** GHc
Gherla **6** FGc
Ghor, El– **22** Efg
Ghugri (riv.) **19** Ij
Ghurdaqah, Al– **25** Db
Gialoúsa **22** DEe
Giandža (Kirovabad) **13** De
Giant's Causeway **7** Cd
Giarre **10** Ef
Gibara **35** Ca
Gibeon **26** Ad
Gibraltar **9** Cd
Gibraltar, Strait of– **24** Ba
Gibson Desert **29** CDc
Gidole **25** Dd
Gien **8** Ed
Gießen **5** Bc
Gifu **16** Ic
Giglio (i.) **10** Cc
Gijón **9** Ca
Gila (riv.) **33** Bc
Gila Bend **33** Bc
Gilbāna **25** map no.1
Gilbert River **29** Gb
Gilgit **20** Da
Gillingham **7** Gf
Gineifa **25** map no.1
Gingoog (mt.) **18** FGc
Ginir **25** Ed
Gioia del Colle **10** Fd
Gióna Óros (mt.) **11** Ed
Giovi, Passo dei– (p.) **10** Bb
Girardot **37** Bb
Giresun **21** Ba
Giresun dağları (mts.) **22** FGb
Giridih **19** Ij
Gironde (riv. m.) **8** Ce
Gisborne **27** Dd
Giulianova **10** DEc
Giurgiu **6** Gde

Givet **8** Fb
Givors **8** Fe
Giza **25** CDab
Gižiga **14** IJc
Giżycko **5** Hab
Gjirokastra **11** CDc
Gjoia Haven **31** Fb
Gjøvik **4** Bc
Gjuhës, Kep i– **11** Cc
Glace Bay **32** Fa
Gladstone **29** Ic
Gláma (mt.) **4** map no.1
Gláma (riv.) **4** Bcd
Glasgow [U.K.] **7** DEd
Glasgow [U.S.] **33** Cb
Glauchau **5** Dc
Glazov **13** Ed
Glendale **33** Bc
Glendive **33** Cb
Glenelg River **29** Gf
Glen Innes **29** Id
Glen More (phys. reg.) **7** Dc
Glens Falls **32** Da
Glenwood Springs **33** Cbc
Glina **10** Fb
Glittertind (mt.) **4** Bc
Gliwice (mt.) **5** Gc
Globe **33** BCc
Głogów **5** EFc
Glomfjord **4** Cb
Glommersträsk **4** DEb
Glorieuses, Îles– **26** map no.1
Gloucester **7** EFf
Głuchołazy **5** Fc
Glückstadt **5** Bb
Gluhov **12** Ec
Gmünd **5** Ed
Gmunden **5** DEe
Gniezno **5** Fb
Gnjilane **11** Db
Gnowangerup **29** Be
Goa (State) **20** De
Goalpara **19** Jj
Goba **25** DEd
Gobabis **23** DEh
Gobernador Gregores **40** ABb
Gobi Desert **14** De
Gobijski Altaj **16** ABab
Gobò **17** Dgh
Goce Delčev **11** EFc
Godavari (riv.) **20** Ee
Godhavn / Qeqertarsuaq **30** MNc
Godhra **20** Dd
Godolló **6** Dc
Godoy Cruz **39** Bc
Godthåb / Nuuk **30** MNc
Gō–Gawa (riv.) **17** Cg
Gogland, ostrov– (i.) **4** Fc
Goiana **38** Db
Goiânia **39** CDa
Goiás (State) **38** Cc
Goiás **39** Ca
Gökçeada (i.) **11** Fc
Gökırmak (riv.) **22** Eb
Göksu [Tur.] (riv.) **22** Bb
Göksu [Tur.] (riv.) **22** Dd
Göksu [Tur.] (riv.) **22** EFd
Göksun **22** Fc
Gol **4** Bc
Golburn Islands **29** Ea
Golčiha **13** Hb

Gölcük **22** BCb
Goľđap **5** Ia
Gold Coast (phys. reg.) **24** Bd
Gold Coast **29** IJd
Golden **31** Bc
Goléa, El– **24** Ca
Goleniów **5** Eb
Golfito **35** Bc
Golija (mt.) **11** CDb
Goljam Perelik (mt.) **11** EFc
Golmud **15** Df
Golo (riv.) **8** map no.1
Golpāyegān **21** DEc
Golspie **7** Ebc
Goma **25** Ce
Gomati (riv.) **19** Hj
Gombe **24** Dc
Gomel **13** Cd
Gomera (i.) **24** Ab
Gómez Palacio **34** Bb
Gomo **20** Gb
Gonābād **21** FGc
Gonaïves **35** Cb
Gonâve, Isla de la– (i.) **35** Cb
Gonbad–e–Qabus **21** EFb
Gonda **19** Hj
Gonder **25** Dc
Gondia **20** EFd
Gönen **11** Gc
Gong'an **16** Dde
Gongbo'gyamda **19** Bbc
Gongga Shan (mt.) **16** Be
Gonghe **16** ABc
Good Hope, Cape of– **26** Ae
Goodland **33** Cc
Goomalling **29** Be
Goondiwindi **29** HId
Goose Bay **31** Jc
Gorakhpur **20** FGc
Gördes **11** Hd
Gordonvale **29** Hb
Gore **27** Be
Goré [Chad] **25** Bd
Goré [Eth.] **25** Dd
Gorgān **21** EFb
Gorgogna, Isla– (i.) **37** Bb
Gorgora **25** Dc
Gorizia **10** Dab
Gorki **12** Dc
Gorki → Nižni Novgorod **13** Dd
Gorlice **5** Hd
Görlitz **5** Ec
Gorlovka **13** CDe
Gorna Orjahovica **11** FGb
Gornjacki **13** Fc
Gornji Vakuf **6** Ce
Gorno Altajsk **13** Hd
Gornozavodsk **14** GHe
Gorny **17** CDb
Gorodec **12** Fb
Gorodenka **6** Gb
Gorodišče **12** Dd
Gorodnica **6** Ha
Gorodok [Mold.] **6** Hb
Gorodok [Ukr.] **12** Cd
Gorohov **6** Ga
Gorontalo **18** Fd
Goryn (riv.) **12** Cc
Gorzów Wielkopolski **5** Eb
Goshogawara **17** FGd
Goslar **5** Cc
Gospić **6** Bd

Gosport **7** Ff
Gostivar **11** Dc
Gostyń **5** Fc
Gostynin **5** Gb
Göta älv (riv.) **4** Cd
Göta kanal **4** CDd
Götaland **4** Cd
Göteborg **4** BCd
Gotel Mountains **24** Dd
Gotha **5** Cc
Gotland (i.) **4** Dd
Gotō–Rettō **16** Gd
Gotska Sandön (i.) **4** Dd
Göttingen **5** BCc
Gough (i.) **23** ABj
Gouin, Réservoir– (res.) **31** Hd
Goulburn **29** HIef
Goulette, La– **10** Cf
Gouménissa **11** Ec
Goundam **24** Bc
Gourdon **8** De
Gouré **24** Dc
Gouro **25** BCc
Govāter **20** Bc
Gove Peninsula **29** Fa
Goverla, gora– (mt.) **6** Gb
Governador Valadares **39** Da
Goya **39** Cb
Göynük **22** Cb
Gozo (i.) **10** Ef
Graaff Reinet **26** Be
Gračac **6** BCd
Gracias a Dios, Cabo– **35** Bb
Gradaús **38** Bb
Gradaús, Serra dos– (mts.) **38** Bb
Grafton **29** Id
Grafton, Cape– **29** Hb
Graham Island **31** Bc
Graham Land **42** grid square no.1
Grahamstown **26** Be
Grain Coast **24** ABd
Grajaú **38** Cb
Grajewo **5** Ib
Grampian Mountains **7** DEc
Granada [Nic.] **35** Bb
Granada [Sp.] **9** Dd
Gran Arber (mt.) **5** Dd
Granby **31** Hd
Gran Canaria (i.) **24** Ab
Gran Chaco (phys. reg.) **39** BCb
Grand Bahama Island **32** Dc
Grand Ballon **8** Gd
Grand–Bassam **24** Bd
Grand Canal **7** Ce
Grand Canyon (v.) **33** Bc
Grand Canyon **33** Bc
Grand Cayman (i.) **35** Bb
Grand'Combe, La– **8** EFe
Grande, Rio– [Bol.] (riv.) **39** Ba
Grande, Rio– [Braz.] (riv.) **39** Dab
Grande, Rio– [Braz.] (riv.) **38** Cc
Grande, Rio– [N. Amer.] (riv.) **33** CDd
Grande, Rio– [Nic.] (riv.) **35** Bb
Grande Comore (i.) **26** Dc

H

Hab - Hek

Hekla (mt.) **4** map no.1
Hel **5** Ga
Helagsfjället (gl.) **4** BCc
Helan Shan (mts.) **16** Cc
Helena [Ar.–U.S.] **32** BCb
Helena [Mt.–U.S.] **33** Bb
Helen Reef (i.) **27** Bb
Helgeland (phys. reg.) **4** Cb
Helgoland (i.) **5** Aa
Hellin **9** Ec
Hell Ville **23** GHg
Helmand (riv.) **20** Bb
Helmsdale **7** Eb
Helmstedt **5** Cb
Helsingborg **4** BCde
Helsingfors / Helsinki **4** Fcd
Helsingør **5** CDa
Helsinki / Helsingfors **4** Fcd
Henan (prov.) **16** Dd
Henares (riv.) **9** Db
Henbury **29** Ec
Henderson **33** Bc
Henderson Island **28** Cd
Hengchun **16** EFf
Hengelo **8** Ga
Hengxian **16** Cf
Hengyang **15** Dg
Hénin–Liétard **8** Eb
Hennebont **8** Bd
Henzada **19** BCe
Hepu **16** Cf
Heras, Colonia de– **36** CDh
Herät **15** Cf
Hercegnovi **11** Cbc
Heredia **35** Bbc
Hereford **7** Ee
Hereheretule Atoll **28** Bc
Hereke **22** BCb
Herford **5** Bb
Herma Ness (cap.) **7** Fa
Hermanus **26** Ae
Hermón (mt.) **22** Ef
Hermosillo **34** Ab
Hernandarias **39** Cb
Herning **4** Bd
Herrera del Duque **9** Cc
Herson **13** Ce
Hertford **7** FGf
Hervás **9** BCb
Hervey Bay **29** Icd
Hervey Bay (g.) **29** Icd
Herzegovina (phys. reg.) **11** BCb
Hessen (State) **5** Bc
Heta (riv.) **14** Cb
Heves **6** Ec
Hexian **16** Df
Heyuan **16** Df
Hibbing **32** Ba
Hida (mts.) **17** Efg
Hidaka–Sanmyaku (mts.) **17** Hc
Hidalgo del Parral **34** Bb
Hierro (i.) **24** Ab
Higashine **17** FGe
High River **31** Dc
Highs Atlas (mts.) **24** Ba
Hiiumaa (i.) **4** Ed
Híjar **9** Eb
Híjāz, Al– (hist. reg.) **21** BCde
Hikone **17** DEg
Hildesheim **5** BCb

Hilla, El– **25** Cc
Ḥillah, Al– **21** CDc
Hillsboro **32** Bb
Hilo **28** map no.1
Hilok (riv.) **16** Da
Hilok **14** Ed
Hilversum **8** Fa
Himachal Pradesh (State) **20** Eb
Himalayas (mts.) **20** EHbc
Himara **11** CDc
Himeji **16** Hcd
Himi **17** Ef
Himki **12** Eb
Ḥinākīyah, Al– **21** Ce
Hinche **35** Cb
Hinchinbrook Island **29** Hb
Hindukush (mts.) **20** CDa
Hindustan (phys. reg.) **20** DGc
Hingol (riv.) **20** Cc
Hinnøya (i.) **4** CDa
Hınzır Burun **22** Ed
Hiou (i.) **28** map no.4
Hirado **17** Ah
Hīräkud **16** Cf
Hiratsuka **17** Fg
Hirfanlı Barajı **22** DEc
Hirgis–Nur (l.) **14** Ce
Hiroo **17** Hc
Hirosaki **16** Jb
Hiroshima **16** Hd
Hirson **8** Fc
Hīrşova **6** Hld
Hisär **20** DEc
Hispaniola (Haiti) (i.) **35** CDb
Hita **17** Bh
Hitachi **16** Jc
Hitiaa **28** map no.2
Hitoyoshi **17** Bh
Hitra (i.) **4** ABc
Hiva **13** Fe
Hiva Oa, Île– (i.) **28** Cc
Hjälmaren (l.) **4** CDd
Hjørring **4** Bd
Hkakabo Razi (mt.) **19** Cc
Hmelnicki **6** Hb
Hmelnik **6** Hlb
Ho **24** Cd
Hoa Binh **19** DEd
Hobart **29** map no.1
Hobbs **33** Cc
Hobbs Coast **42** grid square no.3
Hobyo **25** Ed
Hochgolling (mt.) **5** DEe
Ho Chi Minh **15** Dhi
Hodaka–Dake (mt.) **17** Ef
Hodh (phys. reg.) **24** Bc
Hódmezővásárhely **6** Ec
Hodonín **5** Fd
Hodorov **6** Gb
Hodžejli **13** Ee
Hodžent (Leninabad) **13** Fe
Hoek van Holland, Rotterdam– **8** EFb
Hof **5** CDc
Höfn **4** map no.1
Hofrat en Nahas **25** Cd
Hofsjökull (gl.) **4** map no.1
Höfu **17** Bgh
Hohe Tavern (mts.) **5** De
Hohhot **16** Db

Hoi An **19** Ee
Hojniki **12** CDc
Hokitika **27** De
Hokkaidō (i.) **16** JKb
Holbæk **5** Cb
Holguín **35** Ca
Hollywood, Los Angeles– **33** ABc
Holm **12** Db
Holman Island **31** CDa
Holmsk **14** He
Holmsund **4** Ec
Holon **22** Efg
Holstebro **4** ABd
Holsteinsborg / Sisimiut **31** Jb
Holyhead **7** De
Homalin **19** BCcd
Hombori **24** Bc
Home Bay **31** Ib
Home Hill **29** Hbc
Homestead **32** Cc
Homoljske planina (mts.) **6** EFd
Homs **21** Bc
Honaz dağı **22** Bd
Honbetsu **17** Hc
Hondo (riv.) **34** Dc
Honduras (Ind. St.) **30** Jh
Honduras, Golfo de– **34** Dc
Honghu **16** De
Hong Kong **15** Dg
Hongshui He **16** Cef
Honguedo, Détroit d'– **32** Ea
Hongze Hu (l.) **16** Ed
Honiara **27** CDc
Honjō **17** Fge
Honningsvag **4** EFa
Honokaa **28** map no.1
Honolulu **28** map no.1
Honshū (i.) **16** Hlbc
Honu **14** Hc
Hood, Mount– **33** Ab
Hoogeveen **8** Ga
Hooker, Bîr– **22** BCg
Hoolehua **28** map no.1
Hoover Dam (dam) **33** Bc
Hopedale **31** IJc
Hopen (i.) **13** Bb
Hopër (riv.) **12** Fc
Hopetoun **29** Ce
Hopkins, Lake– **29** Dc
Hor (riv.) **16** Ia
Hor **14** Ge
Horlick Mountains **42** grid square no.3
Hormigas **34** Bb
Hormuz, Strait of– **21** Fd
Horn (cap.) **4** map no.1
Horn **5** Ed
Horn, Cabo– **40** Bc
Horn, Cape– **36** Di
Hornavan (l.) **4** Db
Horn Islands **27** DEc
Horog **13** Gf
Horqin Youyi Qianqi **16** EFa
Horqueta **39** Cb
Horsens **4** Bde
Horsham **29** Gf
Horten **4** Bd
Hospet **20** Fe
Hospitalet de Llobregat **9** Gb
Hoste, Isla– (i.) **40** ABc
Hotan **20** EFa

Hotin **6** Hb
Hot Springs [Ar.–U.S.] **32** Bb
Hot Springs [S.D.–U.S.] **33** Cb
Houaïlou **28** map no.4
Houei Sai **19** Dd
Houlton **32** Ea
Houma **32** Bc
Houston **32** Bc
Houtman Abrolhos (is.) **29** Ad
Hovran Gölü **22** Cc
Howar **25** Cc
Howe, Cape– **29** Hlf
Howe, West Cape– (cap.) **29** Bf
Howland Island **28** Ab
Hoy (i.) **7** Eb
Høyanger **4** Ac
Hoyos **9** Bb
Hradec Králové **5** EFc
Hristinovka **6** IJb
Hromtau **12** Ic
Hron (riv.) **5** Gd
Hrubieszów **5** Ic
Ḥsakah **21** BCb
Hsinchu **16** Ff
Huachacalla **39** Ba
Huacho **37** Bd
Huai He (riv.) **16** Ed
Huailai **16** Eb
Huainan **16** Ed
Hualien **16** Ff
Huallaga (riv.) **37** Bc
Huambo **26** Ac
Huanan **17** Ba
Huancane **39** ABa
Huancavelica **37** Bd
Huancayo **36** Ce
Huang Hai → Yellow Sea **16** Fc
Huang He **16** Ed
Huang He (riv.) **16** DEc
Huangshi **16** DEde
Huang Shui (riv.) **16** Bc
Huangyan **16** Fe
Huangyuan **16** Bc
Huánuco **37** Bc
Huaráz **37** Bc
Huascarán, Nevado– (mt.) **37** Bc
Hubei **16** Dd
Hubli **15** Ch
Hubsugul (l.) **14** Dd
Ḥudaydah, Al– **21** Cfg
Huddersfield **7** Fe
Hudiksvall **4** Dc
Hudson (riv.) **32** Da
Hudson Bay **31** Gbc
Hudson Strait **31** Hlb
Hue **15** Dh
Huedin **6** Fc
Huehuetenango **35** Ab
Huelma **9** Dd
Huelva **9** Bd
Huércal–Overa **9** DEd
Huesca **9** Ea
Huéscar **9** Dd
Huete **9** Db
Hufūf, Al– **21** DEd
Hughenden **29** Gc
Huila, Nevado del– (mt.) **37** Bb
Huili **16** Be

Iracoubo 37 Db
Irafshān 21 Gd
Iráklia (i.) 11 Fe
İráklion 11 Ff
Iran (Ind. St.) 15 Bf
Iran, Penunungan– 18 Dd
Iránshahr 21 Gd
Irapuato 34 Bb
Iraq (Ind. St.) 15 Bf
Irati 39 Cb
Irazú, Volcán– (mt.) 35 Bc
Irbid 22 Ef
Irbit 12 Jb
Ireland (Ind. St.) 3 BCb
Irgiz 13 Fe
Irian Jaya (prov.) 27 Bc
Irian Jaya 27 Bc
Iringa 26 Cb
Iriomote–Jima (i.) 16 Ff
Iriri (riv.) 38 Bb
Irish Sea 7 De
Irkutsk 14 Dd
Iroise (b.) 8 Ac
Iron Gate (p.) 6 Fd
Iron Knob 29 Fe
Iron Mountain 32 BCa
Ironwood 32 BCa
Irpen 6 Ja
'Irqah, Al– 21 Dg
Irrawaddv, Mouths of the– 19 BCe
Irrawaddy (riv.) 19 Ccd
Irtyš (riv.) 13 Gd
Irún 9 DEa
Isabela, Isla– (i.) 36 Ad
Isafjörður 4 map no.1
Isahaya 17 ABh
Isar (riv.) 5 Dd
Ischia (i.) 10 Dd
Ise 17 Eg
Iseo 10 Cb
Iseo, Lago d'– (l.) 10 Cb
Isère (riv.) 8 Fe
Iserlohn 5 Ac
Isernia 10 Ed
Ise–Wan 17 Eg
Iseyin 24 Cd
İsfendiyar → Küre dağları (mts.) 22 DEb
Ishigaki–Jima (i.) 16 FGf
Ishikari–Gawa (riv.) 17 Hc
Ishikari–Wan 17 Gc
Ishinomaki 16 Jc
Ishizuchi–Yama (mt.) 17 Ch
Ishurdi 20 Gd
Işik dăg (mt.) 22 Db
Isilkul 13 Gd
İšim (riv.) 13 Fd
Išim 13 Fd
Isimbaj 12 Ic
Isiro 26 Ba
Iskar (riv.) 11 EFb
İskenderun 22 Fd
İskenderun Körfezi 22 EFd
İskilip 22 DEb
İskitim 13 Hd
Isla–Cristina 9 Bd
Islâhiye 22 Fd
Islamabad 15 Cf
Island Lagoon 29 Fe
Islay (i.) 7 Cd
Isle (riv.) 8 De
Ismailia 25 Da

Isna 25 Db
Isoka 26 Cc
Isola del Liri 10 Dd
Isparta 22 Cd
Isperih 11 Gb
Israel (Ind. St.) 15 Bf
Issoire 8 Ee
Issoudun 8 DEd
Issyk–Kul (Rybačje) 13 Ge
Issyk–Kul, ozero– (l.) 13 Ge
İstanbul (Constantinople) 22 Bb
Istanbul–Üsküdar 22 Bb
Istiaía 11 Ed
Istmina 37 Bb
Istra 6 ABd
Itabaiana 38 Dc
Itaberaba 38 Cc
Itabira 39 Da
Itabuna 38 Dc
Itacaiúnas (riv.) 38 BCb
Itacoatiara 38 Bb
Itagüí 37 Bb
Itaituba 38 Bb
Itajaí 39 Db
Itajubá 39 Db
Italia, Cerro– 40 Bc
Italy (Ind. St.) 3 Ec
Itambé, Pico de– (mt.) 39 Da
Itaperuna 39 Db
Itapetinga 38 CDc
Itapeva 39 Db
Itapicuru [Braz.] (riv.) 38 Cb
Itapicuru [Braz.] (riv.) 38 Dc
Itapipoca 38 Db
Itaqui 39 Cb
Itararé 39 Db
Itarsi 20 Ed
Itea 11 Ed
Ithaca 32 Da
Ithaca (i.) 11 Dd
Itoigawa 17 Ef
Itseqqortoormit / Scoresbysund 30 PQb
Ituí (riv.) 37 Bc
Itumbiara 39 Da
Iturup, ostrov– / Etorofu Tō (i.) 14 He
Ituxi (Iquiri) (riv.) 37 Cc
Itzehoe 5 Bb
Iultin 14 KLc
Ival (riv.) 39 Cb
Ivalo 4 FGa
Ivalojoki (riv.) 4 Fa
Ivangorod 4 Gd
Ivanhoe 29 GHe
Ivankov 6 Ia
Ivano–Frankovsk 6 Gb
Ivanovo 3 GHb
Ivdel 13 EFc
Ivittuut 31 Kb
Ivory Coast (Ind. St.) 23 Be
Ivory Coast (phys. reg.) 24 Bd
Ivrea 10 Ab
Ivujvik 31 Hb
Iwaki 16 Jc
Iwakuni 17 BCg
Iwamisawa 17 Gc
Iwanai 17 Fc
Iwanuma 17 Gef
Iwate–San (mt.) 17 Gde
Iwo 24 Cd

Ixtlán del Rio 34 Bb
Iyadh 21 Dfg
Izamal 34 Db
Izberbaš 21 Da
Iževsk 13 Ed
Izjaslav 6 Ha
Izjum 12 Ed
Izki 21 Fe
Izmail 6 Id
İzmir 22 Ac
Izmir Bay 22 Ac
Izmit 22 BCb
Iznalloz 9 Dd
Iznik 22 BCb
İznik Gölü 22 Bb
Izozog, Bañados del– 39 Ba
Izúcar de Matamoros 34 Cc
Izu–Hantō 17 Fg
Izumo 17 Cg
Izu–Shotō 16 IJd
Izvesti C.I.K., ostrova– 13 GHb

J

Jabal Iweibid 25 map no.1
Jabalón (riv.) 9 Dc
Jabalpur 15 Cg
Jablah 22 Ee
Jablanica (mt.) 11 Dc
Jablanica 10 Fc
Jablonec–nad–Nisou 5 Ec
Jablonicki, pereval– 6 FGb
Jablunkovsky prusmyk 5 Gd
Jaboatão 38 Db
Jabor 28 map no.3
Jaburu 37 Cc
Jaca 9 Ea
Jacarézinho 39 CDb
Jaciparaná 37 Cc
Jackson [Mi.–U.S.] 32 Ca
Jackson [Ms.–U.S.] 32 BCb
Jackson [Tn.–U.S.] 32 Ca
Jacksonville 32 CDb
Jacobabad 20 Cc
Jacobina 38 Cc
Jacques Cartier, Détroit de– (str.) 32 Eab
Jacuí 39 Cbc
Jadida, El– 24 ABa
Jaén [Peru] 37 Bc
Jaén [Sp.] 9 Dd
Jaffna 15 Chi
Jafr, Al– 22 Fg
Jagdalpur 20 Fe
Jaghbūb, Al– 24 Eab
Jaguarão 39 Cc
Jaguariaíva 39 CDb
Jaguaribe (riv.) 38 Db
Jahrom 21 Ed
Jaipur 15 Cg
Jaisalmer 20 Dc
Jajce 6 Ed
Jajva 6 Ib
Jakarta 18 Cf
Jakobstad 4 Ec
Jakutsk 14 Fc
Jakuvlevca (mt.) 17 Cb
Jalalabad 20 CDb
Jalālah al Baḥrāyah, Jabal– (mt.) 22 CDh

Jalālah al Qibliah, Jabal– (mt.) 22 CDh
Jalandhar 20 Eb
Jalapa Enriquez 34 Cbc
Jalgaon 20 DEd
Jalingo 24 Dd
Jalna 20 Ee
Jalón (riv.) 9 Eb
Jalpaiguri 19 Jj
Jalta 13 Ce
Jālū, Wāḥāt– 24 Eb
Jaluit Atoll 27 Db
Jaluit Atoll (at.) 28 map no.3
Jalutorovsk 13 Fd
Jamaame 25 Ee
Jamaica (Ind. St.) 30 JKh
Jamaica Channel 35 Cb
Jamalpur [Bngl.] 20 GHcd
Jamalpur [India] 19 Ij
Jamantau, gora– (mt.) 13 Ed
Jamanxim (riv.) 38 Bb
Jambol 11 Gb
Jambongan, Pulau– (i.) 18 Ec
James (riv.) 32 Ba
James Bay 30 JKd
James Ross Island 42 grid square no.1
Jamestown [N.D.–U.S.] 33 CDb
Jamestown [N.Y.–U.S.] 32 Da
Jammu 20 DEb
Jammu e Kashmir (State) 20 DEab
Jamnagar 15 Cg
Jampol [Ukr.] 6 GHb
Jampol [Ukr.] 6 Ib
Jämsä 4 Fc
Jamshedpur 20 FGd
Jamsk 14 Id
Jana (riv.) 14 Gc
Janaúba 39 Da
Janesville 32 Ca
Janghai 19 Hj
Janin 22 Ef
Janisjärvi, ozero– 4 Gc
Jan Mayen (i.) 30 Rbc
Jánoshalma 6 Dc
Janski 14 Gc
Jantra (riv.) 11 FGb
Januária 39 Da
Japan (Ind. St.) 15 Ef
Japan, Sea of– / East Sea 16 HIbc
Japurá (riv.) 37 Cc
Japurá 37 Cc
Jar 12 Hb
Jarābulus 22 FGd
Jaramillo 40 Bb
Jaransk 12 Gb
Jarcevo [Russia] 14 BCcd
Jarcevo [Russia] 12 Db
Jardines de la Reina (i.) 35 BCa
Jari (riv.) 38 Bab
Jarīd, Shaṭṭ al– (l.) 24 Ca
Jarocin 5 FGbc
Jaroslavl 13 Cd
Jarosław 5 Icd
Järpen 4 Cc
Jarub 21 Ef
Järvenpää 4 Fc
Jarvis Island 28 Abc
Jäsk 21 Fd

Kahoolawe (i.) **28** map no.1
Kahovka **12** Dd
Kahovskoje vodohranilišče **12** DEd
Kahramanmaras **21** Bb
Kahuku Point **28** map no.1
Kai, Kepulauan– **27** Bc
Kaiama **24** Cd
Kaieteur Falls **37** Db
Kaifeng **16** DEcd
Kaikoura **27** De
Kailua **28** map no.1
Kainji Reservoir **24** Ccd
Kaiserslautern **5** ABd
Kaishantun **17** ABc
Kaiwi Channel **28** map no.1
Kaiyuan [China] **16** Fb
Kaiyuan [China] **16** Bf
Kajaani **4** Fb
Kajabbi **29** FGbc
Kakamas **26** ABd
Kakegawa **17** EFg
Kakinada **20** Fe
Kala, El– **10** Bf
Kalabáka **11** DEd
Kalabo **26** Bc
Kalač **12** Fc
Kalač–na–Donu **12** Fd
Ka Lae (cap.) **28** map no.1
Kalahari Desert **26** Bd
Kalakan **14** Ed
Kalámai **11** DEe
Kalamazoo **32** Ca
Kalamunda **29** ABe
Kalannie **29** Be
Kalao, Pulau– (i.) **18** EFf
Kalaotoa, Pulau– (is.) **18** Ff
Kalapana **28** map no.1
Kalaraš **6** Hlc
Kalat **20** Cc
Kalaus (riv.) **12** Fd
Kalavarda **22** ABd
Kalávrita **11** Ed
Kale [Tur.] **22** BCd
Kale [Tur.] **22** Bd
Kalecik **22** Db
Kalemie **26** Bb
Kalevala **4** Gb
Kalewa **19** BCd
Kalgoorlie **29** Ce
Kaliakra, Nos– **11** Hb
Kalibo **18** Fb
Kalimantan → Borneo (i.) **18** DEd
Kálimnos (i.) **11** Ge
Kalimpong **19** Jj
Kalinin → Tver **13** Cd
Kaliningrad **13** ABd
Kalininsk **12** FGc
Kalinkoviči **3** FGb
Kalinovka **6** Ib
Kalispell **33** Bb
Kalisz **5** Gc
Kalixälven (riv.) **4** Eb
Kaljazin **12** Eb
Kalkfontein **26** Bd
Kallavesi (l.) **4** Fc
Kallsjön (l.) **4** Cc
Kalmar **4** CDd
Kalmyk (Aut. Rep.) **13** De
Kalmykovo **12** Hd
Kalocsa **6** Dc
Kalpa **20** Eb

Kalpeni Island **20** Dfg
Kalpi **20** EFc
Kaluga **13** Cd
Kalumburu **29** Da
Kalundborg **5** Ca
Kaluš **6** Gb
Kalvarija **5** Ia
Kalyan **20** De
Kama (riv.) **12** Hb
Kamaishi **17** GHe
Kamarän **21** Cf
Kambalda **29** Ce
Kambarka **12** Hlb
Kambove **26** Bc
Kamčatka (riv.) **14** Id
Kamchatka Peninsula **14** Id
Kamčija (riv.) **6** He
Kamenec–Podolski **6** Hb
Kamenjak, Rt– **6** Ad
Kamenka [Russia] **17** DEb
Kamenka [Russia] **12** Fc
Kamenka–Bugskaja **6** Ga
Kamen Kaširski **12** BCc
Kamen–na–Obi **13** GHd
Kamen–Rybolov **17** BCb
Kamenskoje **14** Jc
Kamenskoje (Dneprodzeržinsk) **12** Dd
Kamenskoje vodohranilišče **12** Ib
Kamensk–Šahtinski **12** Fd
Kamensk–Uralski **13** Fd
Kamenz **5** Ec
Kamień Pomorski **5** Eab
Kamina **23** Ef
Kamino–Shima (i.) **17** Ag
Kamloops **33** Aa
Kampala **25** Dde
Kampar (riv.) **18** Bde
Kampar **19** Dh
Kampen **8** Fa
Kâmpóng Chhnăng **19** Df
Kâmpóng Saôm **19** Df
Kampot **19** Df
Kamyšin **13** Dde
Kananga **26** Bb
Kanaš **12** Gb
Kanazawa **16** Ic
Kanchanaburi **19** Cf
Kanchenjunga (mt.) **19** IJj
Kānchipuram **20** EFf
Kandalakša **13** BCc
Kandangan **18** Ee
Kandavu Island **27** Dc
Kandavu Passage (str.) **28** map no.6
Kandi **24** Cc
Kandıra **22** Cb
Kandla **20** CDd
Kandy **20** EFg
Kanem (phys. reg.) **25** Bc
Kaneohe **28** map no.1
Kang **20** Bb
Kangaatsiaq / Kangâtsiaq **31** Jb
Kangaba **24** Bc
Kangâmiut **31** Jb
Kangân **21** Ed
Kangar **19** Dg
Kangaroo Island **29** Ff
Kangaruma **37** Db
Kangâtsiaq / Kangaatsiaq **31** Jb

Kangding **16** Bde
Kangean, Kepulauan– **18** Ef
Kangean, Pulau– (i.) **18** Ef
Kanggye **16** Gb
Kangmar **19** Ji
Kangnüng **16** Gc
Kangto (mt.) **19** Bc
Kaniama **26** Bb
Kanin, Poluostrov– **13** Dc
Kanin Nos, mys– **13** Dc
Kanjiža **6** Ec
Kankan **24** Bc
Kankossa **24** ABc
Kannauj **19** GHj
Kano **24** Cc
Kanoya **17** Bi
Kanpur **15** Cg
Kansas (riv.) **32** Bb
Kansas (State) **32** Bb
Kansas City **32** Bb
Kansk **14** Cd
Känthi **19** Ik
Kantō–Heiya (phys. reg.) **17** FGf
Kanton Atoll **28** Ac
Kanye **26** Bd
Kaohsiung **16** EFf
Kaolack **24** Ac
Kaoma **26** Bc
Kapaa **28** map no.1
Kapanga **26** Bb
Kapčagaj **13** Ge
Kapela (mt.) **6** Bd
Kapfenberg **5** Ec
Kapidağı, Yarimadasi– **11** GHc
Kapingamarangi, Atoll– **27** CDb
Kapisigdlit / Kapisillit **31** JKb
Kapisillit / Kapisigdlit **31** JKb
Kapit **18** Dd
Kaposvár **6** Cc
Kapsukas → Marijampolė **5** Ia
Kapuas (riv.) **18** Def
Kapuas Hulu, Pegunungan– **18** Dd
Kapuskasing **31** GHd
Kapuvár **6** Cc
Kara **24** Cc
Karaağaç **11** Gc
Karababa dağı (riv.) **22** EFc
Karabaš **12** IJb
Karabiga **11** Gc
Kara–Bogaz–Gol, zaliv– (b.) **13** Ee
Karabük **22** Db
Karacabey **22** Bb
Karacaköy **11** Hc
Karačev **12** Ec
Karachi **15** Cg
Kara Dağ (mt.) **22** Dd
Karagajly **13** Ge
Karaganda **13** Ge
Karaginski, ostrov– (i.) **14** Jd
Karagöl dağ (mt.) **22** Gb
Karaisali **22** Ed
Karaj **21** Eb
Karak, Al– **22** Eg
Kara–Kolpak (Aut. Rep.) **13** Ee
Karakoram (mts.) **20** Eab
Karakoram Pass **20** Ea

Karaköse–Ağri **21** Cab
Karakumski Kanal **13** EFf
Karakumy (phys. reg.) **13** EFef
Karaman **22** Dd
Karamay **15** Ce
Karamiran Shankou **20** Ga
Karapınar **22** Dd
Karasburg **26** Ad
Kara Sea **41** grid square no.3
Karasjok **4** Fa
Kara Strait **41** grid square no.3
Karasu **22** Cb
Karasuk **13** Gd
Karatas **22** Ed
Karatau, Hrebet– (mts.) **13** FGe
Karatsu **17** ABh
Karaul **13** Hb
Karauli **19** Gj
Karáva (mt.) **11** Dd
Karažal **13** FGe
Karbalā' **21** Cc
Karcag **6** Ec
Kardhitsa **11** DEd
Kärdla **4** Ed
Kärdžali **11** Fc
Karekelong, Pulau– (i.) **18** Gd
Karelia (phys. reg.) **13** Cc
Karelia (Aut. Rep.) **13** Cc
Karen (State) **19** Ce
Kargopol **12** Ea
Karhula **4** Fc
Kariai **11** EFc
Kariba **26** Bc
Kariba, Lake– **26** Bc
Karibib **26** Ad
Karimata Islands **18** Ce
Karimata Strait **18** Ce
Karimnagar **20** EFe
Karimunjawa Islands **18** CDf
Karin **25** Ec
Karis **4** Ec
Karisimbi (mt.) **26** Bb
Karkheh (riv.) **21** Dc
Karkinitski zaliv **12** Dd
Karlobag **6** Bd
Karlovac **6** BCd
Karlovo **11** Fb
Karlovy Vary **5** Dc
Karlshamn **4** Cd
Karlskoga **4** Cd
Karlskrona **4** CDd
Karlsruhe **5** ABd
Karlstad **4** Cd
Karmah **25** Dc
Karnali (riv.) **20** Fc
Karnataka (State) **20** DEf
Karnobat **11** Gb
Karonga **26** Cbc
Karoo (phys. reg.) **26** Be
Karora **25** Dc
Káros (i.) **11** Fe
Kárpathos (i.) **11** Gf
Kárpathos **11** Gf
Karpaty (mts.) **12** BCd
Karpenision **11** DEd
Karpinsk **12** IJab
Karpuzlu **22** ABd
Kars **21** Ca
Karsakpaj **13** Fe
Karši **13** Ff

Kartal 22 Bb
Kartaly 13 Fd
Karumba 29 Gb
Kärun (riv.) 21 Dc
Karvinà 5 Gd
Karwar 20 Df
Karymskoje 14 Ed
Kaş 22 Bd
Kasai (riv.) 26 ABb
Kasai Occidental (reg.) 26 Bb
Kasai Oriental (reg.) 26 Bb
Kasama 26 Cbc
Kasane 26 Bc
Kasba Lake 31 Eb
Kasempa 26 Bc
Kasenga 26 Bc
Kasese 25 CDde
Kasganj 19 Gj
Käshän 21 Ec
Kashi 15 Cf
Kashipur 19 Gi
Kashiwazaki 17 EFf
Käshmar 21 Fb
Kashmir 20 Eb
Kasimov 12 Fc
Kašira 12 Ec
Kasiruta, Pulau– (i.) 18 Ge
Kaskö 4 Ec
Käson, Stenón– 11 Gf
Kasongo 26 Bb
Kásos (i.) 11 Gf
Kaspijski 12 Gd
Kasr, Ra's– 25 Dc
Kassala 25 Dc
Kassándra (pen.) 11 Ecd
Kassándra, Gulf of– 11 Ecd
Kassel 5 Bc
Kasserine 24 Ca
Kassubia (hist. reg.) 5 FGab
Kastamonu 22 DEb
Kastéllion 11 Ef
Kastoria 11 Dc
Kastornoje 12 Ec
Kasur 20 Db
Katanga (hist. reg.) 26 Bb
Katangli 14 Hd
Katanning 29 Be
Katarnian Ghat 19 Hi
Katav–Ivanovsk 12 Ic
Katchall (i.) 19 Bg
Katerini 11 Ec
Katha 19 Cd
Katherine 29 Ea
Kathgodam 19 Gi
Kathiawar (phys. reg.) 20 CDd
Kathmandu 15 Cg
Katihar 19 Ij
Katingan (riv.) 18 De
Katiola 24 Bd
Káto Akhaïa 11 Dde
Katoomba 29 Ie
Katowice 5 Gc
Kätrinä, Jabal– (mt.) 25 Db
Katrineholm 4 CDd
Katsina 24 Cc
Kattakurgan 13 Ff
Kattegat (str.) 4 BCd
Katun (riv.) 13 Hd
Kau 18 Gd
Kauai (i.) 28 Ba
Kauai Channel 28 map no.1

Kauhajoki 4 Ec
Kaula (i.) 28 map no.1
Kaulakahi Channel 28 map no.1
Kauliranta 4 EFb
Kaunas 4 EFe
Kaura Namoda 24 Cc
Kautokeino 4 EFa
Kavacık 22 Bc
Kavaja 11 Cc
Kavála 11 Fc
Kavalerovo 17 Db
Kavaratti (i.) 20 Df
Kavarna 11 Hb
Kawagoe 17 Ffg
Kawaguchi 17 FGfg
Kawaikini (mt.) 28 map no.1
Kawasaki 16 IJc
Kawio, Kepulauan– 18 FGd
Kawm 25 Db
Kawthaung 19 Cfg
Kaya 24 Bc
Kayah (State) 19 Ce
Kayan (riv.) 18 Ed
Kayes 24 Ac
Kayoa, Pulau– (i.) 18 Gde
Kayseri (Cesarea Mazaca) 22 EFc
Kazaçje 14 Gb
Kazakhstan (Ind. St.) 13 EGe
Kazalinsk 13 EFe
Kazan 13 Dd
Kazan (riv.) 31 Eb
Kazanlák 11 Fb
Kazatin 6 Ib
Kaz daği (mt.) 22 Ac
Käzerun 21 Ed
Kažim 12 Ha
Käzimiyah, Al– 21 Cc
Kazincbarcika 6 Eb
Kéa (i.) 11 Fe
Kearney 33 CDb
Kebir (riv.) 22 Fe
Kebnekaise (mt.) 4 Dab
Kecskemét 6 Dc
Kédainiai 4 Ee
Kediri 18 Df
Kédougou 24 Ac
Keele Peak 31 Bb
Keelung 16 Fef
Keetmanshoop 23 DEh
Keewatin, District of– 31 Fb
Kefa (phys. reg.) 25 Cd
Keflavík 4 map no.1
Kehl 5 ABd
Keitele (l.) 4 Fc
Keith 29 Gf
Kelang 18 Bd
Kelang, Pulau– (i.) 18 Ge
Kelasa, Selat– 18 Ce
Kelkit (riv.) 22 Fb
Kéllé 26 Ab
Kelloselkä 4 FGb
Kelowna 31 Dcd
Keltepe (mt.) 22 Db
Keluang 18 Bd
Kem 13 Cc
Kemerovo 13 Hd
Kemi 4 Fb
Kemijärvi (l.) 4 Fb
Kemijärvi 4 Fb
Kemijoki (riv.) 4 Gb
Kempsey 29 Ie

Kempten im Allgäu 5 Ce
Ken (riv.) 20 Ed
Kendal 7 Ed
Kendari 18 Fe
Kenema 24 Ad
Kenge 26 Ab
Kengtung 19 Cd
Kenhardt 26 Bd
Kéniéba 24 ABc
Kénitra 24 Ba
Kenmare 7 Bf
Kenmare River 7 ABf
Kennedy, Cape– →
  Canaveral, Cape– 32 CDc
Keno Hill 31 Bb
Kenora 31 Fcd
Kent (co.) 7 Gf
Kent 24 Ad
Kentau 13 FGe
Kent Peninsula 31 Eb
Kentucky (State) 32 Cb
Kenya (Ind. St.) 23 Fe
Kenya (mt.) 25 De
Keokuk 32 Ba
Keonjhargarh 20 Gd
Kerala (State) 20 Efg
Kerama–Rettō 16 Ge
Kerč 13 Ce
Kerčensky Poluostrov 12 Ed
Kerempe Burun 22 Da
Keren 25 Dc
Kerguelen, Îles– (is.) 2
Kerinci, Gunung– (mt.) 18 Be
Kerkennah Islands 24 Da
Kerki 13 Ff
Kerkíras, Stenón– (str.) 11 CDd
Kermadec Islands 27 Ed
Kermán 21 Fc
Kermänshäh 21 Dc
Kerme Körfezi 11 GHe
Kérouané 24 ABd
Kerulen (riv.) 14 Ee
Keşan 11 Gc
Keşap 22 Gb
Kesennuma 17 GHe
Keshan 16 FGa
Kestenga 4 Gb
Kestep 22 Bd
Keszthely 6 Cc
Kéta 24 Cd
Ketapang 18 CDe
Ketchikan 31 BCc
Ketoj, ostrov– (i.) 14 Ie
Ketrzyn 5 Ha
Kettering 7 Fe
Keuruu 4 Fc
Keweenaw Peninsula 32 Ca
Key West 32 Cc
Kezel Owzan (riv.) 21 Db
Kežma 14 CDd
Khäbüra, Al– 21 Fe
Khairpur 20 Cc
Khalíg el Tína (g.) 25 map no.1
Khálki (i.) 11 Ge
Khalkís 11 EFd
Khalüf 21 Fe
Khamasin, Al– 21 CDe
Khambhät 20 Dd
Khambhät, Gulf of– 20 Dd
Khamir 21 Cf
Khamis Mushayt 21 Cf

Khamsa 25 map no.1
Khanabad 20 CDa
Khanaqin 21 CDc
Khandaq, Al– (str.) 25 CDc
Khandwa 20 Ed
Khanewal 20 Db
Khanh Hung 19 Eg
Khánia 11 EFf
Khaníon, Kólpos– 11 EFf
Khanpur 20 Dc
Khän Yūnus 22 DEg
Kharagpur 15 Cg
Kharga Oasis 25 CDb
Khárijah, Al– 25 CDb
Khärk, Jazireh– ye– (i.) 21 DEd
Khartoum 25 Dc
Khartoum North 25 Dc
Khäsh 21 Gd
Khashm al Qirbah 25 Dc
Khasi–Jaintia Hill 16 Ee
Khawr al Fakkän 21 Fd
Khaybar 21 BCd
Khíos 22 Ac
Kholm 20 Ca
Khong 19 Ef
Khong Sedon 19 Ee
Khon Kaen 19 De
Khoräsän (phys. reg.) 21 Fbc
Khóra Sfakíon 11 Ff
Khorat → Nakhon
  Ratchasima 19 Def
Khorixas 26 Ad
Khorramäbäd 21 Dc
Khorramshahr 21 DEc
Khouribga 24 Ba
Khrisí (i.) 11 Ff
Khufrah, Al– 24 Cc
Khulna 20 GHd
Khums, Al– 24 Da
Khuríyä Muríya, Jazä'ir– 21 Ff
Khurmah, Al– 21 Ce
Khuzdar 20 Cc
Khvoy 21 CDb
Khyber Pass 20 Db
Kiantajärvi 4 Gb
Kibombo 26 Bb
Kibondo 26 Cb
Kičevo 11 Dc
Kidal 24 Cc
Kidderminster 7 Ee
Kidira 24 Ac
Kiel 4 Be
Kiel Canal 5 Bab
Kielce 5 Hc
Kieler Bucht 5 Ca
Kieta 27 Cc
Kiev 13 Cd
Kiffa 24 Ac
Kifísiá 11 EFd
Kigali 26 BCb
Kigoma 23 EFf
Kii–Hantō 17 Eh
Kii–Suidō 17 Dh
Kijevskoje vodohranilišče 12 CDc
Kikai–Jima (i.) 16 GHe
Kikinda 6 Ed
Kikonai 17 FGd
Kikori 27 Cc
Kikwit 26 Ab
Kil 4 Cd

Kon - Kur

Kongolo **26** Bb
Kongor **25** Dd
Kongsberg **4** Bcd
Kongsvinger **4** BCc
Kongur Shan (mt.) **13** Gf
Konin **5** Gb
Konjic **6** CDe
Konoša **13** CDc
Konotop **13** Cd
Końskie **5** GHc
Konstantinovka **12** Ed
Konstanz **5** Be
Kontagora **24** Cc
Kontiomäki **4** Gb
Kontum (Cong Tum) **19** Ef
Konya **22** Dd
Konžakovski Kamen, gora–
  (mt.) **12** IJb
Kootenay (riv.) **33** Bb
Kopaonik (mts.) **11** Db
Kópavogur **4** map no.1
Kopejsk **13** Fd
Kopervik **4** Ad
Kopetdag, Hrebet– (mts.) **21**
  Fb
Köping **4** CDd
Koprivnica **6** Cc
Köprü (riv.) **22** Cd
Korab (mt.) **11** Dc
Koraput **20** Fe
Korba **20** Fd
Korça **11** Dc
Korčula (i.) **11** Bb
Korea Strait **16** Gd
Korec **6** Ha
Korf **14** Jc
Korhogo **24** Bd
Kórinthos **11** Ee
Kõriyama **16** Jc
Korjakskaja Sopka, vulkan–
  (mt.) **14** IJd
Korkino **3** Jb
Korkuteli **22** BCd
Kornati **6** Be
Köroğlu dağları (mts.) **22** CDb
Köroğlu tepe (mt.) **22** CDb
Korogwe **26** Cb
Koro Island **28** map no.6
Koror **27** Bb
Körös (riv.) **6** Ec
Korosten **13** Bd
Korostyšev **6** Ia
Korsakov **14** He
Korsør **5** Ca
Kortrijk **8** Eb
Kos **11** Ge
Kos (i.) **11** Ge
Kosa Arabatskaja Strelko
  (pen.) **12** DEd
Koščagyl **12** Hd
Kościan **5** Fb
Kościerzyna **5** FGa
Kosciusko, Mount– **29** Hf
Kösedağ (mt.) **22** FGbc
Koshiki–Rettõ **17** Ai
Kosi (riv.) **20** Gc
Košice **5** Hd
Kosmet **11** Db
Kosöng **16** Gc
Kosovo polje (phys. reg.) **11**
  Db
Kosovska Mitrovica **11** Db
Kosrae (i.) **27** Db

Kostajnica **6** BCd
Kostopol **6** Ha
Kostroma **13** Dd
Kostrzyn **5** Eb
Koszalin **5** Fa
Kőszeg **6** Cc
Kota **20** Ecd
Kotaagung **18** Bf
Kota Baharu **19** Dg
Kotabaru **18** Ee
Kota Kinabalu **18** Ec
Kotel **11** Gb
Kotelnič **13** DEd
Kotelnikovo **12** Fd
Kotelny, ostrov– (i.) **14** Gb
Kotka **4** Fc
Kotlas **13** Dc
Kotor **11** Cb
Kotorska, Boka– **11** BCb
Kotor Varoš **6** Cd
Kotovsk [Mold.] **6** Ic
Kotovsk [Russia] **12** Fc
Kotovsk [Ukr.] **6** IJc
Kotri **20** Cc
Kottagudem **20** EFe
Kotto (riv.) **25** Cd
Kotuj (str.) **14** Dc
Kotzebue **30** BCc
Koudougou **24** Bc
Koufonísion **11** Gf
Koulamoutou **26** Ab
Koulikoro **24** Bc
Koumac **28** map no.4
Kourou **37** Db
Kouroussa **24** Bc
Koury **24** Bc
Koutiala **24** Bc
Kouvola **4** Fc
Kovdor **4** Gb
Kovel **12** Bc
Kovrov **13** Dd
Kovylkino **12** Fc
Kowloon **16** DEf
Kowön **16** Gc
Köyceğiz Gölü **22** Bd
Kozan **22** EFd
Kozáni **11** Dc
Kožle **5** Gc
Kozloduj **11** Eb
Kozmodemjansk **12** Gb
Közu–Shima (i.) **17** Fg
Kra, Isthmus of– **19** CDf
Kra Buri **19** Cf
Kragerø **4** Bd
Kragujevac **6** Ede
Kraków **5** GHc
Kraljevo **6** Ee
Král Sněžník (mt.) **5** Fc
Kramatorsk **13** Ce
Kramfors **4** Dc
Kranidhion **11** Ee
Kranj **6** Bc
Krapina **6** BCc
Krasavino **12** Ga
Krasino **13** Eb
Kraskino **14** FGe
Kraśnik **5** Ic
Kraśnik Fabryczny **5** HIc
Krasnodar **13** Ce
Krasnograd **12** Ed
Krasnogvardejskoje **12** Fd
Krasnojarsk **14** Cd
Krasnokamsk **13** Ed

Krasnoperekopsk **12** Dd
Krasnorečenski **17** Db
Krasnoselkup **13** Hc
Krasnoslobodsk **12** FGd
Krasnoturinsk **13** EFcd
Krasnoufimsk **12** Ib
Krasnouralsk **12** IJb
Krasnovišersk **13** Ec
Krasnovodsk **21** Ea
Krasnozatonski **12** Ha
Krasnoznamensk **13** Fd
Krasny Barrikady **12** Gd
Krasny Jar **12** Gd
Krasny Kut **12** Gc
Krasny Liman **12** Ed
Krasny Luč **12** Ed
Krasnystaw **5** Ic
Kratié **19** Ef
Krefeld **5** Ac
Kremenčug **12** Dd
Kremenčugskoje
  vodohranilišče **12** Dd
Kremenec **6** Ga
Krems an der Donau **5** Ed
Kretinga **12** Bb
Kribi **24** CDd
Kričev **12** Dc
Krilon, mys– **16** Ja
Kriós, Ákra– **11** Ef
Krishna (riv.) **20** Ee
Krishnanagar **19** Jk
Kristiansand **4** ABd
Kristianstad **4** Cde
Kristiansund **4** Ac
Kristinehamn **4** Cd
Kristinestad **4** Ec
Kriva Palanka **11** DEb
Krivoj Rog **3** Cc
Križevci **10** Fab
Krk (i.) **6** Bd
Krkonoše **5** EFc
Krnov **5** Fc
Kronoki **14** Jd
Kronprinsesse Martha Kyst
  42 grid square no.1
Kronprins Olav Kyst **42** grid
  square no.2
Kronštadt **4** Gcd
Kroonstad **23** Eh
Kropotkin **13** De
Krosno **5** Hd
Krosno Odrzańskie **5** Eb
Krotoszyn **5** Fc
Krugersdorp **26** Bd
Krui **18** Bef
Kruja **11** Cc
Krung Thep → Bangkok **19**
  Df
Kruševac **6** Ee
Krymskije Gory **12** De
Krzyż **5** EFb
Ksar–el–Boukhari **24** Ca
Ksar–el–Kébir **24** Ba
Kstovo **12** FGb
Kuala Dungun **19** Dgh
Kuala Krai **19** Dg
Kuala Lipis **19** Dh
Kuala Lumpur **15** Di
Kuala Terengganu **19** DEg
Kuantan **19** Dh
Kuban (riv.) **13** Ce
Kučevo **6** EFd
Kuching **15** Di

Kuchinoerabu–Shima (i.) **17**
  ABi
Kuchi–no–Shima (i.) **17** ABi
Kuçova **11** Dc
Kudat **18** Ec
Kudus **18** Df
Kudymkar **13** Ed
Kufra Oasis **24** Eb
Kufstein **5** De
Kuhak **21** Gd
Küh–e Bābā (mts.) **20** Cb
Kuhestak **21** Fd
Kuhmo **4** Gbc
Kuito **26** Ac
Kuivaniemi **4** EFb
Kujawy (phys. reg.) **5** Gb
Kujbyšev → Samara **13** Ed
Kuji **17** GHd
Kujto, ozero– **4** Gb
Kujū–San (mt.) **17** Bh
Kukēsi **11** Dbc
Kukmor **12** Hb
Kula [Bul.] **11** Eb
Kula [Yugo.] **6** Dd
Kuldiga **12** Bb
Kulebaki **12** Fb
Kulgera **29** Ed
Kuljab **13** FGf
Kulsary **13** Ee
Kulti **19** Ik
Kulu **22** Dc
Kulunda **13** GHd
Kuma (riv.) **12** Gde
Kumai **18** De
Kumamoto **16** GHd
Kumanovo **11** Db
Kumasi **24** Bd
Kumayri (Leninakan) **13** De
Kumbakonam **20** EFf
Kumbo **24** CDd
Kum–Dag **13** Ef
Kume–Jima (i.) **16** Ge
Kumertau **12** HIc
Kumo–Manyčski kanal (riv.)
  12 FGd
Kunasir, ostrov– / Kunashiri–
  Tõ (i.) **17** Ibc
Kunda **4** Fd
Kund Rasmussen Land **31**
  ILab
Kunene (riv.) **26** Ac
Kungälv **4** Bd
Kungrad **13** Ee
Kungur **13** Ed
Kunlong **19** Cd
Kunlun Shan **20** FGab
Kunming **15** Dg
Kunsan **16** Gc
Kuntilla, El– **22** Eg
Kununurra **29** Db
Kuopio **4** FGc
Kupa (riv.) **6** Bd
Kupang **18** Ffg
Kupino **13** Gd
Kupjansk **12** Ed
Kuqa **13** He
Kura (riv.) **13** DEf
Kurashiki **17** Cg
Kuraymah **25** Dc
Kurayoshi **17** CDg
Kurdistan (phys. reg.) **21** CDb
Kurdufān (State) **25** CDc
Kure **16** Hd

Küre dağları (İsfendiyar) (mts.) **22** DEb
Kure Island (Ocean) **27** DEa
Kurejka (riv.) **14** Cc
Kuressaare (Kingissepp) **4** Ed
Kurgan **13** Fd
Kuri Bay **29** Cb
Kuril Islands **14** Hle
Kurilsk **14** He
Kurnool **20** Ee
Kuro–Shima (i.) **17** Ai
Kuršėnai **4** Ede
Kursk **13** Cd
Kurski Zaliv (l.) **4** Ee
Kuršumlija **11** Db
Kuru (riv.) **25** Cd
Kuruman **26** Bd
Kurume **16** Hd
Kurunegala **20** Fg
Kuşada Körfezi **22** Acd
Kuşadası **11** Ge
Kusagaki–Guntō **17** Ai
Kuş Gölü **22** Ab
Kushima **17** Bi
Kushiro **16** Jb
Kushtia **19** Jk
Kuška **15** Cf
Kussaro–Ko **17** Hlc
Kustanaj **13** Fd
Küsti **25** Dc
Kušva **13** EFd
Küt, Al– **21** Dc
Kut, Ko– (i.) **19** Df
Kütahya **22** Bc
Kutaisi **21** Ca
Kutch (phys. reg.) **20** CDd
Kutch, Gulf of– **20** Cd
Kutch, Rann of– **20** CDd
Kutina **6** Cd
Kutno **5** Gb
Kutu **26** Ab
Kutum **25** Cc
Kuusamo **4** Gb
Kuusankoski **4** Fc
Kuvandyk **12** lc
Kuwait (Ind. St.) **15** Bfg
Kuzneck **12** Gc
Kvaløy (i.) **4** Da
Kvarner (g.) **6** ABd
Kvarnerić (g.) **6** Bd
Kvikkjokk **4** Db
Kvitøya **13** Ca
Kwa (riv.) **26** Ab
Kwajalein Atoll **27** Db
Kwando (riv.) **26** Bc
Kwango (riv.) **26** Ab
Kwangsi **15** Dg
Kwekwe **26** Bc
Kwenge (riv.) **26** Ab
Kwidzyn **5** Gb
Kwilu (riv.) **26** Ab
Kyangin **19** BCe
Kyaukpadaung **19** BCd
Kyaukpyu **19** Be
Kyaukse **19** Cd
Kyle of Lochalsh **7** CDc
Kynuna **29** Gc
Kyoga, Lake– **25** Dd
Kyōga–Misaki **17** Dg
Kyŏngju **17** ABg
Kyŏngsŏng **17** ABd
Kyōto **16** lcd

Kyrēnia **22** De
Kyrgyzstan (Ind. St.) **13** Ge
Kyštym **12** Jb
Kyūshū (i.) **16** Hd
Kyushū–Sanchi **17** Bh
Kyzyl **14** Cd
Kyzylkum (phys. reg.) **13** Fe
Kzyl–Orda **13** Fe

L

Labé **24** Ac
Labouheyre **8** Ce
Laboulaye **39** Bc
Labrador **31** Hlc
Labrador, Coast of– **31** IJc
Labrador City **31** lc
Labrador Sea **31** Jc
Lábrea **37** Cc
Labuan, Pulau– **18** Dc
Labuha **18** Ge
Labytnangi **13** Fc
Lacaune, Monts de– (mts.) **8** Ef
Laccadive Islands **20** Df
Lacepede Islands **29** Cb
Lachlan River **29** GHe
Lac la Biche **31** DEc
Laconia, Gulf of– **11** Ee
Lacq **8** Df
Ladakh Range **20** EFb
Ladoga, Lake– **13** BCc
Ladysmith **26** BCd
Lae **27** Cc
Lærdalsøyri **4** Ac
Læsø (i.) **4** Bd
Lafayette **32** Bbc
Lafia **24** Cd
Laghouat **24** Ca
Lagos [Nig.] **24** Cd
Lagos [Port.] **9** Ad
Lagos de Moreno **34** Bb
Lagrange **29** Cb
Laguna **39** Db
Lahad Datu **18** Ecd
Lahaina **28** map no.1
Lahat **18** Be
Laḥḏj **21** CDg
Lähijän **21** Eb
Lahn **5** Bc
Lahn (riv.) **5** ABc
Laholm **4** Cd
Lahore **15** Cf
Lahti **4** Fc
Laï **25** Bd
Lai Chau **19** Dd
Laingsburg **26** ABe
Lainioälven (riv.) **4** Ea
Lairg **7** Dbc
Laixi (Shuiji) **16** Fc
Lajas, Las– **39** ABc
Lajes **39** CDb
Lajkovac **6** DEd
Lake Charles **32** Bb
Lake City **32** Cbc
Lake Constance **5** BCe
Lake Harbour **31** Ib
Lakeland **32** Cc
Lakemba (i.) **28** map no.6
Lake Nash **29** Fc
Lakewood **32** Ca

Lakhimpur **19** Hj
Lak Sao **19** DEe
Laksefjord (b.) **4** Fa
Lakselv **4** Fa
Lakshadweep **20** Dfg
Lalapaşa **22** Ab
Lalin **9** ABa
Lalitpur **19** Gj
Lamar **33** Cc
Lambaréné **24** De
Lambasa **28** map no.6
Lambert Glacier **42** grid square no.2
Lamego **9** Bb
Lamezia Terme **10** Fe
Lamia **11** Ed
Lamon Bay **18** Fb
Lampang **19** Ce
Lampedusa (i.) **10** Dg
Lamphun **19** CDe
Lamu **26** Db
Lanai (i.) **28** map no.1
Lanbi Kyun (i.) **19** Cf
Lancang Jiang (riv.) **19** CDd
Lancaster [Can.] **31** Id
Lancaster [Ca.–U.S.] **33** Bc
Lancaster [Pa.–U.S.] **9** Hd
Lancaster [U.K.] **7** Ed
Lancelin **29** ABe
Lanciano **10** Ec
Lańcut **5** Ic
Landeck **5** Ce
Landenpohja **4** Gc
Landerneau **8** Ac
Lander River **29** Ec
Landes (phys. reg.) **8** Cef
Land's End (cap.) **7** CDf
Landshut **5** Dd
Landskrona **4** Cde
Langeland (i.) **5** Ca
Langjökull (gl.) **4** map no.1
Langkawi, Pulau– (i.) **19** Cg
Langon **8** Ce
Langøya (i.) **4** Ca
Langreo **9** Ca
Langres **8** Ca
Langres, Plateau de– (plat.) **8** Fd
Langsa **18** Ad
Lang Son **19** Ed
Languedoc (phys. reg.) **8** EFef
Lan Hsu (Hungtao Yu) (is.) **16** Ff
Lannion **8** Bc
Lansing **32** Ca
Lanusei **10** Be
Lanzarote (i.) **24** Ab
Lanzhou **16** BCc
Laoag **15** DEh
Laoang **18** FGb
Lao Cai **19** Dd
Laodicea → Latakia **22** Ee
Laoha He (riv.) **16** EFb
Laon **8** Ec
Laos (Ind. St.) **15** Dh
Lapalisse **8** Ed
La Pérouse Strait **16** Ja
Lapland (phys. reg.) **4** EGab
Lappeenranta **4** FGc
Lâpseki **11** Gc
Laptev Sea **41** grid square no.4

Lapua **4** Ec
Łapy **5** Ib
Lär **21** EFd
Larache **24** Ba
Laramie **33** Cb
Larantuka **18** Ff
Larche, Col de– → Maddalena, Colle della– **10** Ab
Laredo [Sp.] **9** Da
Laredo [U.S.] **32** Bc
Lárestän (phys. reg.) **21** EFd
Larino **10** Ed
Lárisa **11** Ed
Larkana **20** Cc
Lárnaca **22** DEe
Larne **7** Dd
Larrimah **29** Eb
Larsen Ice Shelf **42** grid square no.1
Larvik **4** Bd
Lascaux (c.) **8** De
Lashio **15** Dg
Laskargah **20** BCb
Lastovo (i.) **11** Bb
Latacunga **37** Bc
Latakia (Laodicea) **22** Ee
Late Island **28** Ac
Latina **10** Dd
Latvia (Ind. St.) **4** EFd
Lauca, Rio– (riv.) **39** Ba
Lauenburg an der Elbe **5** Cb
Lau Group **27** Ec
Launceston **29** map no.1
Laura **29** Gb
Laurel [Ms.–U.S.] **32** BCb
Laurel [Mt.–U.S.] **33** BCb
Lauria **10** Ed
Lausanne **10** Aa
Lausitz (hist. reg.) **5** DEc
Laut, Pulau– (i.) **19** Eh
Laut Kecil, Kepulauan– **18** Ee
Lautoka **28** map no.6
Laval **8** Cc
Lavaur **8** Df
Laverton **29** Cd
Lavras **39** Db
Lávrion **11** EFe
Lavumisa **26** Cd
Lawdar **21** Dg
Lawrence **32** Bb
Lawton **32** Bb
Lawz, Jabal al– (mt.) **21** Bd
Laylá **21** De
Laysan Island **28** Aa
Lazio (reg.) **10** CDcd
Leaf (riv.) **31** Hc
Learmouth **29** Ac
Łeba **5** Fa
Lebanon (mts.) **22** EFef
Lebanon (Ind. St.) **15** Bf
Lebedin **12** DEc
Lębork **5** Fa
Lebrija **9** Bd
Łebsko, Jezioro– **5** Fa
Lebu **39** Ac
Lecce **10** Gd
Lecco **10** Bb
Lech (riv.) **5** Cd
Lectoure **8** Df
Leczyca **5** Gb
Ledesma **9** BCb
Ledjanaja, gora– (mt.) **14** Kc

M

Ma (riv.) **19** Ed
Maalaea **28** map no.1
Ma'än **22** Eg
Maanselkä (mts.) **4** FGab
Ma'arrat an Nu'män **22** Fe
Maas (riv.) **5** Ac
Maastricht **8** Fb
Mabaruma **37** CDb
Mabote **26** Cd
Macaé **39** Db
McAlester **32** Bb
McAllen **32** Bc
Macao **15** Dg
Macapá **36** Ec
Macas **37** Bc
Macau **38** Db
Macauley Island **27** DEd
McCall **33** Bb
McClintock Channel **31** Ea
McCook **33** CDbc
Macdonald, Lake– **29** Dc
Macdonnell Ranges **29** EFc
Macedonia (phys. reg.) **11** DEc
Macedonia (Ind. St.) **11** DEc
Macedonia (reg.) **11** DFc
Maceió **36** Gd
Mcensk **12** Ec
Macenta **24** Bd
Macerata **10** Dc
Machala **37** ABc
Machaneng **26** Bd
Machilipatnam **20** Fe
Machiques **37** Bab
Machupicchu (r.) **37** Bd
Măcin **6** Id
Macina (phys. reg.) **24** Bc
Macintyre River **29** HId
Mackay [Austl.] **29** HIc
Mackay [U.S.] **33** Bb
Mackay, Lake– **29** Dc
Mckean Atoll **28** Ac
Mackenzie (riv.) **30** EFc
Mackenzie, District of– **31** CEb
Mackenzie Bay **31** ABab
Mackenzie Mountains **31** BCb
Mackenzie River **29** Hc
Mackinaw City **32** Ca
McKinley, Mount– **41** grid square no.2
Maclear **26** BCe
McLennan **31** Dc
McLeod, Lake– **29** Ac
McMurdo **42** grid square no.4
McMurdo Sound **42** grid square no.4
McMurray **30** GHd
Macon **32** Cb
Mâcon **8** Fd
Macquarie (i.) **2**
Macquarie River **29** He
Mac Robertson Land **42** grid square no.2
Macumba, Thе– (riv.) **29** Fd
Madagascar (Ind. St.) **23** Ggh
Madama **24** Db
Madan **11** Fc
Madang **27** Cc
Madaniyïn **24** CDa
Madaripur **19** Jk

Maddalena, Colle della– (Larche, Col de–) (p.) **10** Ab
Maddalena, La– (i.) **10** Bd
Madden Dam **35** map no.1
Madden Lake **35** map no.1
Madeira (i.) **24** Aa
Madeira (riv.) **38** Ab
Madeira Islands **24** Aa
Madeleine, Île de la– (i.) **32** Ea
Madhubani **19** Ij
Madhya Pradesh (State) **20** EFd
Madina do Boé **24** Ac
Madinat ash Sha'b **21** Cg
Madingo–Kayes **26** Ab
Madingou **26** Ab
Madison **32** BCa
Madisonville **32** Cb
Madiun **18** Df
Madonie, Le– (mts.) **10** DEf
Madra daği (mt.) **11** Gd
Madrakah, Ra's al– **21** Ff
Madran dağ (mt.) **22** Bd
Madras **15** Ch
Madre, Laguna– **34** Cb
Madre, Sierra– [Mex.] (mts.) **34** Cc
Madre, Sierra– [Phil.] (mts.) **18** Fa
Madre de Dios, Isla– **40** Abc
Madre de Dios, Río– (riv.) **37** BCd
Madre del Sud, Sierra– (mts.) **34** BCc
Madre Occidental, Sierra– (mts.) **34** Bb
Madre Oriental, Sierra– (mts.) **34** BCb
Madrid **9** CDb
Madrid–Villaverde **9** Db
Madura, Pulau– (i.) **18** Df
Madurai **15** Chi
Madyan (phys. reg.) **21** Bd
Maebashi **16** Ic
Mae Hong Son **19** Ce
Mae Sai **19** Cd
Maestra, Sierra– (mts.) **35** Cab
Maevatanana **26** map no.1
Maéwo, Île– (i.) **28** map no.4
Mafia Island **26** CDb
Mafikeng **26** Bd
Mafra **39** CDb
Mafraq, Al– **22** Ff
Magadan **14** Id
Magadi **25** Dc
Magangué **37** Bb
Magdagači **14** Fd
Magdalena (riv.) **37** Bb
Magdalena [Bol.] **39** Ba
Magdalena [Mex.] **34** ABa
Magdalena, Isla– **40** Ab
Magdeburg **5** CDb
Magelang **18** CDf
Magellan, Strait of– **36** BCi
Magellan, Strait of– / Magellanes, Estrecho de– **40** ABc
Magellanes, Estrecho de– / Magellan, Strait of– **40** ABc
Magerøya (i.) **4** EFa
Maggiore, Lago– (Verbano) (l.) **10** Bab

Maglić (mt.) **11** Cb
Maglie **10** Gd
Magna, Fossa– **17** EFfg
Magnitogorsk **13** EFd
Magua **27** map no.1
Magude **26** Cd
Magwe **19** BCd
Mahäbäd **21** CDb
Mahabharat Range **19** HIi
Mahačkala **13** DEe
Mahajanga **23** Gg
Mahakam (riv.) **18** Ede
Mahalapye **26** Bd
Maḥallah al Kubrá, Al– **25** Da
Mahambet **12** Hd
Mähän **21** Fc
Mahanadi (riv.) **20** Fd
Mahanoro **26** map no.1
Maharashtra (State) **20** DEe
Mahdïyah, Al– **24** Da
Mahé (i.) **15** Bg
Mahe **20** DEf
Mahenge **26** Cb
Mahesäna **20** Dd
Mahoba **19** GHj
Mahón **9** GHc
Mahrah, Al– (phys. reg.) **21** DEf
Maiana Atoll **27** Db
Maicuru (riv.) **38** Bab
Maidstone **7** FGf
Maiduguri **24** Dc
Maiella, La– (mt.) **10** Ec
Maigualida, Sierra– (mts.) **37** Cb
Maihar **19** Hj
Maijdi **19** Jk
Main (riv.) **5** Bcd
Maï–Ndombe, Lake– **26** ABb
Maine (State) **32** DEa
Maine (hist. reg.) **8** CDc
Maingkwan **19** BCc
Mainland (i.) **7** Fa
Mainland (Pomona) (i.) **7** DEb
Mainpuri **19** Gj
Maintirano **26** map no.1
Mainz **5** Bcd
Maipo, Volcán– (mt.) **39** ABc
Maipú **39** Dc
Maiquetía **37** Ca
Maitland **29** Ie
Maiz, Islas del– **35** Bb
Maizuru **16** HIc
Maja (riv.) **14** Gd
Majabat el Kubra (phys. reg.) **24** Bbc
Majardah, Wadi– (riv.) **10** Bf
Majene **18** Ee
Majevica (mts.) **6** Dd
Maji **25** Dd
Majja **14** Gc
Majkop **13** CDe
Majma'ah **21** Dd
Majorca (r.) **9** Gc
Majuro Atoll **27** Db
Makabana **26** Ab
Makalehi, Pulau– (i.) **18** FGd
Makarjev **12** FGb
Makarov **14** He
Makarska **11** Bb
Makasar → Ujung Pandang **18** Eef
Makassar Strait **15** Dij

Makat **12** Hd
Makatea, Île– (i.) **28** Bc
Makejevka **13** CDe
Makemo Atoll **28** Bc
Makeni **24** Ad
Makgadikgadi Pans **26** Bd
Makhfar al Ḥamman **21** Bb
Makian, Pulau– (i.) **18** Gd
Makinsk **13** Gd
Makó **6** Ec
Makokou **24** Dd
Makoua **24** Dde
Makran (phys. reg.) **21** FGd
Makrónisos (i.) **11** Fe
Maksimovka **17** EFab
Makurazaki **17** ABi
Makurdi **24** Cd
Malabar Coast **20** DEfg
Malabo **24** Cd
Malacca **15** Di
Malacca → Melaka **18** Bd
Malacca, Strait of– **15** Di
Málaga **9** Cd
Malaita Island **27** Dc
Malaja Višera **12** Db
Malakal **25** Dd
Malang **18** Df
Malanje **23** Df
Malanville **24** Cc
Mälaren (l.) **4** Dd
Malargüe **39** Bc
Malaspina Glacier **31** ABbc
Malatya **22** FGc
Malawi (Ind. St.) **23** Fg
Malawi, Lake– (Nyasa, Lake–) **26** Cc
Malaybalay **18** Gc
Maläyer **21** DEc
Malaysia (Ind. St.) **15** Di
Malbork **5** Db
Malden Island **28** Bb
Malditos, Montes– **9** Fa
Maldives (Ind. St.) **15** Ci
Maldonado **39** Cc
Male **20** Dh
Malea, Cape– **11** Ee
Male Atoll **20** Dh
Malebo, Pool– **26** Ab
Malegaon **20** DEd
Malé Karpaty (mts.) **5** Fd
Malékoula, Île– (i.) **28** map no.4
Mali (Ind. St.) **23** Bd
Malik, Wädï al– (riv.) **25** CDc
Malili **18** Fe
Malin **6** Ia
Malindi **26** CDb
Malin Head **7** Cd
Malino, Bukit– (mt.) **18** Fd
Malinovka (riv.) **17** Dgh
Malipo **16** BCf
Malita **18** Gc
Malkara **11** Gc
Malko Tärnovo **11** GHbc
Mallaig **7** CDc
Mallawi **25** CDb
Mallow **7** Be
Malmberget **4** Eb
Malmédy **8** FGb
Malmesbury **26** Ae
Malmö **4** Ce
Malo (i.) **28** map no.4
Maloelap Atoll **27** Db

Mar - Mer

Marvdasht **21** Ed
Marx **12** Gc
Mary **13** Ff
Maryborough **29** Id
Maryland (State) **32** Db
Masaka **25** De
Masan **16** Gcd
Masasi **23** Fg
Masaya **35** Bb
Masbate **18** Fb
Masbate (i.) **18** Fb
Mascara **24** Ca
Mascarene Islands **23** map no.1
Masela (i.) **17** Hlg
Maseru **23** Eh
Mashhad **21** FGb
Mashike **17** Gc
Mashkel (riv.) **20** Bc
Mashra'ar Raqq **25** CDd
Masīlah, Wādī al– **21** DEf
Masindi **25** Dd
Maşīrah, Jazīrat– (i.) **21** FGe
Maşīrah, Khalīj– **21** Fef
Masjed–Soleymān **21** DEc
Mask, Lake– **7** Be
Masoala, Cap– **26** map no.1
Mason City **32** Ba
Massa **10** Cbc
Massachusetts (State) **32** Da
Massa Marittima **10** Cc
Massangena **26** Cd
Massapê **38** CDb
Massat **8** Df
Massawa **25** DEc
Massena **32** Da
Massénya **25** Bc
Masset **31** Bc
Massif Central (mts.) **8** EFe
Massinga **26** Cd
Mastouta **10** Bf
Masuda **17** BCg
Masuku **26** Ab
Masvingo **26** Ccd
Maşyāf **22** Fe
Matadi **26** Ab
Matagalpa **35** Bb
Matagorda Bay **32** Bc
Mataiea **28** map no.2
Matak, Pulau– (i.) **18** Cd
Matala **26** Ac
Matam **24** Ac
Matamoros **30** Ig
Matanzas **35** Ba
Matão, Serra do– (mts.) **38** Bbc
Matapán, Cape– **11** Ee
Mataporquera → Valdeolea **9** CDa
Matara **20** EFg
Mataram **18** Ef
Mataranka **29** Eab
Matariya, El– **25** map no.1
Mataró **9** Gb
Matehuala **34** BCb
Matera **10** Fd
Matese (mts.) **10** Ed
Mátészalka **6** Fc
Mathura **20** Ec
Mati **18** Gc
Mätir **10** Bf
Matočkin Šar **13** EFb
Matočkin Šar, proliv– **13** EFb

Mato Grosso (State) **38** Bc
Mato Grosso **39** BCa
Mato Grosso, Plateau of– **38** Bc
Mato Grosso do Sul (State) **39** Cab
Matopo Hills **26** Bcd
Matosinhos **9** Ab
Mátra **6** DEc
Matrah **21** Fe
Maţrūḩ **25** Ca
Matsue **16** Hc
Matsu Liehtao **16** Fe
Matsumae **17** FGd
Matsumoto **16** Ic
Matsusaka **17** Egh
Matsuyama **16** Hd
Matua, ostrov– (i.) **14** Ie
Matuku Island **28** map no.6
Maturín **37** Cb
Mau **19** Hj
Maubeuge **8** EFb
Maui **28** Ba
Maumere **18** Ff
Maun **26** Bc
Mauna Kea (mt.) **28** map no.1
Mauna Loa (mt.) **28** map no.1
Maungdaw **19** Bd
Maupihaa Atoll **28** Bc
Mau Ranipur **19** Gg
Mauriac **8** Ee
Mauritania (Ind. St.) **23** ABcd
Mauritius (Ind. St.) **23** map no.1
Mawchi **19** Ce
Mawlaik **19** BCd
Mawson **42** grid square no.2
Mayaguana Island **32** Dc
Mayagüez **35** Db
Maydh **25** Ec
Maydi **21** Cf
Mayenne **8** Cc
Mayenne (riv.) **8** Cd
Maynas (phys. reg.) **37** Bc
Mayo **31** Bb
Mayor, Puig– (mt.) **9** Gc
Mayotte (i.) **23** Gg
May Pen **35** Cb
Mayumba **26** Ab
Mayum La (p.) **20** Fb
Mazabuka **26** Bc
Mazagão **38** Bb
Mazamet **8** Ef
Mazara del Vallo **10** Df
Mazār–e Sharīf **15** Cf
Mazarrón **9** Ed
Mazaruni (riv.) **37** CDb
Maztlán **30** Hg
Mažeikiai **12** Bb
Mazirbe **12** Bb
Mazovia (phys. reg.) **5** GHb
Mbabane **26** Cd
Mbaiki **25** Bd
Mbala (Abercorn) **26** Cb
Mbale **26** Ca
Mbalmayo **24** Dd
Mbandaka **26** Aab
M'banza Congo **26** Ab
Mbanza–Ngungu **26** Ab
Mbeya **23** Ff
Mbinda **26** Ab
Mbini (phys. reg.) **24** CDd
Mbomou (riv.) **26** Ba

Mbout **24** Ac
M'Bridge (riv.) **26** Ab
Mbuji–Mayi **26** Bb
Mbulu **26** Cb
Mburucuya **39** Cb
Mead, Lake– **33** Bc
Meadow Lake **31** DEc
Mealháda **9** ABb
Mearim (riv.) **38** Cb
Meaux **8** Ec
Mecca **21** BCe
Mechelen **8** Fb
Mecklenburg (hist. reg.) **5** CDb
Mecklenburger Bucht **5** Ca
Mecsek (mt.) **6** Dc
Medan **15** Di
Medellín **36** Cc
Mederdra **24** Ac
Medford **33** Ab
Medgidia **6** Id
Media Agua **39** Bc
Mediaş **6** Gc
Medicine Hat **33** BCab
Medina **21** BCe
Medinaceli **9** Db
Medina del Campo **9** Cb
Medina del Rioseco **9** Cb
Medina–Sidonia **9** Cd
Medinipur **20** Gd
Mediterranean Sea **23** CEb
Medjerda, Montes de la– **10** ABf
Medjez el–Bab **10** Bf
Mednogorsk **12** Ic
Medny, ostrov– **14** Jd
Médoc (phys. reg.) **8** Ce
Medvedica (riv.) **12** Fc
Medveži, ostrova– **14** Jb
Medvežjegorsk **13** Cc
Medyado Atoll **28** map no.3
Medyai Atoll **28** map no.3
Medžibož **6** Hb
Meekatharra **29** Bd
Meerut **20** Ec
Mega **25** Dd
Mega, Pulau– (i.) **18** Be
Megara **11** Ede
Meghalaya (State) **19** Bc
Meghna (riv.) **19** Jjk
Meia Ponte (riv.) **39** Da
Meiganga **24** Dd
Meiktila **19** Cd
Meiningen **5** Cc
Meissen **5** Dc
Meixian **16** Ef
Mejillones **39** Ab
Mékambo **24** Dd
Mekele **25** DEc
Meknès **24** Ba
Mekong (riv.) **19** Eef
Mekong Delta **19** Efg
Mekongga, Gunung– (mt.) **18** Fe
Melaka (Malacca) **18** Bd
Melalap **18** Ec
Melanesia (is.) **27** BDbc
Melawi (riv.) **18** Dde
Melchor Ocampo **34** Bc
Melenki **12** Fb
Meleuz **12** Hlc
Melfi [Chad] **25** Bc

Melfi [It.] **10** Ed
Melilla **24** Ba
Mèlito di Porto Salvo **10** Ef
Melitopol **12** DEd
Mělník **5** Ec
Melo **39** Cc
Melrhir, Chott– (l.) **24** Ca
Melun **8** Ec
Melville **33** Ca
Melville, Cape– **29** GHa
Melville Bay **29** Fa
Melville Island [Austl.] **29** Ea
Melville Island [Can.] **41** grid square no.2
Melville Peninsula **31** Gb
Memmingen **5** Cde
Mempawah **18** Cd
Memphis **32** Cb
Menai Strait **7** De
Ménaka **24** Cc
Mende **8** Ee
Mendocino, Cape– **33** Ab
Mendoza **39** Bc
Menemen **22** Ac
Meneng Point **27** map no.2
Mengdingjie **19** CDd
Menggala **18** Ce
Menglian **19** CDd
Mengzi **16** Bf
Menindee **29** Ge
Meningie **29** Ff
Menongue **26** Ac
Menphis (r.) **22** Ch
Mentakab **18** Bd
Mentawai, Selat– **18** ABde
Mentawai Islands **18** Ae
Mentok **18** BCe
Menzies **29** Cde
Menzies, Mount– **42** grid square no.2
Meppel **8** FGa
Meppen **5** Ab
Mequinanza, Embalse de– (l.) **9** EFb
Merabéllou, Kólpos– **11** FGf
Merak **18** Cf
Méralab (i.) **28** map no.4
Merano **10** Ca
Meratus, Pegunungan– **18** Ee
Merauke **27** BCc
Merced **33** ABc
Mercedes [Arg.] **39** Cc
Mercedes [Arg.] **39** Cb
Mercedes [Arg.] **39** Bc
Mercedes [Ur.] **39** Cc
Merceg **25** Ed
Merefa **12** Ed
Mergenevo **12** Hd
Mergui **19** Cf
Mergui Archipelago **19** Cf
Meriç (riv.) **11** Gc
Mérida [Mex.] **30** IJg
Mérida [Sp.] **9** Bc
Mérida (riv.) **37** Bb
Mérida, Cordillera de– (mts.) **37** BCb
Meridian **32** Cb
Mérignac **8** Ce
Merir (r.) **27** Bb
Merksem **5** Cc
Merredin **29** Be
Merrick (mt.) **7** Dd

Merritt 31 CDc
Merriwa 29 Ie
Mersa Fatma 21 Cg
Merseburg 5 CDc
Mersey (riv.) 7 Ee
Mersin 22 Ed
Merta Road 20 Dc
Merthyr Tydfil 7 Ef
Merzifon 22 Eb
Mesa 33 Bc
Mesagne 10 Fd
Mesola 10 Db
Mesolóngion 11 Dd
Mesopotamia [Arg.] (phys. reg.) 39 Cbc
Mesopotamia [Iraq] (phys. reg.) 21 CDbc
Messalo (riv.) 26 Cc
Messaoud, Hassi– 24 Ca
Messina [It.] 10 Ee
Messina [S. Afr.] 23 EFh
Messina, Gulf of– 11 Ee
Messina, Stretto di– 10 Ee
Messini 11 DEe
Mesta (Néstos) (riv.) 11 Fc
Mestghanem 24 BCa
Meta (riv.) 37 Bb
Meta, La– (mt.) 10 DEd
Metán 39 Bb
Metauro (riv.) 10 Dc
Metković 11 BCb
Metrz Glacier 42 grid square no.4
Métsovon 11 Dd
Metz 8 Gc
Meulaboh 18 ABd
Meurthe (riv.) 8 Gc
Meuse (riv.) 8 Fc
Mexiana, Ilha– 38 Cab
Mexicali 34 Aa
Mexico (Ind. St.) 30 HIgh
Mexico, Gulf of– 34 CDb
Mexico City 30 Igh
Meyísti (i.) 22 Bd
Meymaneh 20 BCa
Mezdra 11 EFb
Mezen (riv.) 13 Dc
Mezen 13 Dc
Mézenc, Mont– (mt.) 8 Fe
Mezőkövesd 6 Ec
Mezőtúr 6 Ec
Mhow 20 Ed
Miami 32 Cc
Miandrivazo 26 map no.1
Miäneh 21 Db
Miangas, Pulau– (is.) 18 Gc
Mianwali 20 Db
Mianyang 16 BCd
Miaodao Qundao 16 EFc
Miarinarivo 26 map no.1
Miass 13 EFd
Miastko 5 Fab
Micenae (r.) 11 Ee
Michalovce 5 HId
Michigan (State) 32 Ca
Michigan, Lake– 32 Ca
Michigan City 32 Ca
Michipicoten 31 Gd
Micrónesia (is.) 27 BDbc
Mičurin 11 GHb
Mičurinsk 12 Fc
Midar 24 Ba
Middelburg [S. Afr.] 26 BCd

Middelburg [S. Afr.] 26 Be
Middelfart 5 BCa
Middle Andaman (i.) 19 BCf
Middle Atlas (mts.) 24 Ba
Middlesbrough 7 FGd
Midi, Canal du– 8 DEf
Midi d'Ossau, Pic du– (mt.) 8 Cf
Midland 33 Ca
Midway Islands 28 Aa
Midžor (mt.) 11 Fe
Miechów 5 GHc
Międzyrzec Podlaski 5 Ibc
Międzyrzecz 5 EFb
Mielec 5 Hc
Miercurea Ciuc 6 GHc
Mieres 9 BCa
Miguel Alves 38 Cb
Mihajlovgrad 11 Fe
Mihajlovka 13 Dd
Mikkeli 4 FGc
MiKonos (i.) 11 Fe
Mikun 13 DEc
Mikuni–Sanmyaku (mts.) 17 Ff
Mikura–Jima (i.) 17 FGh
Miladummadulu Atoll 20 DEg
Milagro, El– 39 Bc
Milan 10 Bb
Milás 22 ABd
Milazzo 10 Ee
Mildura 29 Ge
Miles 29 HId
Miles City 33 Cb
Miletus (r.) 22 Ad
Milfort Haven 7 Df
Miliana 9 FGd
Milikapiti 29 Ea
Miling 29 Bde
Milk (riv.) 33 Cb
Millau 8 Ee
Millerovo 12 Fd
Millevaches, Plateau de– (plat.) 8 DEe
Millicent 29 FGf
Mîlos (i.) 11 Fe
Milparinka 29 Gde
Milwaukee 32 Ca
Milwaukee Depth 35 Dab
Mimizan 8 Ce
Mimmaya 17 FGd
Mîna' al 'Aḥmadī 21 Dd
Minahassa 18 Fd
Minamata 17 ABh
Minami–Daitö–Jima (i.) 16 He
Minami–Iö–Jima 27 BCa
Minas 39 Cc
Minas–cué 39 Cb
Minas de Ríotinto 9 BCd
Minas de São Domingos 9 ABd
Minas Gerais (State) 39 Da
Minatitlán 34 Cc
Minbu 19 Bde
Minbya 19 Bd
Minchinmávida, Volcán– (mt.) 40 Ab
Mindanao (i.) 15 Ei
Minden 5 Bb
Mindoro (i.) 15 DEh
Mindoro Strait 18 EFb
Mineiros 39 Ca
Mineralnyje Vody 12 Fe

Minervino Murge 10 Fd
Minfeng 20 Fa
Mingan 31 Ic
Minhe 16 Bc
Minho (riv.) 9 Aab
Minho (hist. reg.) 9 Ab
Minicoy Island 20 Dg
Minigwal, Lake– 29 Cd
Minilya 29 Ac
Minjar 12 Ib
Min Jiang (riv.) 16 Ee
Minna 24 Cd
Minneapolis 32 Ba
Minnesota (State) 32 Ba
Minnipa 29 EFe
Miño (riv.) 9 Ba
Minorca (i.) 9 GHc
Minot 33 Cb
Minqin 16 Bc
Min Shan (mts.) 16 Bd
Minsk 13 Bd
Mińsk Mazowiecki 5 HIb
Minto, Lac– 31 Hc
Minusinsk 14 Cd
Minxian 16 Bd
Minyä, Al– 25 CDb
Miquelon (i.) 31 Jd
Mira (riv.) 9 Ad
Miracema do Tocantins 38 Cbc
Miraflores 37 Bb
Miraflores Locks 35 map no.1
Miraj 20 DEe
Miramar 39 Cc
Miranda 39 Cb
Miranda de Ebro 9 Da
Miranda do Douro 9 Bb
Mirande 8 CDf
Mirandela 9 Bb
Mirandola 10 Cb
Mirbat 21 EFf
Mirecourt 8 FGc
Mirgorod 12 Dd
Miri 18 Dd
Mirim, Lagoa– (lag.) 39 Cc
Mirina 11 Fd
Mirny [Ant.] 42 grid square no.4
Mirny [Russia] 14 Ec
Mirpur Khas 20 CDc
Miryang 17 Ag
Mirzapur 20 Fcd
Mishan 16 Ha
Mi–Shima (i.) 17 Bg
Misiones, Sierra de– (mts.) 39 Cb
Miskitos, Cayos– (is.) 35 Bb
Miskolc 6 Eb
Mismär 21 Bf
Mismîyah, Al– 22 Ff
Misool, Pulau– (i.) 18 He
Mississauga 31 GHd
Mississippi (riv.) 32 Bb
Mississippi (State) 32 BCb
Missoula 33 Bb
Missouri (State) 32 Bb
Missouri (riv.) 32 Ba
Mistassini, Lac– 31 Eb
Mistelbach an der Zaya 5 Fd
Misti, Volcán– (volc.) 39 Aa
Misurata 24 Da
Mitchell [Austl.] 29 Hd
Mitchell [U.S.] 32 Ba

Mitchell, Mount– 32 Cb
Mitchell River 29 Gb
Mitchell River (riv.) 29 Gb
Mit Ghamr 22 Cg
Mithimna 11 FGd
Mitiaro Island 28 Bc
Mitilini 22 Ac
Mitilinis, Stenón– 11 Gd
Mitla Pass 25 map no.2
Mito 17 Gf
Mittellandkanal (can.) 5 ABb
Mitú 37 BCb
Mitumba, Monts– 26 Bbc
Mitwaba 26 Bb
Mitzic 24 Dd
Miyake–Jima (i.) 17 FGg
Miyako 16 Jc
Miyako–Jima (i.) 16 Gef
Miyakonojö 16 Hd
Miyanoura–Dake (mt.) 17 Bi
Miyazaki 16 Hd
Miyun 16 Eb
Mizdah 24 Da
Mizen Head 7 ABf
Mizil 6 Hd
Mizoč 6 GHa
Mizoram (State) 19 Bd
Mizuho 42 grid square no.2
Mizusawa 17 Ge
Mjölby 4 Cd
Mjøsa (l.) 4 Bc
Mkuze 26 Cd
Mladá Boleslav 5 Ec
Mladenovac 6 Ed
Mława 5 GHb
Mljet (i.) 11 Bb
Mo 4 Cb
Moa (riv.) 24 Ad
Moa, Pulau– (i.) 18 Gf
Moala (i.) 28 map no.6
Moanda 26 Ab
Moba 26 Bb
Mobaye 26 Ba
Mobayi–Mbongo 26 Ba
Mobile 32 Cb
Mobridge 33 Cb
Moçambique 23 FGg
Mocha, Isla– (i.) 39 Ac
Mochis, Los– 34 ABb
Mochudi 26 Bd
Mocímboa da Praia 26 Dc
Môco, Serra– (mts.) 26 Ac
Mocoa 37 Bb
Mocuba 23 Fg
Modane 8 Ge
Módena 10 Cb
Modica 10 Ef
Modřany 5 Ecd
Moe 29 Hf
Mogadishu 25 Ed
Mogaung 19 Cc
Mogi das Cruzes 39 Db
Mogilev 13 Cd
Mogilev–Podolski 6 Hb
Mogoča 14 EFd
Mogok 19 Cd
Mogrein 24 ABb
Moguer 9 Bd
Mohács 6 Dd
Mohanganj 19 Jj
Mohenjo Daro (r.) 20 Cc
Moinesti 6 Hc
Moissac 8 De

Mojave 33 Bc
Mojave Desert 33 Bc
Mojynty 13 Ge
Mokolo 24 Dc
Mokp'o 14 Ff
Mola di Bari 10 Fd
Moldav (riv.) 5 Ed
Moldavia (phys. reg.) 6 Hcd
Molde 4 Ac
Moldefjorden (b.) 4 Ac
Moldova (Ind. St.) 6 Ic
Moldova Nouă 6 Ed
Moldoveanu, Vîrful– (mt.) 6 Gd
Molepolole 26 Bd
Molfetta 10 Fd
Molise (reg.) 10 Ed
Mollendo 39 Aa
Mölndal 4 BCd
Molodečno 12 Cc
Molodežnaja 42 grid square
  no.2
Mologa (riv.) 12 Eb
Molokai (i.) 28 Ba
Molopo (w.) 26 Bd
Moluccas (is.) 18 GHde
Molucca Sea 18 Gef
Moma 26 CDc
Mombasa 23 FGf
Mombetsu 16 Jb
Momboyo (riv.) 25 BCe
Momčilgrad 11 Fc
Møn (i.) 5 Da
Mona, Isla– (i.) 35 Db
Monaco (Ind. St.) 10 Ac
Monaghan 7 Cd
Mona Passage (str.) 35 Db
Moncayo, Sierra del– (mts.) 9
  DEb
Mončegorsk 13 Cc
Mönchengladbach 5 CDc
Monclova 34 Bb
Moncton 31 Id
Mondego (riv.) 9 ABb
Mondego, Cape– 9 Ab
Mondello 10 De
Mondovi 10 Ab
Monemvasia 11 Ee
Moneron, ostrov– (i.) 17 Ga
Monfalcone 10 Db
Monforte de Lemos 9 Ba
Monga 26 Ba
Mongalla 25 Dd
Mong Cai 19 Ed
Monger, Lake– 29 Bd
Monghpayak 19 CDd
Mongnai 16 Af
Mongo 25 BCc
Mongolia (Ind. St.) 15 De
Mongolski Altaj (mts.) 14 Ce
Mongororo 25 Cc
Mongu 26 Bc
Monkoto 25 BCe
Monmouth 7 Ef
Monopoli 10 Fd
Monor 6 Dc
Monreale 10 De
Monrovia 24 Ad
Mons 8 EFb
Monselice 10 Cb
Montagne Noire (mt.) 8 Ef
Montalbán 9 Eb
Montana (State) 33 BCb

Montaña, La– (phys. reg.) 37
  Bcd
Montánchez 9 Bc
Montargis 8 Ed
Montauban 8 DEef
Montbard 8 Fd
Montbéliard 8 Gd
Montceau–les–Mines 8 EFd
Mont–de–Marsan 8 CDef
Montdidier 8 Ec
Monteagudo 39 Ba
Monte Albán (r.) 34 Cc
Monte Alegre 38 Bb
Monte Azul 39 Da
Monte Bello Islands 29 ABc
Monte Caseros 39 Cbc
Montecatini Terme 10 Cc
Monte Comán 39 Bc
Montecristo (i.) 10 Cc
Montefiascone 10 Dc
Montego Bay 35 Cb
Monteiro 38 Db
Montélimar 8 Fe
Monte Lindo (riv.) 39 BCb
Monte Lirio 35 map no.1
Montemorelos 34 Cb
Montenegro 11 Cb
Montepuez 26 Cc
Montepulciano 10 Cc
Montereau–Faut–Yonne 8 Ec
Monterey 33 Ac
Monteria 37 Bb
Monterós 39 Bb
Monterrey 34 BCb
Monte Sant'Angelo 10 Ed
Montes Claros 39 Da
Montevideo 39 Cc
Montgenèvre (p.) 10 Ab
Montgomery [U.K.] 7 Ee
Montgomery [U.S.] 32 Cb
Montigny–lès–Metz 8 Gc
Montijo [Port.] 9 Ac
Montijo [Sp.] 9 Bc
Montilla 9 Cd
Mont–Joli 32 Ea
Mont–Laurier 32 Da
Montluçon 8 Ed
Montmagny 31 Hd
Montmorillon 8 Dd
Monto 29 Icd
Montoro 9 Ccd
Montpelier 32 Da
Montpellier 8 EFf
Montréal 31 Hd
Montreux 10 Aa
Montrose [U.K.] 7 EFc
Montrose [U.S.] 33 Cc
Mont–Saint–Michel, Le– 8 Cc
Montserrat (i.) 35 Db
Monywa 19 BCd
Monza 10 Bb
Monzón 9 Fb
Moonie 29 Id
Moonta 29 Fe
Moora 29 Be
Moore, Lake– 29 Bde
Moorea (i.) 28 map no.2
Moorhead 32 Ba
Moose (riv.) 32 Ca
Moose Jaw 33 Cab
Moosonee 31 Db
Mopti 24 Bc

Moquegua 39 ABa
Mora [Port.] 9 Ac
Mora [Sp.] 9 CDc
Mora [Swe.] 4 Cc
Moradabad 15 Cg
Mora de Rubielos 9 Eb
Moratalla 9 DEc
Morava 5 Fd
Morava, Južna– 11 DEb
Moravia (phys. reg.) 5 Fd
Morawa 29 Bd
Morawhanna 37 Db
Moray Firth (b.) 7 Ec
Morcenx 8 Cef
Mordvinia (Aut. Rep.) 13 Dd
Morecambe Bay 7 Ede
Moree 29 Hld
Morelia 34 Bc
Morella 9 EFb
Morena 19 Gj
Morena, Sierra– (mts.) 9 BDc
Morenci 33 Cc
Moresby Island 31 Bc
Moreton 29 Ga
Moreton Bay 29 Id
Moreton Island 29 Id
Mórfou 22 De
Morgan 29 FGe
Mori 17 Gc
Morioka 16 Jc
Morlaix 8 ABc
Mornington Island 29 FGb
Morocco (Ind. St.) 23 Bbc
Morogoro 23 Ff
Moro Gulf 18 Fc
Morombe 26 map no.1
Morón 35 Ca
Morondava 23 Gh
Morón de la Frontera 9 Cd
Moroni 26 Dc
Morotai, Pulau– 18 Gd
Morotai, Selat– 18 Gd
Moroto 26 Ca
Morozovsk 12 Fd
Morphou Bay 22 De
Morris Jesup, Kap– 41 grid
  square no.1
Morrumbene 26 Cd
Moršansk 12 Fc
Mortara 10 Bb
Mortes, Rio das– (riv.) 38 Bc
Mortlock Islands 27 Cb
Morvan, Monts du– 8 EFd
Morven (mt.) 7 Eb
Morven 29 Hd
Morvi 20 Dd
Morwell 29 Hf
Moscow 13 Cd
Mosel (riv.) 5 Acd
Moselle (riv.) 5 Acd
Moshi 26 Cb
Mosjøen 4 Cb
Moskenesøya (i.) 4 BCb
Moskva (riv.) 12 Eb
Mosonmagyaróvár 5 Fe
Mosqueiro 38 Cb
Mosquitia (phys. reg.) 35 Bb
Mosquitos, Costa de 35 Bb
Mosquitos, Golfo de los– 35
  Bbc
Moss 4 Bd
Mossaka 24 De
Mosselbaai 23 Ei

Mossendjo 26 Ab
Mossman 29 Hb
Mossoró 38 Db
Moss Vale 29 Hle
Most 5 Dc
Mostar 11 BCb
Mostiska 5 Id
Mosty 12 Bc
Mosul 21 Cb
Motagua (riv.) 35 ABb
Motala 4 Cd
Motherwell 7 Ed
Motihari 20 FGc
Motril 9 Dd
Motu One Atoll 28 Bc
Moudjéria 24 Ac
Moúdros 11 Fd
Mouila 26 Ab
Mould Bay 41 grid square
  no.2
Moulins 8 Ed
Moulmein 15 Dh
Moulouya (riv.) 24 Ba
Moultrie 32 Cb
Moundou 25 Bd
Mountain Nile (riv.) 25 Dd
Mount Barker 29 Bef
Mount Douglas 29 Hc
Mount Gambier 29 FGf
Mount Garnet 29 GHb
Mount Isa 29 Fc
Mount Magnet 29 Bd
Mount Morgan 29 Hlc
Mount Vernon 32 Cb
Moura [Austl.] 29 Hc
Moura [Braz.] 37 Cc
Moura [Port.] 9 Bc
Mourne Mountains 7 CDd
Mouscron 8 Eb
Moussoro 25 Bc
Moyale 25 Dd
Moyo, Pulau– (i.) 18 Ef
Moyobamba 37 Bc
Mozambique (Ind. St.) 23 Fgh
Mozambique Channel 26
  CDcd
Možga 12 Hb
Mozyr 12 Cc
Mpanda 26 Cb
Mpika 26 Cc
Mragowo 5 Hb
Mreïti, El– 24 Bb
Mreyyé, El– (phys. reg.) 24 Bc
Mtwara 23 FGfg
Muang Pakxan 19 De
Muang Sing 19 Dd
Muang Xaignabouri 19 De
Muang Xépôn 19 Ee
Muar 18 Bd
Muarasiberut 18 Ae
Muaratebo 18 Be
Muaratewe 18 Ef
Mubarraz, Al– 21 Dd
Mubi 24 Dc
Muchinga Mountains 26 Cc
Mudan Jiang (riv.) 17 Ab
Mudanjiang 16 GHb
Mudanya 22 Bb
Mudawwarah, Al– 22 Fh
Mueda 26 Cc
Muende 26 Cc
Mufulira 26 Bc
Mugi 17 Dh

Muğla **22** Bd
Muglad, Al– **25** Cc
Mugodžary (mts.) **13** Ee
Muḩammad Qawl **25** Db
Mühldorf am Inn **5** CDd
Mühlhausen **5** Cc
Mühlig–Hofmann Gebirge **42** grid square no.1
Muhu (i.) **4** Ed
Muisne **37** ABb
Mujnak **13** Ee
Mukačevo **5** Id
Mukalla, Al– **21** Dg
Mukhā, Al– **21** Cg
Mukinbudin **29** Be
Mula **9** Ec
Mulhacén (mt.) **9** Dd
Mulhouse **8** Gd
Muling **17** Bb
Muling He (riv.) **17** Bbc
Mull, Island of– **7** CDc
Mullewa **29** Bd
Mullingar **7** Ce
Mulobezi **26** Bc
Mulock Glacier **42** grid square no.4
Multan **15** Cfg
Mumbwa **26** Bc
Mun (riv.) **19** De
Muna, Pulau– (i.) **18** Fef
Münden **5** Bc
Mundiwindi **29** BCc
Mundo Novo **38** Cc
Mundubbera **29** Hld
Mungbere **25** Cd
Mungindi **29** Hd
Munger **20** Gcd
Munich **5** CDd
Munku–Sardyk, gora– (mt.) **14** CDd
Muñoz Gamero, Península– **40** Ac
Munster (prov.) **7** BCe
Münster **5** ABbc
Muntele Mare, Vîrful– (mt.) **6** Fc
Muntenia (phys. reg.) **6** GHd
Muong Sen **19** DEe
Muonio **4** EFb
Muonioälven (riv.) **4** Ea
Mur (riv.) **5** Ee
Mura (riv.) **6** Cc
Murakami **17** Fe
Murallón, Cerro– (mt.) **40** Ab
Muraši **13** Dd
Murat (riv.) **21** Cb
Murat daği (mt.) **22** Bc
Muratlı **22** Ab
Murchison River **29** Bd
Murcia **9** Ed
Murcia (phys. reg.) **9** Ec
Muren **14** CDe
Mureş (riv.) **6** FGc
Muret **8** Df
Murgab **16** Ac
Murge, Le– (mts.) **10** Fd
Murghab (riv.) **20** BCa
Murgon **29** Id
Müritz (l.) **5** Db
Murmansk **13** Cc
Murmaši **4** GHa
Muro Lucano **10** Ed
Murom **12** Fb

Muroran **16** Jb
Muros **9** Aa
Muroto **17** Dh
Muroto–Zaki **17** Dh
Murray Bridge **29** FGf
Murray River **29** Hf
Murrumbidgee River **29** GHe
Murud, Gunong– (mt.) **18** Ed
Mururoa Atoll **28** BCd
Murwara **20** Fd
Murwillumbah **29** IJd
Murzuq **24** Db
Mürzzuschlag **5** EFe
Muş **21** Cb
Musala (mt.) **11** Eb
Musan **16** Gb
Muscat (phys. reg.) **21** Fe
Muscat **21** Fe
Musgrave **29** Ga
Musgrave Ranges **29** Ed
Mus–Haja, gora– (mt.) **14** Hc
Mushie **26** Ab
Musi (riv.) **18** Be
Muskegon **32** Ca
Muskogee **32** Bb
Musoma **25** De
Mussende **26** Ac
Mustafa–Kemalpaşa **22** Bbc
Mustang **19** Hli
Mustvee **4** Fd
Muswellbrook **29** Hle
Mut **25** Cb
Mutarara **26** Cc
Mutare **26** Cc
Mutatá **37** Bb
Mutsu **16** Jb
Mutsu–Wan **17** Gd
Muwayh, Al– **21** Ce
Muxima **26** Ab
Muyinga **26** BCb
Muzaffarpur **20** Gc
Muztag (mt.) **20** Fa
Mvolo **25** Cd
Mwali (i.) **26** Dc
Mwanza **26** Cb
Mweelrea (mt.) **7** Be
Mwene Ditu **26** Bb
Mweru, Lake– **26** Bb
Mwinilunga **26** Bc
Myanmar (Burma) (Ind. St.) **15** Dg
Myaungmya **19** Be
Myingyan **19** Cd
Myitkyina **15** Dg
Mymensingh **20** Hd
Myoshi **17** Cg
Myrdalsjökl (gl.) **4** map no.1
Mysore **15** Ch
Mys Šmidta **14** KLc
My Tho **19** Efg
Mytišči **12** Eb
Mzimba **26** Cc
Mzuzu **26** Cc

N

Naab (riv.) **5** Dd
Naalehu **28** map no.1
Naantali **4** Ec
Naas **7** Ce
Nabadwip **19** Jk

Naberežnyje Čelny **13** DEd
Nabesna **31** Ab
Nabire **27** Bc
Nabk, An– **22** Fef
Nablus **22** Ef
Nābul **10** Cf
Nacala **26** Dc
Nacala–a–Velha **26** CDc
Nacaome **35** Bb
Nachingwea **26** Cbc
Náchod **5** EFc
Nacozari de García **34** Bab
Nadiad **20** Dd
Nádusa **11** Dc
Nadvornaja **6** Gb
Næstved **4** Bc
Nafīdah, An– **10** Cf
Nafūd, Al– (phys. reg.) **21** BCd
Naga **18** Fb
Nagaland (State) **19** Bc
Nagano **16** Ic
Nagaoka **16** Ic
Nagappattinam **20** EFf
Nagasaki **16** Gd
Nagato **17** Bg
Nagda **20** Ed
Nagercoil **20** Eg
Nagorny **14** Fd
Nagoya **16** Ic
Nagpur **15** Cg
Nagqu **19** Bb
Nagyatád **6** Cc
Nagykanizsa **6** Cc
Nagykörös **6** DEc
Naha **16** Ge
Nahodka **14** Ge
Nahuel Huapi, Lago– **40** Ab
Nain **31** Ic
Nā'īn **21** Ec
Nairn **7** Ec
Nairobi **25** De
Naivasha **26** Cb
Najafābād **21** Ec
Najd (hist. reg.) **21** CDe
Najin **16** Hb
Najran **21** CDf
Nakadöri–Jima (i.) **17** Ah
Naka–Iō–Jima (i.) **27** BCa
Nakaminato **17** Gf
Naka–no–Shima (i.) **17** ABj
Nakashibetsu **17** Ic
Nakatsu **17** Bh
Nakhichevan (Aut. Rep.) **13** De
Nakhl, An– **22** DEf
Nakhon Pathom **19** CDf
Nakhon Phanom **19** De
Nakhon Ratchasima (Khorat) **19** Def
Nakhon Sawan **19** CDe
Nakhon Si Thammarat **19** CDg
Nakina **31** Gc
Nakło nad Noteć **5** Fb
Nakonde **26** Cb
Nakskov **5** Ca
Naktong–gang (riv.) **17** Ag
Nakuru **25** De
Nal (riv.) **20** Cc
Nalčik **13** De
Nalut **24** Da
Namak, Daryācheh– ye– **21** Ec

Namakzār (l.) **20** Bb
Namakzar–e–Shandād **21** Fcd
Namangan **13** Ge
Namapa **26** CDc
Nambour **29** Id
Nambucca Heads **29** IJe
Namcha Barwa (mt.) **19** BCc
Namche Bazar **19** Ij
Nam Co (l.) **19** Bb
Namdalen (phys. reg.) **4** Cb
Nam Dinh **19** Ed
Namib Desert **26** Acd
Namibe **23** CDg
Namibia (Ind. St.) **23** Dh
Naminga **14** EFd
Namlea **18** Ge
Namoi River **29** Hle
Namonuito Atoll **27** Cb
Namorik Atoll **27** Db
Nampa **33** Bb
Nampala **24** Bc
Namp'o **16** FGc
Nampula **26** Cc
Namsos **4** Bb
Nam Tha **19** Dd
Namtu **19** Cd
Namur **8** Fb
Namuruputh **26** Ca
Namwala **26** Bc
Nan (riv.) **19** De
Nan **19** De
Nanaimo **33** Ab
Nanao **17** Ef
Nanatsu–Shima **17** Ef
Nancha **16** Ga
Nanchang **15** DEg
Nancheng **16** Ee
Nanchong **16** Cd
Nancy **8** Gc
Nanda Devi (mt.) **20** EFb
Nānded **20** Ee
Nandi [Fiji] **28** map no.6
Nandi [Zimb.] **26** Cd
Nanga Parbat (mt.) **20** Dab
Nangapinoh **18** De
Nangatayap **18** De
Nanjing (Nanking) **16** Ed
Nanking → Nanjing **16** Ed
Nan Ling (mts.) **16** Def
Nanning **15** Dg
Nanortalik **31** Kbc
Nanping **16** Ee
Nansei–Shotō → Ryukyu Islands **16** FGef
Nanshan Islands **18** Dcd
Nanterre **8** DEc
Nantes **8** Cd
Nantes–Brest, Canal– **8** Bcd
Nantong **16** Fd
Nanumea Atoll **27** Dc
Nanuque **39** DEa
Nanusa, Pulau– Pulau– **18** Gd
Nanxiong **16** DEef
Nanyang **16** Dd
Nanyuki **25** Dde
Nanzhang **16** Dd
Não, Cabo de la– (cap.) **9** Fc
Napier **27** Id
Napier Mountains **42** grid square no.2
Naples **10** Ed

Nida (riv.) **5** Hc
Niedere Tavern (mts.) **5** DEe
Nieder–Österreich (phys. reg.) **5** DFd
Niedersachsen **5** ACb
Nienburg an der Weser **5** Bb
Nieuw Amsterdam **37** Db
Nieuw Nickerie **38** Ba
Niğde **22** Ecd
Niger (Ind. St.) **23** CDd
Niger (riv.) **24** Cd
Niger Delta **24** Cd
Nigeria (Ind. St.) **23** CDe
Nigrita **11** Ec
Nihoa (i.) **28** ABa
Niigata **16** Ic
Niihama **17** Cgh
Niihau (i.) **28** Aa
Nii–Jima (i.) **17** Fg
Niimi **17** Cg
Niitsu **17** Ff
Nijar **9** DEd
Nijmegen **8** Fb
Nikel **13** BCc
Nikki **24** Ccd
Nikkö **17** Ff
Nikolajev **13** Ce
Nikolajevsk **12** Gd
Nikolajevsk–na–Amure **14** GHd
Nikólaos, Áyios– **11** FGf
Nikolsk [Russia] **12** Gb
Nikolsk [Russia] **12** Gc
Nikopol [Bul.] **11** Fb
Nikopol [Ukr.] **12** Dd
Niksar **22** Fb
Nikshahr **21** Gd
Nikšić **11** Cb
Nikumaroro (i.) **28** Ac
Nila, Pulau– (i.) **18** Gf
Nilande Atoll **20** Dh
Nile (riv.) **25** Db
Nilphamari **19** Jj
Nimba Mountains **24** Bd
Nîmes **8** EFf
Nimrod Glacier **42** grid square no.4
Nimule **25** Dd
Nine Degree Channel **20** Dg
Nineveh (r.) **21** Cb
Ning'an **16** Gb
Ningbo **15** Eg
Ningde **16** EFe
Ningdu **16** Ee
Ningsia **15** Df
Ningwu **16** Dc
Ninigo Group **27** Cc
Ninnis Glacier **42** grid square no.4
Niobrara (riv.) **33** Cb
Nioro du Sahel **24** Bc
Niort **8** Cd
Nipigon **31** Gd
Nipigon, Lake– **31** Gcd
Nipissing, Lake– **31** GHd
Niquelândia **38** Cc
Niš **11** DEb
Nisa **9** Bc
Nisab **21** Dg
Nišava (riv.) **11** Eb
Niscemi **10** Ef
Nishinoomote **17** Bi
Nishino–Shima (i.) **27** BCa

Nísiros (i.) **11** Ge
Niterói **39** Db
Nith (riv.) **7** DEd
Nitra **5** Gd
Nittilling Lake **31** Hlb
Niuafo'ou Island **28** Ac
Niue (i.) **28** Ac
Niu'erhe **14** Fd
Niulakita Island **27** DEc
Nivernais (phys. reg.) **8** Ed
Nivski **4** GHb
Nizamabad **20** Ee
Nizina Podlaska (hist. reg.) **5** Ib
Nizip **22** Fd
Nízke Tatry (mts.) **5** Gd
Nižneangarsk **14** DEd
Nižnejansk **14** GHb
Nižnekamsk **12** GHb
Nižne–Leninskoje **14** Ge
Nižneudinsk **14** CDd
Nižnevartovsk **13** GHc
Nižnij Novgorod (Gorki) **13** Dd
Nižnij Novgorod vodohranilišče **12** Fb
Nižni Lomov **12** Fc
Nižni Tagil **13** EFd
Nižnjaja Pojma **14** CDd
Nižnjaja Tura **12** IJb
Nizzana (r.) **22** Eg
Njandoma **12** Fa
Njazepetrovsk **12** Ib
Njombe **26** Cb
Njurba **14** Ec
Njurunda **4** Dc
Nkhata Bay **26** Cc
Nkhota–Kota **26** Cc
Nkongsamba **24** CDd
Nobeoka **16** Hd
Nogales **33** Bc
Nogent–le–Rotrou **8** Dc
Noginsk **12** Eb
Noheji **17** Gd
Nojima–Kaki **17** FGg
Nokia **4** Ec
Nok Kundi **20** Bc
Nolinsk **12** GHb
Nome **30** Bc
Nong'an **16** FGb
Nong Khai **15** Dh
Nonouti Atoll **27** Dc
Nontron **8** De
Noqui **26** Ab
Noranda **32** Da
Nord **30** Qa
Nordaustlandet **41** grid square no.3
Norden **5** Ab
Nordenham **5** Bb
Nordenskjolda, ostrova– **14** BCb
Nordfjord (b.) **4** Ac
Nordhausen **5** Cc
Nordkinn (cap.) **4** FGa
Nordmaling **4** Dc
Nordvik **14** Eb
Nore (riv.) **7** Ce
Norfolk (co.) **7** Ge

Norfolk [Nb.–U.S.] **32** Ba
Norfolk [Va.–U.S.] **32** Db
Norfolk Island **27** Dd
Norilsk **14** BCc
Normandie, Collines de– (mts.) **8** Cc
Normandy (phys. reg.) **8** CDc
Norman River **29** Gb
Normanton **29** Gb
Norman Wells **31** BCb
Nørresundby **4** Bd
Norrköping **4** Dd
Norrland (phys. reg.) **4** CDb
Norrtälje **4** Dd
Norseman **29** Ce
Norte, Cabo– **38** Ca
Norte, Submeseta– (phys. reg.) **9** Cab
Northallerton **7** EFd
Northam **29** Be
Northampton [Austl.] **29** ABd
Northampton [U.K.] **7** FGe
North Andaman (i.) **19** BCf
North Battleford **31** Ec
North Bay **31** Hd
North Cape [Nor.] **4** Fa
North Cape [N.Z.] **27** Dd
North Carolina (State) **32** CDb
North Channel **7** CDd
North Dakota (State) **33** CDb
Northeast Pass (str.) **28** map no.3
Northeim **5** BCc
Northern Dvina (riv.) **13** Dc
Northern Ireland (reg.) **7** Cd
Northern Mariana Islands **27** Cb
Northern Territory (State) **29** EFbc
North Foreland **7** GHf
North Frisian Islands **5** ABa
North Island **27** Dd
North Korea (Ind. St.) **15** Eef
North Lakhimpur **19** Bc
North Little Rock **32** Bb
North Magnetic Pole (1980) **41** grid square no.2
North Minch (str.) **7** CDb
North Ossetia (Aut. Rep.) **13** De
North Platte **33** CDb
North Platte (riv.) **33** Cb
North Pole **41** grid square no.1
North Rona (i.) **7** Db
North Saskatchewan (riv.) **31** Ab
North Sea **7** Gc
North Uist (i.) **7** BCc
Northumberland Islands **29** Ic
North West Cape **29** Ac
North West Highlands (mts.) **7** Dbc
North West River **31** IJc
Northwest Territories **31** CHb
Norway (Ind. St.) **3** DEa
Norway, Kapp– **42** grid square no.1
Norway House **31** Cb
Norwegian Sea **4** ABb

Noshiro **16** IJb
Nossob (riv.) **26** Bd
Nosy–Bé (i.) **26** map no.1
Nosy Boraha (i.) **26** map no.1
Nota (riv.) **4** Ga
Noteć (riv.) **5** Eb
Nótios Evvoïkós, Kólpos– **11** EFd
Noto **10** Ef
Notodden **4** Bd
Noto–Hantō **17** DEf
Nottingham **7** Fe
Nottingham Island **31** GHb
Nouakchott **24** Ac
Nouméa **28** map no.4
Nova Cruz **38** Db
Nova Friburgo **39** Db
Nova Gaia **26** Ac
Nova Gorica **6** Acd
Nova Gradiška **6** Cd
Nova Iguaçu **39** Db
Novaja Kahovka **12** Dd
Novaja Ljalja **12** Jb
Novaja Zemlja (i.) **13** DEb
Nova Mambone **26** Cd
Novara **10** Bb
Nova Scotia (prov.) **31** Id
Nova Varoš **11** CDb
Nova Zagora **11** FGb
Nové Zámky **5** Gd
Novgorod **13** Cd
Novi Bečej **6** Ed
Novi Ligure **10** Bb
Novi Pazar [Bul.] **11** Gb
Novi Pazar [Yugo.] **11** Db
Novi Sad **6** DEd
Novi Vinodolski **6** Bd
Novoaltajsk **13** Hd
Novoanninski **12** Fc
Nôvo Aripuanã **37** CDc
Novočerkassk **12** Fd
Novograd–Volynski **6** Ha
Nôvo Hamburgo **39** Db
Novokazalinsk **13** Fe
Novokujbyševsk **13** Ed
Novokuzneck **13** Hd
Novolazarevskaja **42** grid square no.4
Novo Mesto **6** Bd
Novopokrovka **17** Db
Novopolock **12** Cb
Novorossijsk **13** Ce
Novošahtinsk **12** Ed
Novosergijevka **12** Hlc
Novosibirsk **13** Hd
Novosibirsk–Akademgorodok **13** GHd
Novoskovsk → Bobriki **13** CDd
Novotroick **13** Ed
Novoukrainka **12** Dd
Novouzensk **12** Gc
Novovjatsk **12** GHb
Novovolynsk **6** Ga
Novozybkov **12** Dc
Novska **6** Cd
Novy Port **13** FGc
Novy Uzen **13** Ee
Nowa Huta **5** Hcd
Nowa Sól **5** Ec
Nowe **5** Gb
Nowgong **19** Bc
Nowra **29** Ief

Ontario, Lake– **32** Da
Onteniente **9** Ec
Ontong Java Atoll **27** CDc
Ooa Atoll **28** map no.3
Oodnadatta **29** EFd
Ooldea **29** Ee
Oostende **8** Eb
Opala **25** Ce
Oparino **12** Gb
Opava **5** Fd
Opelika **32** Cb
Opobo **24** Cd
Opočka **12** Cb
Opole **5** FGc
Opuwo **26** Ac
Or (riv.) **12** Id
Oradea **6** EFc
Oraefajökull (gl.) **4** map no.1
Orai **19** Gj
Oran **24** BCa
Orange (prov.) **26** Bd
Orange [Austl.] **29** HIe
Orange [Fr.] **8** Fe
Orange [U.S.] **32** Bbc
Orange, Cabo– **38** Ba
Oranienburg **5** Db
Oranje (riv.) **26** Be
Oranjemund **26** Ad
Oranžerej **12** Gd
Orbetello **10** Cc
Orbost **29** Hf
Orcadas **42** grid square no.1
Orcera **9** Dc
Orchej **6** Ic
Orchila, Isla– (i.) **35** Db
Ord, Mount– **29** Db
Ordos (phys. reg.) **16** Cc
Ord River (riv.) **29** Db
Ord River **29** Db
Ordu **22** FGb
Ordžonikidze **12** Dd
Ordžonikidze → Vladikavkaz **13** De
Örebro **4** CDd
Oregon (State) **33** ABb
Öregrund **4** Dc
Orehovo–Zujevo **13** CDd
Orel **13** Cd
Orem **33** Bb
Ore Mountains **5** Dc
Ören **11** GHe
Orenburg **13** Ed
Orense **9** Ba
Orestiás **11** Gc
Øresund **5** Dab
Orhangazi **11** Hc
Orhei (Orgejev) **6** Ic
Orhon (riv.) **14** De
Orihuela **9** Ec
Orinoco (riv.) **37** Cb
Orinoco, Mouths of the– **37** CDb
Orissa (State) **20** FGd
Oristano **10** Be
Oristano, Golfo di– **10** Be
Orivesi (l.) **4** Gc
Orizaba **34** Cc
Orjahovo **11** EFb
Orjen (mt.) **11** Cb
Orjiva **9** Dd
Orkanger **4** Bc
Orkney Islands **7** EFb
Orlando **32** Cc

Orléanais (hist. reg.) **8** DEcd
Orléans **8** DEd
Ormara **20** BCc
Ormoc **18** Fb
Orne (riv.) **8** Cc
Örnsköldsvik **4** DEc
Orohena (mt.) **28** map no.2
Oroluk Atoll **27** Cb
Oroqen Zizhiqi **14** Fd
Orosei, Golfo di– **10** Bd
Orosháza **6** Ec
Oroya, La– **37** Bd
Orsa **4** Cc
Orša **13** BCd
Orsk **13** EFd
Orşova **6** EFd
Ortegal, Cabo– **9** ABa
Orthez **8** Cf
Ortigueira **9** ABa
Ortles (mt.) **10** Ca
Orümîyeh **21** CDb
Oruro **39** Ba
Orust (i.) **4** Bd
Orvieto **10** Dc
Oš **13** Ge
Os **4** Ac
Osa **12** Ib
Osa, Peninsula de– **35** Bc
Ōsaka **16** Id
Osakov, ostrov– (i.) **13** GHa
Osăm (riv.) **11** Fb
Oshawa **31** Hd
Oshika–Hantō **17** GHe
Ō–Shima **17** Fd
Ō–Shima (i.) **17** Fg
Oshima–Hantō **17** FGcd
Oshkosh **32** BCa
Oshogbo **24** Cd
Oshwe **26** ABb
Osijek **6** Dd
Osinniki **13** Hd
Osipoviči **12** Cc
Oskarshamn **4** Dd
Oslo **4** Bd
Oslofjorden (b.) **4** Bd
Osmaniye **22** Fd
Osnabrück **5** Bb
Osogovske planina **11** Eb
Osorno [Chile] **40** ABc
Osorno [Sp.] **9** Ca
Osprey Reef (i.) **29** Ha
Óssa (mt.) **11** Ed
Ossa, Mount– **29** map no.1
Ossora **14** Jd
Ostaškov **12** Db
Østerdalen (v.) **4** Bc
Östersund **4** Cc
Östhammar **4** Cc
Ostia (r.) **10** Dd
Ostrava **5** FGd
Ostróda **5** GHb
Ostrog **6** Ha
Ostrogožsk **12** Ec
Ostrołeka **5** Hb
Ostrov [Czech Rep.] **5** Dc
Ostrov [Russia] **4** FGd
Ostrowiec Świętokrzyski **5** Hc
Ostrów Mazowiecka **5** HIb
Ostrów Wielkopolski **5** Fc
Ostuni **10** Fd
Ōsumi–Hantō **17** Bi
Ōsumi–Kaikyō **16** Hd
Ōsumi–Shotō **16** GHd

Osuna **9** Cd
Oświęcim **5** Gcd
Ota–Porto **8** map no.1
Otaru **16** Jb
Otavalo **37** Bb
Otavi **26** Ac
Ōtawara **17** FGf
Othonoi (i.) **11** Cd
Óthrys (mt.) **11** Ed
Otish, Monts– **31** EFb
Otjiwarongo **26** Ad
Otočac **6** Bd
Otoineppu **17** Hb
Otra (riv.) **4** Ad
Otradny **12** Hc
Otranto, Capo d'– **10** Gd
Otranto, Strait of– **11** Ccd
Ōtsu **17** DEg
Ottawa **32** Bb
Ottawa (riv.) **32** Da
Ottawa [Can.] **31** Hd
Ottumwa **32** Ba
Otway, Cape– **29** Gf
Otwock **5** Hb
Ou (riv.) **19** Dd
Ouachita Mountains **32** Bb
Ouadane **24** Ab
Ouadda **25** Cd
Ouaddaï (phys. reg.) **25** BCc
Ouagadougou **24** Bc
Ouahigouya **24** Bc
Oualata **24** Bc
Ouanda–Djallé **25** Cd
Ouargla **24** Cb
Oubangui (riv.) **25** ABd
Oudtshoorn **26** Be
Oued, El– **24** Ca
Oued ben Tili **24** Bb
Oued–Zem **24** Ba
Ouessant, Ile d'– (i.) **8** Ac
Ouesso **24** Dd
Oujda **24** Ba
Oulainen **4** Fb
Oullins **8** Fe
Oulu **4** Fb
Oulujärvi **4** Fb
Oulujoki (riv.) **4** Fb
Oum Chalouba **25** Cc
Oum er–Rbia (riv.) **24** Ba
Ou Neua **19** Dd
Ounianga Kébir **25** Cc
Ourinhos **39** CDb
Ourique **9** ABd
Ouro Prêto **39** Db
Ōu–Sanmyaku (mts.) **17** Gde
Ouse [Eng.–U.K.] (riv.) **7** Fe
Ouse [Eng.–U.K.] (riv.) **7** Fe
Oust (riv.) **8** Bd
Outjo **26** Acd
Outokumpu **4** Gc
Ouvéa, Île– (i.) **27** Dcd
Ouyen **29** Gf
Ovalle **39** Ac
Ovamboland (hist. reg.) **26** Ac
Ovar **9** Ab
Övertorneå **4** Eb
Ovidiopol **6** Jc
Oviedo **9** Ca
Øvre Årdal **4** ABc
Ovruč **12** Cc
Owando **24** De

Owase **17** Eg
Owensboro **32** Cb
Owen Sound **32** Ca
Owerri **24** Cd
Oxapampa **37** Bd
Oxelösund **4** Dd
Oxford **7** Ff
Oxnard **33** ABc
Oyama **17** FGf
Oyapock (riv.) **38** Ba
Oyem **24** Dd
Oyo **24** Cd
Oyonnax **8** Fd
Øy Peter Island **42** grid square no.3
Ozamis **18** Fc
Ozark Plateau **32** Bb
Ózd **6** DEb
Ozernovski **14** Id
Ozersk **5** Ia
Ozerski **17** Ha
Ozery **12** Ec
Ozieri **10** Bd
Ozinki **12** GHc
Ozorków **5** Gbc

P

Paamiut / Frederikshåb **31** JKb
Paarl **26** Ae
Paauilo **28** map no.1
Pabianice **5** GHc
Pabna **19** Jjk
Pab Range **20** Cc
Pacaás Novos, Serra de– (mts.) **37** Cd
Pacajá (riv.) **38** Bb
Pacaraima, Sierra– (mts.) **37** Cb
Pacasmayo **37** ABc
Pachino **10** Ef
Pachitea (riv.) **37** Bc
Pachuca de Soto **34** Cbc
Pacific Ocean **2**
Pacitan **18** Df
Padang **15** Dj
Paderborn **5** Bc
Padre Island **32** Bc
Padua **10** Cb
Paducah **32** Cb
Páea **28** map no.2
Paestum (r.) **10** Ed
Páfos **22** De
Pag (i.) **6** Bd
Pagadian **18** Fc
Pagai, Kepuluan– **18** Ae
Pagai Selantan (i.) **18** ABe
Pagai Utara (i.) **18** ABe
Pagan Island **27** Cb
Pagasitikós Kólpos **11** Ed
Page **33** Bc
Paget, Mount– **40** Ec
Pagoda Point **19** Be
Pago Pago **28** Ac
Pahkaning Bum **19** Cc
Pahoa **28** map no.1
Paia **28** map no.1
Paide **4** Fd
Paijänne (l.) **4** Fc
Pailolo Channel **28** map no.1

Paisley **7** Dd
Paistunturit (mt.) **4** FGa
Paita **37** Ac
Pajala **4** Eb
Pajaros, Farallon de– (i.) **27** Ca
Pakanbaru **18** Bd
Pakistan (Ind. St.) **15** Cg
Pakokku **19** Bd
Pak Phanang **19** Dg
Paks **6** Dc
Pakxé **19** Ee
Pala **25** Bd
Palagruža **11** Bb
Palana **14** IJd
Palangkaraya **18** De
Palanpur **20** Dd
Palapye **26** Bd
Palau **10** Bd
Palau Islands **27** Bb
Palauli **28** map no.5
Palaw **19** Cf
Palawan (i.) **15** Dhi
Palayankottai **20** Eg
Paldiski **4** EFd
Paleleh **18** Fd
Palembang **15** Dj
Palencia **9** CDab
Palermo **10** De
Palestina **39** ABb
Palestine (phys. reg.) **22** Efg
Paletwa **19** Bd
Palghat **20** Ef
Pali **20** Dc
Palikir **27** Cb
Palinuro, Capo– **10** Ed
Palk Strait **20** EFfg
Pallasovka **12** Gc
Pallastunturi (mt.) **4** EFa
Palles, Bisthí i– **11** Cc
Palma **9** Gc
Palma, La– **35** Cc
Palma, La– (i.) **24** Ab
Palmas, Cape– **24** Bd
Palmas, Las– **24** Ab
Palma Soriano **35** Cab
Palmeira dos Indios **38** Db
Palmer Land **42** grid square no.1
Palmer Station (sc. stat.) **42** grid square no.1
Palmerston Atoll **28** Ac
Palmi **10** Ef
Palmira **37** Bb
Palm Springs **33** Bc
Palmyra **21** Bc
Palmyra Atoll **28** Ab
Paloma, La– **39** Cc
Palomani, Nevado– (mt.) **39** Ba
Palomar Mountain (mt.) **33** Bc
Palopo **18** EFe
Palos, Cabo de– (cap.) **9** Ed
Palu **18** EFe
Pamekasan **18** Df
Pamiers **8** DEf
Pamir (plat.) **13** Gf
Pamlico Sound **32** Db
Pampa **33** CDc
Pampas (phys. reg.) **39** Bc
Pamplona [Col.] **37** Bb
Pamplona [Sp.] **9** DEa
Panagjurište **11** Fb

Panaitan, Pulau– (i.) **18** BCf
Panaji (Nova Goa) **20** De
Panamá (Ind. St.) **30** JKi
Panamá **36** Cbc
Panama, Gulf of– **35** Cc
Panama City **32** Cbc
Panaro (riv.) **10** Cb
Panay (i.) **15** Eh
Pančevo **6** Ed
Panciu **6** Hd
Panevėžys **4** Fe
Panfilov **13** GHe
Pangaion Óros (mts.) **11** EFc
Pangi **26** Bb
Pangkalanberandan **18** Ad
Pangkalpinang **18** Ce
Pangnirtung **31** Ib
Pangutaran Group **18** EFc
Panié, Mont– (mt.) **28** map no.4
Panjgur **20** Bc
Panna **19** Hj
Pannawonica **29** Bc
Panorama **39** Cb
Pantanal (sw.) **39** Ca
Pantar, Pulau– (i.) **18** Ff
Pantelleria (i.) **10** CDf
Pánuco (riv.) **34** Cb
Pao, El– **37** Cb
Pão de Açúcar **38** Db
Paola **10** Fe
Papa **28** map no.3
Pápa **6** Cc
Papaikou **28** map no.1
Papeete **28** map no.2
Papenoo **28** map no.2
Papetoai **28** map no.2
Papua, Gulf of– **27** Cc
Papua New Guinea (Ind. St.) **27** Cc
Papuk (mts.) **6** Cd
Papun **19** Ce
Pará (State) **38** Bb
Pará (riv.) **38** BCb
Paraburdoo **29** Bc
Paracatu (riv.) **39** Da
Paracatu **39** Da
Paracel Islands **15** Dh
Paraguá (riv.) **39** Ba
Paragua (riv.) **37** Cb
Paragua, La– **37** Cb
Paraguaí (riv.) **38** Bc
Paraguaipoa **37** Ba
Paraguaná, Península de– (pen.) **37** Ca
Paraguay (riv.) **39** Cb
Paraguay (Ind. St.) **36** DEf
Paraíba (State) **38** Db
Paraíba do Sul (riv.) **39** Db
Paraíso **35** map no.1
Parakou **24** Cd
Paramaribo **36** Ec
Paramonga **37** Bd
Paramušir, ostrov– (i.) **14** Id
Paraná **39** BCc
Paraná **38** Cc
Paraná (riv.) **38** Cc
Paraná (riv.) **39** Cb
Paraná (State) **39** Cb
Paranaguá **39** Db
Paranaíba **39** Cab
Paranaíba (riv.) **39** Da
Paranapanema (riv.) **39** Cb

Paranapiacaba, Serra do– (mts.) **39** CDb
Paranavaí **39** Cb
Parepeti (riv.) **39** Bab
Paray–le–Monial **8** Fd
Parbati (riv.) **20** Ed
Parbhani **20** Ee
Parchim **5** Cb
Parczew **5** Ic
Pardo [Braz.] (riv.) **38** CDc
Pardo [Braz.] (riv.) **39** Db
Pardubice **5** EFcd
Parecis, Chapada dos– (mts.) **38** ABc
Parepare **18** Ee
Párga **11** Dd
Paria, Golfo de– **37** Ca
Pariaman **18** ABe
Parika **37** Db
Parima, Sierra– (mts.) **37** Cb
Pariñas, Punta– (cap.) **37** Ac
Paríngul Mare, Vîrful– (mt.) **6** FGd
Parintins **38** Bb
Paris [Fr.] **8** Ec
Paris [U.S.] **32** Bb
Parkersburg **32** CDb
Parkes **29** He
Park Range **33** Cbc
Parma **10** Cb
Parnaguá **38** Cbc
Parnaíba **36** FGd
Parnaíba (riv.) **38** Cb
Parnassós Óros (mt.) **11** Ed
Párnon Óros (mts.) **11** Ee
Pärnu **13** Bd
Paroo Channel (riv.) **29** Gde
Paroo River **29** GHd
Paropamisus (mts.) **20** BCab
Páros (i.) **11** Fe
Parral **39** Ac
Parras **34** Bb
Parry, Cape– **31** Cab
Parry Islands **41** grid square no.2
Parry Sound **31** GHd
Parṣeta (riv.) **5** Fb
Parsons **32** Bb
Parthenay **8** CDd
Partinico **10** De
Partizansk **14** Ge
Paru (riv.) **38** Bb
Párvomaj **11** Fb
Pas, The– **31** Db
Pasadena [Ca.–U.S.] **33** Bc
Pasadena [Tx.–U.S.] **32** Bc
Pa Sak (riv.) **19** Def
Paşcani **6** Hc
Pasco **33** Bb
Pascoal, Monte– **38** CDc
Pasewalk **5** DEb
Pasir Mas **19** Dg
Pasni **20** Bc
Paso, El– **33** Cc
Paso de Indios **40** Bb
Paso de los Libres **39** Cb
Paso de los Toros **39** Cc
Passau **5** Dd
Passero, Capo– **10** Ef
Passo Fundo **39** Cb
Passos **39** Db
Pastaza (riv.) **37** Bc
Pasto **36** Cc

Pastos Bons **38** Cb
Pasvik (riv.) **4** Ga
Patagonia (phys. reg.) **40** ABbc
Patagonica, Cordillera– (mts.) **40** Aab
Patan [India] **20** Dd
Patan [Nep.] **20** Gc
Paternò **10** Ef
Paterson **32** Da
Pathankot **20** Eb
Pati **18** Df
Patía **37** Bb
Patía (riv.) **37** Bb
Patiala **20** Ebc
Pátmos (i.) **11** Ge
Patna **15** Cg
Patomskoje Negorje **14** Ed
Patos **38** Db
Patos, Lagoa dos– (lag.) **39** Cc
Patos de Minas **39** Da
Patquía **39** Bbc
Pátrai **11** DEd
Patraïkós Kólpos **11** Dd
Patrocínio **39** Da
Pattani **19** Dg
Patti **10** Ef
Patuakhali **19** Jk
Patuca (riv.) **35** Bb
Patuca, Punta– (cap.) **35** Bb
Pau **8** Cf
Pau d'Arco **38** Cb
Pau dos Ferros **38** Db
Pauillac **8** Ce
Pauini **37** Cc
Pauini (riv.) **37** Cc
Paulatuk **31** Cb
Paulista **38** Db
Paulistana **38** Cb
Paulo Afonso, Cachoeira de– **38** Db
Pavia **10** Bb
Pavlodar **13** Gd
Pavlovo **12** Fb
Pavlovsk **12** EFc
Pavlovskaja **12** EFd
Paxoí (i.) **11** CDd
Payne Bay → Bellin **31** Hlbc
Payne's Find **29** Bd
Paysandú **39** Cc
Pays de Caux (phys. reg.) **8** Dc
Paz, La– [Arg.] **39** Cc
Paz, La– [Arg.] **39** Cc
Paz, La– [Bol.] **39** Ba
Paz, La– [Mex.] **34** Ab
Pazardžik **11** EFb
Peace River (riv.) **31** Dc
Peace River **31** Dc
Peak Hill **29** Bd
Pearl Harbor **28** map no.1
Peary Land **41** grid square no.1
Pebane **26** Cc
Pebas **37** Bc
Peć **11** Db
Peçanha **39** Da
Pečenga **13** Cbc
Pečora (riv.) **13** Ec
Pečora **13** Ec
Pecoraro, Monte– **10** Fe
Pečory **4** Fd

Pecos (riv.) **33** Cc
Pecos **33** Cc
Pécs **6** CDc
Pedra Azul **39** Da
Pedreiras **38** Cb
Pedrera, La– **37** BCc
Pedro Afonso **38** Cb
Pedro Cays (is.) **35** Cb
Pedro de Valdivia **39** ABb
Pedro II, Ilha– **37** Cb
Pedro Juan Caballero **39** Cb
Pedro Miguel **35** map no.1
Pedro Miguel Locks **35** map no.1
Peebles **7** Ed
Pee Dee (riv.) **32** CDb
Peel Sound **31** Fa
Peene (riv.) **5** Db
Pegai **11** Dd
Pegu **19** Ce
Pegu Yoma **19** Cde
Pehuajó **39** Bc
Peipus, Lake– **13** Bd
Peixe **38** Cc
Pekalongan **18** CDf
Peking → Beijing **16** Ebc
Pelagie, Isole– **10** Dg
Pélagos (i.) **11** EFd
Pelat, Mont– (mt.) **8** Ge
Peleaga, Vîrful– (mt.) **6** Fd
Pelechuco **39** Ba
Peleduj **14** Ed
Peleng, Pulau– (i.) **18** Fe
Peljesac (pen.) **11** Bb
Pello **4** EFb
Pelly (riv.) **31** Bb
Pelly Bay **31** FGb
Pelopónnisos (phys. reg.) **11** DEe
Peloritani (mts.) **10** Eef
Peloro o Punta del Faro, Capo– (cap.) **10** Ee
Pelotas **39** Cc
Pelotas, Rio– (riv.) **39** Cb
Pelusium (r.) **25** map no.1
Pelvoux, Massif du– (mt.) **8** Ge
Pelym (riv.) **12** Ja
Pematangsiantar **18** ABd
Pemba **26** Dc
Pemba (i.) **26** CDb
Pemberton **29** Be
Pembroke [Can.] **32** Da
Pembroke [U.K.] **7** Df
Pembuang (riv.) **18** De
Penafiel **9** ABb
Peñafiel **9** CDb
Peñalara (mt.) **9** CDb
Penambo Range **18** Ed
Peña Nevada, Cerro– (mt.) **34** BCb
Peña Prieta (mt.) **9** Ca
Peñaranda de Bracamonte **9** Cb
Peñarroya–Pueblonuevo **9** Cc
Peñas, Cabo de– (cap.) **9** Ca
Penas, Golfo de– (b.) **40** Ab
Peña Ubiña (mt.) **9** BCa
Pendembu **24** ABd
Pendleton **33** ABb
Peneda (mt.) **9** Ab
Penedo **38** Dc
Penganga (riv.) **20** Ede

Peniche **9** Ac
Peñíscola **9** Fb
Penitente, Serra do– (mts.) **38** Cb
Penju, Kepulauan– **18** Gf
Penne **10** Dc
Penner (riv.) **20** Ef
Pennine Alps **10** Aab
Pennines **7** EFde
Pennsylvania (State) **32** Da
Peno **12** Db
Penong **29** Ee
Penonomé **35** Bc
Penrhyn Atoll **28** ABc
Penrith **29** Ie
Pensacola **32** Cb
Pentecôte, Île– (i.) **28** map no.4
Penticton **33** ABb
Pentland Firth **7** Eb
Penza **13** Dd
Penzance **7** CDf
Penžina (riv.) **14** Jc
Penžinskaja guba **14** Jc
Peoria **32** Ca
Pequiri (riv.) **39** Ca
Perabumulih **18** BCe
Perche, Col de la– (p.) **8** Ef
Perche, Collines du– (mts.) **8** Dc
Percival Lakes **29** CDc
Perdido, Monte– **9** EFa
Perecin **5** Id
Pereira **37** Bb
Pereslavl–Zalesski **12** Eb
Pergamino **39** BCc
Pergamum → Bergama **22** Ac
Peribonca (riv.) **32** Da
Périgord (phys. reg.) **8** De
Périgueux **8** De
Perija, Sierra de– (mts.) **37** Bab
Peristéri (mt.) **11** Dd
Perito Moreno **40** Ab
Perlas, Archipiélago de las– (is.) **35** Cc
Perm **13** Ed
Përmeti **11** Dc
Pernambuco (State) **38** Db
Pernik **11** Eb
Péronne **8** Ec
Pérouse Pinnacle, La– (i.) **28** Aa
Perpignan **8** Ef
Perry Island **31** Eb
Persepolis (r.) **21** Ecd
Persian Gulf **21** DEd
Perth [Austl.] **29** ABe
Perth [U.K.] **7** Ec
Perthus, Col de– **9** Ga
Pertusato, Capo– **8** map no.1
Perú (Ind. St.) **36** Cde
Peru, Altiplano del– **37** Bd
Perugia **10** Dc
Peruibe **39** Db
Pervomajsk [Russia] **12** Fc
Pervomajsk [Ukr.] **12** CDd
Pervouralsk **13** EFd
Pesaro **10** Dc
Pescadores (is.) **16** EFf
Pescara **10** Ec
Peschici **10** Fd

Peshāwar **15** Cf
Peshkopia **11** Dc
Peskovka [Russia] **12** Hb
Peskovka [Ukr.] **6** IJa
Pesqueira **38** Db
Pessac **8** Ce
Peštera **11** Fbc
Pestovo **12** Eb
Petah Tiqwa **22** Ef
Petalioi, Gulf of– **11** Fde
Petauke **26** Cc
Peterborough [Austl.] **29** FGe
Peterborough [Can.] **32** Da
Peterborough [U.K.] **7** FGe
Peterhead **7** Fc
Petermann Ranges **29** DEcd
Petersburg [Ak.–U.S.] **31** Bc
Petersburg [Va.–U.S.] **32** Db
Peter's Mine **37** CDb
Peter the Great Bay **16** Hb
Peto **34** Dbc
Petrel **42** grid square no.1
Petrič **11** Ec
Petrila **6** Fd
Petrolândia **38** Db
Petrolina **38** Cb
Petropavlovsk **13** FGd
Petropavlovsk Kamčatski **14** IJd
Petrópolis **39** Db
Petroşani **6** Fd
Petrovsk **12** Gc
Petrovsk–Zabaikalski **14** Dd
Petrozavodsk **13** BCc
Petuhovo **13** Fd
Peureulak **18** Ad
Pevek **14** Kc
Pforzheim **5** Bd
Phalodi **20** Dc
Phangan, Ko– (i.) **19** CDg
Phang–nga **19** Cg
Phan Rang **18** CDb
Phan Thiet **19** Ef
Phatthalung **19** CDg
Phet Buri **19** CDf
Phetchabun **19** De
Philadelphia **32** Dab
Philippines (Ind. St.) **15** Ehi
Philippine Sea **27** Bb
Phitsanulok **19** De
Phnum Pénh **15** Dh
Phoenix (i.) **28** Ac
Phoenix **33** Bc
Phoenix Islands **28** Ac
Phöngsali **19** Dd
Phrae **19** De
Phu Bia (mt.) **19** De
Phuket **19** Cg
Phu Miang (mt.) **19** De
Phu Qui **19** Ee
Phu Quoc, Dao– (i.) **19** Df
Piacenza **10** Bb
Pianosa (i.) **10** Cc
Piaozero, ozero– **4** Gb
Piaseczno **5** Hbc
Piatra Neamţ **6** Hc
Piauí (riv.) **38** Cb
Piauí (State) **38** Cb
Piave (riv.) **10** Da
Piazza Armerina **10** Ef
Pibor Post **25** Dd
Picardy (hist. reg.) **8** DEbc
Pichilemu **39** Ac

Pickle Crow **31** FGc
Pico, El– **39** Ba
Picos **38** Cb
Pico Truncado **40** Bb
Picton, Isla– **40** Bc
Pidurutalagala (mt.) **20** Fg
Piedras, Río de las– (riv.) **37** BCd
Piedras Negras **34** Bb
Pieksämäki **4** Fc
Pielavesi **4** Fc
Pielinen (l.) **4** Gc
Piemonte (reg.) **10** Ab
Pierre **33** Cb
Piešťany **5** Fd
Pietermaritzburg **26** Cd
Pietersburg **26** BCd
Pietrasanta **10** Cc
Pietrosu, Vîrful– (mt.) **6** Gc
Pigs, Bay of– **35** Ba
Pikalevo **12** DEb
Pikelot Island **27** Cb
Piła **5** Fb
Pilar **39** Cb
Pilcomayo (riv.) **39** Bb
Pilibhit **20** EFc
Pílica (riv.) **5** Hc
Pilion Óros (mt.) **11** Ed
Pílos **11** De
Pimenta Bueno **37** Cd
Piña **35** map no.1
Pinang (i.) **19** CDg
Pınarbaşı **22** Fc
Pinar del Rio **35** Ba
Pincota **6** EFc
Pindus Mountains **11** Dd
Pine Bluff **32** Bb
Pine Creek **29** Ea
Pine Island Bay **42** grid square no.3
Pine Point **31** Db
Pinerolo **10** Ab
Ping (riv.) **19** Ce
Pingdingshan **16** Dd
Pingelap Atoll **27** Db
Pinglap Atoll **28** map no.3
Pingle **16** CDf
Pingliang **16** Cc
Pingtung **16** Ff
Pingwu **16** Bd
Pingxiang [China] **16** DEe
Pingxiang [China] **16** Cf
Pingyao **16** Dc
Pinheiro **38** Cb
Pini, Pulau– (i.) **18** Ad
Pinios (riv.) **11** DEd
Pinjarra **29** Be
Pinnaroo **29** Gef
Pinotepa Nacional **34** Cc
Pins, Îles des– **27** Cd
Pinsk **13** Bd
Pintados **39** ABb
Pinto **39** Bb
Piombino **10** Cc
Pioner, ostrov– **14** BCab
Pionki **5** Hc
Piotrków Trybunalski **5** Gc
Pipanaco, Salar de– (s. m.) **39** Bb
Piperi (i.) **11** Fd
Piqua **32** Ca
Piracambu, Serra do– (mts.) **38** Cb

Q

Regina [Can.] **31** Ec
Regina [Fr. Gui.] **38** Ba
Registan (phys. reg.) **20** BCb
Regnitz (riv.) **5** Cd
Reguengos de Monsaraz **9** Bc
Rehoboth **26** Ad
Rehovot **22** Eg
Reigate **7** Ff
Reims **8** Fc
Reina Adelaida, Archipiélago–
(is.) **40** Ac
Reindeer Depot **31** Bb
Reindeer Lake **31** Ec
Reinosa **9** Ca
Remanso **38** Cb
Rembang **18** Df
Remiremont **8** Gc
Remscheid **5** Ac
Rendsburg **5** BCa
Rengat **18** Be
Reni **6** Id
Renmark **29** Ge
Rennell Island **27** CDc
Rennes **8** Fc
Rennick Glacier **42** grid
square no.4
Reno (riv.) **10** Cb
Reno **33** ABbc
Reno, El– **32** Bb
Réole, La– **8** CDe
Republican River **32** Bab
Repulse Bay **30** IJc
Requena [Peru] **37** Bc
Requena [Sp.] **9** Ec
Reşadiye Yarimadasi **11** Ge
Resia, Passo di– **10** Ca
Resistencia **39** BCb
Reşiţa (mts.) **6** Ed
Resolute **31** Fa
Resolution Island **31** Ib
Rethel **8** Fc
Réthimmon **11** Ff
Reunion (i.) **23** map no.1
Reus **9** Fb
Reuss (riv.) **5** Be
Reutlingen **5** Bd
Revda **12** IJb
Revelstoke **33** Ba
Revermont (mt.) **8** Fd
Revillagigedo, Islas– **30** GHh
Rewa **20** Fd
Rewari **19** Gij
Rex, Mount– **42** grid square
no.1
Rey **21** Eb
Reykjanes (cap.) **4** map no.1
Reykjavik **4** map no.1
Reynosa **34** Cb
Rež **12** Jb
Reze **8** Cd
Rēzekne **4** Fd
Rezina **6** Ic
Rhein (riv.) **5** Be
Rheine **5** Ab
Rheinland–Pfalz (phys. reg.)
5 Acd
Rhir, Cap– **24** ABa
Rhode Island (State) **32** Da
Rhodes **22** Bd
Rhodes (i.) **22** Bde
Rhodope Mountains **11** EFbc
Rhön (mt.) **5** BCc
Rhône (riv.) **10** Aa

Rhum (i.) **7** Cc
Riaño **9** Ca
Riau, Kepulauan– **18** Bd
Ribadeo **9** Ba
Ribas do Rio Pardo **39** Cb
Ribatejo (phys. reg.) **9** Ac
Ribáué **26** Cc
Ribe **5** Ba
Ribeira (riv.) **39** Db
Ribeira → Santa Eugenia **9** Aa
Ribeirão Prêto **39** Db
Ribérac **8** CDe
Riberalta **37** Cd
Riccione **10** Dc
Richard's Bay **26** Cd
Richardson Mountains **31** Bb
Richard Toll **24** Ac
Richfield **33** Bc
Richland **33** Bb
Richmond [Austl.] **29** Gc
Richmond [In.–U.S.] **32** Cb
Richmond [Ky.–U.S.] **32** Cb
Richmond [Va.–U.S.] **32** Cb
Ried im Innkreis **5** Dd
Riesa **5** Dc
Riesco, Isla– (i.) **40** Ac
Riesi **10** Ef
Rieti **10** Dc
Rif (mts.) **24** Ba
Rifstangi (cap.) **4** map no.1
Rift Valley **26** Cab
Riga **4** Fd
Riga, Gulf of– **4** EFd
Rihand (riv.) **20** Fd
Rihand Sägar **20** Fd
Riihimäki **4** EFc
Riiser–Larsen Halvøya **42**
grid square no.2
Rijeka **6** Bd
Riksgränsen **4** Da
Rila (mts.) **11** Eb
Rimal, Ar– → Rub' al Khali
21 DEef
Rimatara, Île– (i.) **28** Bd
Rimavská Sobota **5** GHd
Rimini **10** Db
Rīmnicu Sārat **6** Hd
Rīmnicu Vilcea **6** Gd
Rimouski **31** Id
Ringebu **4** Bc
Ringerike **4** Bc
Ringsted **5** CDa
Ringus **19** Gj
Ringvassøy (i.) **4** Da
Rinjani, Gunung– (mt.) **18** Ef
Riobamba **37** Bc
Rio Branco **37** Ccd
Rio Brilhante **39** Cb
Rio Claro **39** Db
Rio Colorado **39** Bc
Rio Cuarto **39** Bc
Rio de Janeiro (State) **39** Db
Rio de Janeiro **39** Db
Rio Gallegos **36** Di
Rio Grande **39** Cc
Rio Grande **40** Bc
Rio Grande do Norte (State)
38 Db
Rio Grande do Sul (State) **39**
Cbc
Riohacha **37** Ba
Rioja, La– **39** Bb
Rioja, La– (phys. reg.) **26** DEa

Rio Largo **38** Db
Riom **8** Ee
Rio Mayo **40** ABb
Rio Mulatos **39** Ba
Rio Negro **39** CDb
Rio Negro, Embalse del– (l.)
39 Cc
Rio Tercero **39** Bc
Rio Tinto **38** Db
Rio Verde **39** Ca
Rio Verde de Mato Grosso **39**
Ca
Rishiri–Tō (i.) **16** Jab
Risle (riv.) **8** Dc
Risør **4** Bd
Ritchie's Archipelago **19** Bf
Ritter, Mount– **33** Bc
Riva → Cayağzi **22** Bb
Rivadavia [Arg.] **39** Bb
Rivadavia [Chile] **39** Ab
Riva del Garda **10** Cb
Rivas **35** Bb
Rive–de–Gier **8** Fe
Rivera [Arg.] **39** Bc
Rivera [Ur.] **39** Cc
River Cess **24** ABd
Riverside **33** Bc
Rivière–du–Loup **32** Ea
Rivoli **10** Ab
Riyadh **21** De
Rize **21** Ca
Rizzuto, Capo– **10** Fe
Rjazan **13** CDd
Rjažsk **12** Fc
Rjukan **4** ABd
Roa **9** CDb
Roanne **8** Fde
Roanoke **32** CDb
Roanoke (riv.) **32** Db
Robert English Coast **42** grid
square no.1
Robertsport **24** Ad
Robeson Channel **41** grid
square no.1
Robinvale **29** Ge
Robla, La– **9** BCa
Roboré **39** BCa
Robson, Mount– **31** CDc
Roca, Cabo da– (cap.) **9** Ac
Roca Partida, Isla– (i.) **34** Bb
Rocas, Atol das– (i.) **38** Db
Rocha **39** Cc
Rochechouart **8** De
Rochefort **8** Ce
Rochelle, La– **8** Cd
Rochester [Mn.–U.S.] **32** Ba
Rochester [N.Y.–U.S.] **32** Da
Roche–sur–Yon, La– **8** Cd
Rockefeller Plateau (plat.) **42**
grid square no.3
Rockford **32** Ca
Rockhampton **29** Ic
Rockingham **29** ABe
Rock Island **32** BCa
Rockland **32** Ea
Rock Springs **33** BCb
Rocky Mount **32** Db
Rocky Mountains **31** CDcd
Roda, La– **9** DEc
Rødberg **4** ABc
Rødbyhavn **5** Ca
Rodez **8** Ee
Rodrigues (i.) **23** map no.1

Roebourne **29** Bc
Roebuck Bay **29** Cb
Roermond **8** FGb
Roeselare **8** Eb
Roes Welcome Sound **31** Gb
Rogaguado, Lago– **39** Ba
Rognan **4** Cb
Rohtak **20** Ec
Roi Et **19** De
Roja, La– **36** Dfg
Rojo, Cabo– **34** Cb
Rokan (riv.) **18** Bd
Rolla **32** Bb
Roma **29** Hd
Roman **6** Hc
Romana, La– **35** Db
Romang, Pulau– (i.) **18** Gf
Români **25** map no.1
Romania (Ind. St.) **3** Fc
Romanovka **14** DEd
Romans–sur–Isère **8** Fe
Rome [Ga.–U.S.] **32** Cb
Rome [It.] **10** Dd
Romilly–sur–Seine **8** EFc
Romny **12** Dc
Rømø (i.) **5** Ba
Romorantin–Lanthenay **8**
DEd
Ronas Hill **7** Fa
Ronave **27** map no.2
Roncador, Cayos de– (is.) **35**
BCb
Roncador, Serra do– (mts.)
38 Bc
Roncesvalles **9** Ea
Ronda **9** Cd
Rondane (mt.) **4** Bc
Rondônia **37** Cd
Rondônia (State) **37** Cd
Rondonópolis **39** Ca
Rong, Kaôh– (i.) **19** Df
Ronge, La– **31** Bb
Rongelap Atoll **27** Db
Rønne **4** Ce
Rooniu (mt.) **28** map no.2
Roosendaal **8** Fb
Roosevelt, Rio– (riv.) **38** Ab
Roosevelt Island **42** grid
square no.3
Roosevelt Lake **33** Bb
Roper River **29** Ea
Roper Valley **29** EFa
Roques, Islas los– (is.) **35** Db
Roquetas de Mar **9** Dd
Roraima (State) **37** Cb
Roraima, Monte– **37** CDb
Røros **4** BCc
Rørvik **4** BCb
Ros (riv.) **6** Ib
Rosa, Monte– **10** Ab
Rosário **38** Cb
Rosario [Arg.] **39** Bc
Rosario [Mex.] **34** Bb
Rosario [Mex.] **34** Aab
Rosario de la Frontera **39** Bb
Rosário do Sul **39** Cc
Rosário Oeste **39** Ca
Roseau **35** Db
Rosebery **29** map no.1
Rosebud **29** GHf
Roseburg **33** Ab
Rosenheim **5** CDe
Rosetown **31** Ec

Ros - Sai

Rosignano Marittimo **10** Cc
Roşiori de Vede **6** Gd
Roskilde **5** Da
Roslavl **13** Cd
Rossano **10** Fe
Ross Ice Shelf (gl.) **42** grid
square no.3
Ross Island **42** grid square
no.4
Rosslare **7** CDe
Rosso **24** Ac
Rossoš **12** Ec
Ross River **31** Bb
Ross Sea **42** grid square no.3
Røssvatnet (l.) **4** Cb
Røst (i.) **4** Bb
Rostock **5** Da
Rostock–Warnemünde **5** CDa
Rostov **12** Eb
Rostov–na–Donu **13** CDe
Roswell **33** Cc
Rota Island **27** Cb
Rothaar–Gebirge (mts.) **5** Bc
Rothera (i.) **42** grid square no.1
Rothesay **7** Dd
Roti, Pulau– (i.) **18** Fg
Rotidian Point **27** map no.1
Roto **29** GHe
Rotondo, Monte– **8** map no.1
Rotterdam **8** EFb
Rotterdam–Hoek van Holland
8 EFb
Rottweil **5** Bd
Rotuma Island **27** Dc
Roúbaix **8** Eb
Rouen **8** Dc
Round Mountain, The– (mt.)
29 Ie
Rousay (i.) **7** Eb
Roussillon (phys. reg.) **8** Ef
Rouyn **31** Hd
Rov (riv.) **6** Hb
Rovaniemi **4** Fb
Rovereto **10** Cb
Rovigo **10** Cb
Rovno **13** Bd
Rovuma (riv.) **26** Cc
Rowley Shoals (is.) **29** Bb
Roxas **18** Fb
Royal Canal **7** Ce
Royale, Isle– **32** Ca
Royal Tunbridge Wells **7** Gf
Royan **8** Ce
Roy Hill **29** BCc
Rozewie, Przylądek– (cap.) **4**
De
Rožňava **5** Hd
Roztocze (mts.) **5** Icd
Rtanj (mt.) **6** EFe
Rtiščevo **13** Dd
Ruafa, El– **22** Eg
Ruapehu, Mount– **27** Dd
Rub'al Khali **21** DEef
Rub'al Khali (Ar Rimal) **21** DEef
Rubcovsk **13** Hd
Rubežnoje **12** Ed
Rubinéia **39** CDab
Rubio **37** Bb
Ruda Śląska **5** Gc
Rüdbär **20** Bbc
Rudkøbing **5** Ca
Rudnaja–Pristan **14** Ge
Rudnica **6** Ib

Rudničny **12** Hb
Rudny [Kaz.] **13** Fd
Rudny [Russia] **17** Db
Rudolf, Lake– **25** Dd
Rueil–Malmaison **8** DEc
Rufiji (riv.) **26** Cb
Rufino **39** Bc
Rufisque **24** Ac
Rugby **7** Fe
Rügen (i.) **4** Ce
Rügen → Bergen **5** Da
Ruhea **19** Jj
Ruhr (riv.) **5** Bc
Rui'an **16** Fe
Ruijin **16** Ee
Rujen (mt.) **11** Eb
Ruki (riv.) **26** Aab
Rukwa, Lake– **26** Cb
Ruma **6** Dd
Rumbek **25** Cd
Rum Cay (i.) **32** Dc
Rumia **5** Ga
Rum Jungle **29** DEa
Rummah, Wādī ar– **21** Cd
Rumoi **17** Gbc
Rungwa (riv.) **26** Cb
Rungwa **26** Cb
Ruo Shui (riv.) **16** Bb
Rupununi (riv.) **37** Db
Rurrenabaque **39** Ba
Rurutu, Île– (i.) **28** Bd
Ruşayris, Ar– **25** Dc
Ruse **11** FGb
Russas **38** Db
Russia (Ind. St.) **15** BDc
Russki, Ostrov– **17** BCc
Rustavi **13** De
Ruţbah, Ar– **21** Cc
Ruteng **18** Ff
Ruthenia (phys. reg.) **6** FGb
Rutland **32** Da
Rutland (i.) **19** Bf
Rutog **15** Cf
Ruvuma (riv.) **26** Cc
Ruwenzori (mt.) **25** CDde
Ruzajevka **12** Fc
Ružomberok **5** Gd
Rwanda (Ind. St.) **26** BCb
Rybačje → Issyk–Kul **13** Ge
Rybinsk **13** CDd
Rybinskoje vodohranilišče **13**
Cd
Rybnica **6** Ic
Rybnik **5** Gc
Rylsk **12** DEc
Ryōtsu **17** EFef
Ryukyu Islands (Nansei–
Shotō) **16** FGef
Rzeszów **5** HIc
Ržev **13** Cd

S

Saale (riv.) **5** Cc
Saalfeld **5** Cc
Saar (riv.) **5** Ad
Saarbrücken **5** Ad
Saaremaa (i.) **4** Ed
Saarlouis **5** Ad
Šabac **6** Dd
Sabadell **9** FGb

Sabah (State) **15** Di
Sabalän, Kūhhä– ye– (mt.)
21 Db
Sabanalarga **37** Ba
Sab'Bi' Ār **22** Ff
Sabhā **24** Db
Sabinas **34** Bb
Sabinas Hidalgo **34** BCb
Sabine (riv.) **32** Bb
Sabini, Monti– **10** Dc
Sable, Cape– [Can.] **31** Id
Sable, Cape– [U.S.] **32** Cc
Sable Island **30** LMe
Sables–d'Olonne, Les– **8**
BCd
Sabor (riv.) **9** Bb
Şabrātah **24** Da
Sabrina Coast **42** grid square
no.4
Sabya **21** Cf
Sabzevār **21** Fb
Sabzevārān **21** Fd
Sacajawea Peak **33** Bb
Sacedón **9** Db
Sachs Harbour **31** Ca
Sacramento (riv.) **33** Ac
Sacramento **33** ABc
Sacramento, Pampas del–
(phys. reg.) **37** Bc
Sádaba **9** Ea
Sa' dah **21** Cf
Saddle Island **28** map no.4
Sadiya **19** Dg
Sado (riv.) **9** Ac
Sado–Shima (i.) **16** Ic
Šadrinsk **13** Fd
Şafāqis **24** CDa
Säffle **4** Cd
Safi **24** ABa
Şāfī, Aş– **22** Eg
Safid (riv.) **21** Db
Safonovo **12** Db
Saga [China] **20** FGc
Saga [Jap.] **16** GHd
Sagaing **19** BCd
Sagar **20** Ed
Sagauli **19** Ij
Saginaw **32** Ca
Sagiz (riv.) **12** Hd
Sagiz **12** Hid
Sagra, La– (mt.) **9** Dd
Sagres **9** Ad
Sagua La Grande **35** BCa
Sagunto **9** EFc
Sahagún **9** Ca
Sahara (des.) **24** CDb
Saharan Atlas (mts.) **24** BCa
Saharanpur **20** Ebc
Saharsa **19** Ij
Sahibganj **19** IJj
Sahiwal **20** Db
Šahty **13** De
Šahunja **12** Gb
Sai (riv.) **19** Hj
Sa'īdābād **21** EFd
Saidpur [Bngl.] **19** Jj
Saidpur [India] **19** Hj
Saiki **17** BCh
Saimaa **4** FGc
Saimaan Canal **4** FGc
Saint Affrique **8** Ef

Saint Albans **7** Ff
Saint Amand–Mont–Rond **8**
Ed
Saint André, Cap– (cap.) **26**
map no.1
Saint Andrews **7** Ec
Saint Anthony **31** Jc
Saint Augustine **32** CDbc
Saint Austell **7** Df
Saint Bernard Paß (p.) **10** Ba
Saint Boniface **31** Fcd
Saint Brieuc **8** Bc
Saint Catharines **32** CDa
Saint Céré **8** DEe
Saint Chamond **8** EFe
Saint Charles **32** Bb
Saint Christopher / Saint Kitts
35 Db
Saint–Claude **8** FGd
Saint Cloud **32** Ba
Saint Croix (i.) **35** Db
Saint David's Head (cap.) **7**
Df
Saint Denis [Fr.] **8** Ec
Saint Denis [Reu.] **23** map
no.1
Saint Dié **8** Gc
Saint Dizier **8** Fc
Saint Elias, Mount– **31** ABbc
Saint Elias Mountains **31**
ABbc
Saint Elie **37** Db
Sainte Marie, Cap– (cap.) **26**
map no.1
Saintes **8** Ce
Sainte Savine **8** EFc
Saint Étienne **8** EFe
Saint Étienne–du–Rouvray **8**
Dc
Saint Florent, Golfe de– **8**
map no.1
Saint Flour **8** Ee
Saint Gaudens **8** Df
Saint George [Austl.] **29** Hd
Saint George [U.S.] **33** Bc
Saint Georges (i.) **35** Db
Saint George's **37** Ca
Saint Georges **38** Ba
Saint George's Channel **7**
CDef
Saint Girons **8** Df
Saint Helena (i.) **23** Bg
Saint Helena Bay **26** Ae
Saint Helens **7** Ee
Saint Helier **8** Bc
Saint Hyacinthe **31** Hd
Saint Jean, Lac– (l.) **31** Hd
Saint Jean–d'Angély **8** Cde
Saint Jean–de–Luz **8** Cf
Saint Jean–Pied–de–Port **8**
Cf
Saint John **31** Id
Saint John (riv.) **32** Ea
Saint John's [Atg.] **35** Db
Saint John's [Can.] **31** JKd
Saint Joseph **32** Bab
Saint Jurien **8** De
Saint Kilda (i.) **7** Bc
Saint Kitts / Saint Christopher
(i.) **35** Db
Saint Kitts–Nevis (Ind. St.) **30**
Lh
Saint Laurent **37** Db

San Francisco Javier **9** Fc
San Gallan, Isla– **37** Bd
Sangar **14** FGc
Sangeang, Pulau– (i.) **18** Ef
Sanggau **18** CDde
Sangha (riv.) **24** Dd
Sangihe, Pulau– (i.) **18** FGd
Sangi Islands **18** Gd
San Gil **37** Bb
San Giovanni in Fiore **10** Fe
Sangkulirang **18** Ed
Sangli **20** DEe
San Gottardo (p.) **10** Ba
Sangre de Cristo Mounts **33** Cc
Sangue, Rio do– (riv.) **38** Bc
San Ignacio **39** Ba
San Javier **39** Ba
Sanjō **17** Ff
San Joaquin (riv.) **33** Ac
San Jorge, Golfo– **40** Bb
San José [Bol.] **39** Ba
San José [C.R.] **35** Bc
San José [Guat.] **35** Ab
San Jose [Phil.] **18** Fa
San Jose [Phil.] **18** Fb
San José [U.S.] **33** Ac
San Jose de Buenavista **18** Fb
San José de Jáchal **39** Bbc
San José del Cabo **34** Bb
San José del Guaviare **37** Bb
San José de Mayo **39** Cc
San José de Ocune **37** BCb
San Juan (i.) **30** Lh
San Juan (riv.) **33** BCc
San Juan [Arg.] **39** ABc
San Juan [Peru] **39** Aa
San Juan, Rio– **35** Bb
San Juan Bautista **39** Cb
San Juan de la Maguana **35** Cb
San Juan del Norte **35** Bb
San Juan de los Cayos **37** Ca
San Juan de los Morros **37** Cb
San Julián **36** Dh
San Justo **39** BCc
Sankh (riv.) **19** Ik
Sankosh (riv.) **15** Pj
Sankt Gallen **5** Be
Sankt Moritz **10** Ba
Sankt Pölten **5** Ed
Sankt Veit an der Glan **5** DEe
Sankuru (riv.) **26** Bb
San Lázaro, Cabo– **34** Ab
San Lorenzo **37** Bb
San Lorenzo de El Escorial **9** CDb
Sanlúcar de Barrameda **9** Bd
San Luis [Arg.] **39** Bc
San Luis [Mex.] **33** Cd
San Luis Obispo **33** Ac
San Luis Potosí **30** Hlg
San Marco, Capo– **10** Be
San Marcos **32** Bbc
San Marino **10** Dbc
San Marino (Ind. St.) **10** Dbc
San Martín (sc. stat.) **42** grid square no.1
San Martín **37** Bb
San Martín (riv.) **39** Ba
San Martín, Lago– **40** Ab

San Martín de los Andes **40** ABab
San Martín de Valdeiglesias **9** Cb
San Mateo **33** Ac
San Matias **39** Ca
San Matias, Golfo– **40** Bb
San Miguel (riv.) **39** Ba
San Miguel **35** Bb
San Miguel de Tucumán **39** Bb
San Miguel Islands **18** Ec
Sanmyaku (mts.) **17** EFg
Sannär **25** Dc
Sannicandro Garganico **10** Ed
San Nicolás de los Arroyos **39** Bc
Sanok **5** Hld
San Pablo **18** Fb
San Pedro [Arg.] **39** Bb
San Pedro [I.C.] **24** Bd
San Pedro [Par.] **39** Cb
San Pedro de Arimena **37** Bb
San Pedro de las Bocas **37** Cb
San Pedro de las Colonias **34** Bb
San Pedro Sula **35** Bb
San Pietro **10** Be
Sanquhar **7** DEd
San Quintin **34** Aa
San Rafael [Arg.] **39** Bc
San Rafael [Ven.] **37** Ba
San Ramón de la Nueva Orán **39** Bb
San Remo **10** Ac
San Roque **9** Cd
San Salvador **35** Bb
San Salvador (i.) **32** Dc
San Salvador de Jujuy **39** Bb
Sansanné–Mango **24** Cc
San Sebastián **9** DEa
San Severo **10** Ed
Santa, Rio– (riv.) **37** Bc
Santa Ana [Bol.] **39** Ba
Santa Ana [El Sal.] **35** ABb
Santa Ana [U.S.] **33** Ac
Santa Bárbara **34** Bb
Santa Barbara **33** ABc
Santa Catarina (State) **39** CDb
Santa Clara **35** BCa
Santa Coloma de Gramanet **9** Gb
Santa Cruz (riv.) **40** ABc
Santa Cruz [Phil.] **18** Fb
Santa Cruz [U.S.] **33** Ac
Santa Cruz de la Sierra **39** Ba
Santa Cruz del Sur **35** Ca
Santa Cruz de Moya **9** Ec
Santa Cruz de Tenerife **24** Ab
Santa Cruz do Sul **39** Cb
Santa Cruz Islands **27** Dc
Santa Elena de Uairén **37** CDb
Santa Eugenia (Ribeira) **9** Aa
Santa Eulalia del Río **9** FGc
Santafé **9** Dd
Santa Fe **30** Hf
Santa Fe **36** DEg
Santa Fe de Bogotá **36** Cc
Santa Genoveva (mt.) **34** Ab

Santahar **19** Jj
Santa Inés, Isla– (i.) **40** Ac
Santa Isabel [Arg.] **39** Bc
Santa Isabel [Braz.] **39** Ba
Santa Isabel Island **27** CDc
Santa Maria [Braz.] **39** Cb
Santa Maria [U.S.] **33** Ac
Santa Maria da Vitória **38** Cc
Santa Maria di Leuca, Capo– **10** Ge
Santa María Island **28** map no.4
Santa Marta **37** Ba
Santa Maura → Leucade (i.) **11** Dd
Santa Monica **33** ABc
Santana do Livramento **39** Cc
Santander **9** Da
Sant'Antioco (i.) **10** Be
Santañy **9** Gc
Santarém [Braz.] **36** Ed
Santarém [Port.] **9** Ac
Santa Rosa [Arg.] **39** Bc
Santa Rosa [Braz.] **39** Cb
Santa Rosa [Ca.–U.S.] **33** Ac
Santa Rosa [Hond.] **35** Bb
Santa Rosa [N.M.–U.S.] **33** Cc
Santa Rosalía **34** Ab
Santa Vitória do Palmar **39** Cc
Sant'Eufemia, Golfo di– **10** Fe
Sant Feliu de Guíxols **9** Gb
Santiago (riv.) **37** Bc
Santiago [Chile] **39** ABc
Santiago [Pan.] **35** Bc
Santiago [Sp.] **9** Aa
Santiago, Rio Grande de– (riv.) **34** Bb
Santiago de Cuba **35** Cab
Santiago de la Ribera **9** EFd
Santiago del Estero **39** Bb
Santiago Papasquiaro **34** Bb
Santo Amaro **38** Dc
Santo André **39** Db
Santo Ângelo **39** Cb
Santo Antonio Abad **9** Fc
Santo Antônio de Jesus **38** CDc
Santo Antônio do Içá **37** Cc
Santo Antônio do Leverger **39** Ca
Santo Domingo [Dom. Rep.] **30** KLh
Santo Domingo [Mex.] **34** Bb
Santo Domingo del Pacífico **34** Ab
Santoña **9** Da
Santos **39** Db
Santo Tomé **39** Cb
San Valentin, Cerro– (mt.) **40** Ab
San Vicente **35** Bb
San Vicente de Cañete **37** Bd
San Vicente de la Barquera **9** CDa
San Vito, Capo– **10** De
São Borja **39** Cb
São Félix **38** Bc
São Félix do Xingu **38** Bb
São Francisco (riv.) **38** Cc
São Francisco do Sul **39** Db

São João del Rei **39** Db
São José do Rio Prêto **39** CDb
São Leopoldo **39** CDb
São Lourenço (riv.) **39** Ca
São Luís **38** Cb
São Luís Gonzaga **39** Cb
São Marcos, Baia de– (b.) **38** Cb
São Mateus **39** Ea
Saône (riv.) **8** Fd
São Paulo (State) **39** CDb
São Paulo **39** Db
São Paulo de Olivença **37** Cc
São Pedro e São Paulo, Penedos de– (is.) **36** GHc
São Raimundo Nonato **38** Cb
São Roque, Cabo– **38** Db
São Sebastião, Ilha de– (i.) **39** Db
São Sebastião, Ponta– (cap.) **26** Cd
São Simão **39** CDa
São Tomé (i.) **24** Cde
Sao Tome and Principe (Ind. St.) **23** Ce
Saoura (riv.) **24** Bb
São Vicente, Cabo de– (cap.) **9** Ad
Sapiéntza (i.) **11** De
Sapporo **16** Jb
Sapudi, Pulau– (i.) **18** Df
Saqqez **21** Db
Saraburi **19** Df
Saragossa **9** Eb
Sarajevo **6** DEe
Saraji Mine **29** Hc
Sarakhs **21** Gb
Saraktaš **12** Ic
Saramati (mt.) **19** BCc
Saran **13** Ge
Saranda **11** CDd
Sarangani Islands **18** Gc
Saransk **13** Dd
Sarapul **13** Ed
Sarasota **32** Cc
Saratov **13** Dd
Saratovskoje vodohranilišče **12** Gc
Saravan **19** Ee
Sarawak (State) **15** Di
Saräyä **22** Ee
Sarbisheh **21** FGc
Sardinia (reg.) **10** Bde
Sarektjåkkå (mt.) **4** Db
Sargodha **20** Db
Šargorod **6** Hlb
Sarh **25** BCd
Sāri **21** Eb
Saria (i.) **11** Gf
Sarikei **18** Dd
Sarina **29** Hlc
Sariñena **9** Eb
Sarir **24** Eb
Sariwon **16** Gc
Šarja **13** Dd
Sark (i.) **8** Bc
Šarkişla **22** Fc
Šarköy **22** Ab
Sarlat–la–Canéda **8** De
Sarmiento **40** Bb
Särna **4** Cc
Sarnen **5** ABe

Sarnia 31 Gd
Sarny 13 Bd
Saroako 18 Fe
Saroma–Ko 17 Hlb
Saronikos Kólpos 11 Ee
Saros, Gulf of– 22 Ab
Sárospatak 6 Eb
Šar planina (mts.) 11 Dbc
Sarpsborg 4 BCd
Sarrebourg 8 Gc
Sarreguemines 8 Gc
Sarria 9 Ba
Sars, As– 10 Bf
Sartène 8 map no.1
Sarthe (riv.) 8 Cd
Sárvár 6 Cc
Saryč, mys– 12 De
Saryg–Sep 14 Cd
Sary–Šagan 13 Ge
Sarysu (riv.) 13 Fe
Sary–Taš 13 Gef
Saryžaz 13 GHe
Sasaram 19 Ij
Sasebo 16 Gd
Saskatchewan (prov.) 31 Ec
Saskatchewan (riv.) 31 Bb
Saskatoon 33 Ca
Saskylah 14 Eb
Sasovo 12 Fc
Sassandra (riv.) 24 Bd
Sassandra 24 Bd
Sassari 10 Bd
Sassnitz 4 Ce
Sata–Misaki 17 Bi
Satara 20 De
Satawal Island 27 Cb
Säter 4 CDc
Satka 12 Ibc
Satna 20 Fcd
Sátoraljaújhely 6 Eb
Sätpura Range 20 Ed
Satsuma–Hantō 17 ABi
Sattahip 19 CDf
Satu Mare 6 Fc
Satun 19 Cg
Sauda 4 Ad
Saudárkrókur 4 map no.1
Saudi Arabia (Ind. St.) 15 Bgh
Sauldre (riv.) 8 Ed
Sault Sainte Marie [Can.] 31 Gd
Sault Sainte Marie [U.S.] 32 Ca
Saumur 8 Cd
Saurimo 26 Bbc
Sava (riv.) 6 Dd
Savaiʻi Island 28 Ac
Savannah (riv.) 32 Cb
Savannah 32 CDb
Savannakhet 19 DEe
Savanna–la–Mar 35 Cb
Savaştepe 22 ABc
Savé 24 Cd
Save [Fr.] (riv.) 8 Df
Save [Moz.] (riv.) 26 Cd
Saveh 21 DEb
Savigliano 10 Ab
Savona 10 Bb
Savonlinna 4 Gc
Savoy (hist. reg.) 8 Gde
Savran 6 IJb
Savusavu 28 map no.6
Savu Sea 18 Ffg

Sawahlunto 18 Be
Sawai Madhopur 20 Ec
Sawäkin 25 Dc
Sawhāj 25 Db
Sawqirah 21 Ff
Şawqirah, Ghubbat– 21 Ff
Sawu, Pulau– (i.) 18 Fg
Saxony (phys. reg.) 5 DEc
Say 24 Cc
Sayhut 21 Efg
Sazanit, Ishull i– (i.) 11 Cc
Sázava (riv.) 5 Ed
Scapa Flow (g.) 7 Eb
Scarborough 7 FGd
Scarborough Reef (i.) 18 Ea
Ščekino 12 Ec
Schaffhausen 5 Be
Schefferville 30 Ld
Schelde (riv.) 8 EFb
Schenectady 32 Da
Schleswig 5 Ba
Schleswig–Holstein (State) 5 BCab
Schlüchtern 5 Bc
Schmidta, ostrov– 14 BCa
Schouwen (i.) 8 Eb
Schwaben (phys. reg.) 5 BCde
Schwäbische Alb (mts.) 5 BCd
Schwäbisch Hall 5 BCd
Schwandorf in Bayern 5 Dd
Schwaner, Pegunungan– 18 De
Schwarze Elster (riv.) 5 Dc
Schwedt 5 Eb
Schweinfurt 5 Cc
Schwerin 5 Cb
Sciacca 10 Df
Scicli 10 Ef
Scilly, Isles of– 7 Cg
Scoresby Land 41 grid square no.1
Scoresbysund / Itseqqortoormit 30 PQb
Ščors 12 Dc
Scotland (reg.) 7 DEcd
Scott 42 grid square no.4
Scott, Cape– 31 Cb
Scott, Mount– 33 Ab
Scott Island 42 grid square no.3
Scott Reef (i.) 29 Ca
Scottsbluff 33 Cb
Scottsdale [Austl.] 29 map no.1
Scottsdale [U.S.] 33 Bc
Scranton 32 Da
Ščučinsk 13 Gd
Scunthorpe 7 FGe
Scutari, Lake– 11 Cb
Seabra 38 Cc
Seal, Cape– 26 Be
Seattle 33 Ab
Sebastián Vizcaíno, Bahía– (g.) 34 Ab
Šebekino 12 Ec
Seben 22 Cb
Sebeş 6 Fd
Sebuku, Pulau– (i.) 18 Ee
Secchia (riv.) 10 Cb
Sechura, Bahía de– 37 Ac

Sechura, Desierto de– (des.) 37 ABc
Second Cataract 25 CDb
Sedan 8 Fc
Sederot 22 Eg
Sédhiou 24 Ac
Seeheim 26 Ad
Sefīdar, Kūh– e– (mt.) 21 Ed
Segeža 13 Cc
Ségou 24 Bc
Segovia 9 Cb
Segré 8 Cd
Segre (riv.) 9 Fb
Seguédine 24 Dbc
Séguéla 24 Bd
Seguin 32 Bc
Segura (riv.) 9 DEc
Segura, Sierra de– (mts.) 9 Dcd
Sehwan 20 Cc
Seinäjoki 4 EFc
Seine (riv.) 8 Dc
Seine, Baie de la– 8 Cc
Sejm (riv.) 12 Dc
Sejmčan 14 Ic
Sekondi–Takoradi 24 Bd
Sekota 25 DEc
Šeksna 12 Eb
Šelagski, mys– 14 Kb
Selajar, Pulau– (i.) 18 EFf
Selajar, Selat– 18 EFf
Selatan, Cape– 18 De
Selçuk 11 Gde
Selemdža (riv.) 14 Gd
Selenga (riv.) 14 De
Sélestat 8 Gc
Sélibabi 24 Ac
Selinunte (r.) 10 Df
Selkirk 7 Ed
Selkirk Mountains 33 Bab
Selma 32 Cb
Selvagens, Ilhas– 24 Aab
Selvas (phys. reg.) 37 CDc
Selwyn 29 Gc
Selwyn Range 29 FGc
Semani (riv.) 11 Cc
Semara 24 ABb
Semarang 15 Dj
Semenovka 12 Dc
Semeru, Gunung– (mt.) 18 Df
Semiluki 12 Ec
Semipalatinsk 13 GHd
Semmering (p.) 5 Ee
Semnān 21 Eb
Šemonaiha 13 GHd
Semur–en–Auxois 8 Fd
Senador Pompeu 38 Db
Sena Madureira 37 Cc
Senanga 26 Bc
Sendai [Jap.] 17 ABhi
Sendai [Jap.] 16 Jc
Senegal (riv.) 24 Ac
Senegal (Ind. St.) 23 Ad
Senftenberg 5 Ec
Sengilej 12 Gc
Senhor do Bonfim 38 CDc
Senigallia 10 Dc
Senj 6 Bd
Senja (i.) 4 Da
Senkaku–Shotō 16 Fe
Şenkursk 12 Fa
Senmonorom 19 Ef
Senneterre 31 Hd

Sens 8 Ec
Senta 6 Ecd
Sento Sé 38 Cbc
Senyavin Islands 27 CDb
Seo de Urgel 9 Fa
Seoni 20 Ed
Seoul (Sŏul) 14 Ff
Sepanjang, Pulau– (i.) 18 Ef
Šepetkovo 14 IJc
Šepetovka 6 Ha
Sept–Iles 31 Ic
Serafimovič 12 Fd
Seraing 8 Fb
Serang 18 Cf
Serbia 6 Ede
Serdobsk 12 FGc
Sereflikochisar 22 Dc
Seremban 18 Bd
Serena, La– 39 Ab
Serengeti Plain 26 Cb
Seret (riv.) 6 Gb
Sergeja Kirova, ostrova– 14 BCb
Sergiev Posad (Zagorsk) 13 Cd
Sergino 13 Fc
Sergipe (State) 38 Dc
Seria 18 Dd
Seribu Kepulauan 18 Cf
Sérifos (i.) 11 Fe
Sernyje Vody 12 Hc
Serov 13 Fd
Serowe 26 Bd
Serpa 9 Bd
Serpentine Lakes 29 DEd
Serpuhov 3 Gb
Sérrai 11 Ec
Serrana, Banco de– (is.) 35 BCb
Serranilla, Banco de– (is.) 35 BCb
Serrat, Cap– 10 Bf
Serra Talhada 38 Db
Serrezuela 39 Bc
Serrinha 38 Dc
Sertão (phys. reg.) 38 CDbc
Serua, Pulau– (i.) 18 Hf
Sesfontein 26 Ac
Sesheke 26 Bc
Sesimbra 9 Ac
Sestao 9 Da
Sestroreck 4 Gc
Setana 17 Fc
Sète 8 Ef
Sete Lagoas 39 Da
Sete Quedas, Saltos das– 39 Cb
Sétif 24 Ca
Settat 24 Ba
Setté Cama 26 Ab
Setúbal 9 Ac
Seul, Lac– 31 Fc
Sevan, Lake– 21 Da
Sevastopol 13 Ce
Ševčenko → Aktau 13 Ee
Severn [Can.] (riv.) 31 FGc
Severn [U.K.] (riv.) 7 Ef
Severnaja Zemlja (i.) 41 grid square no.4
Severnyje Uraly (mts.) 12 GHab

Severodvinsk **13** CDe
Severo–Jenisejski **14** Ccd
Severo Krymskij Kanal **12** DEd
Severo–Kurilsk **14** Id
Severomorsk **13** Cc
Severouralsk **13** EFc
Seville **9** Bd
Sevlijevo **11** Fb
Sèvre (riv.) **8** Cd
Seward **30** Dcd
Seychelles (Ind. St.) **15** Bj
Seydişehir **22** Cd
Seyðisfiörður **4** map no.1
Seyhan (riv.) **22** Ed
Seyhan Barajı **22** Ed
Seyitgazi **22** Cc
Seylac **25** Ec
Seymour **29** Hf
Seyne–sur–Mer, La– **8** Ff
Sézanne **8** EFc
Sezze **10** Dd
Sfîntu Gheorghe **6** GHd
Sha'ab, Al– **21** Cg
Shaanxi (prov.) **16** Cd
Shaba (reg.) **26** Bb
Shabunda **26** Bb
Shache **15** Cf
Shackleton Coast **42** grid square no.4
Shackleton Ice Shelf (gl.) **42** grid square no.4
Shag Rocks **40** Dc
Shahdol **20** Fd
Shahganj **19** Hj
Shahjahanpur **20** EFc
Shakawe **26** Bc
Shakotan–Misaki **17** FGc
Shali **19** Jj
Sha'm, Ash– **21** Fd
Shām, Jabal ash– (mt.) **21** Fe
Shammar, Jabal– (mts.) **21** BCd
Shamva **26** Cc
Shan (State) **19** Cd
Shandan **16** Bc
Shandī **25** Dc
Shandong (phys. reg.) **16** Ec
Shandong Bandao (pen.) **16** Ec
Shanghai **15** Ef
Shangqiu **16** Ed
Shangrao **16** Ee
Shangzhi **16** Gab
Shanhaiguan **16** EFb
Shannon (riv.) **7** Be
Shantar Islands **14** GHd
Shantou **16** Ef
Shanxi (prov.) **16** Dc
Shaoguan **16** DEf
Shaowu **16** Ee
Shaoxing **16** EFde
Shaoyang **16** De
Shaqrā **21** Dg
Shaqrā', Ash– **21** CDd
Shāriqah, Ash– **21** EFd
Shark Bay **29** Acd
Sharm ash Shaykh **21** Ad
Sharqāt, Ash– **21** Cb
Shashe (riv.) **26** Bd
Shashi **16** Dd
Shasta, Mount– **33** Ab
Shatt–al–Arab (riv.) **21** Dcd

Shawinigan **31** Hd
Shay Gap **29** Cc
Shaykh 'Uthman **21** Dg
Sheberghan **20** Ca
Sheboygan **32** Ca
Sheffield **7** Fe
Shelby **33** Bb
Shelikhov Gulf **14** IJcd
Shenyang **16** Fb
Sheopur **19** Gj
Shepparton **29** GHf
Sherbro Island **24** Ad
Sherbrooke **31** HId
Sheridan **33** Cb
Sheringham **7** Ge
Sherman **32** Bb
Sherman, Fort– **35** map no.1
Sherridon **31** Ec
Shetland Isles **7** FGa
Shibam **21** Df
Shibata **17** Fef
Shibecha **17** Ic
Shibetsu **17** GHb
Shibin al Kawm **25** CDa
Shidao **16** Fc
Shihr, Ash– **21** DEfg
Shijiazhuang **15** Df
Shikarpur [India] **19** Ij
Shikarpur [Pak.] **20** CDc
Shikoku (i.) **16** Hd
Shilla (mt.) **20** Eb
Shillong **15** Dg
Shimizu **17** EFg
Shimokita–Hantō **17** GHd
Shimonoseki **16** GHd
Shimono–Shima **17** Ag
Shinano–Gawa (riv.) **17** Ff
Shingū **17** DEh
Shinji–Ko **17** Cg
Shinjō **17** FGe
Shinyanga **26** Cb
Shiōgama **17** Ge
Shio–no–Misaki **17** DEh
Shiquan **16** Cd
Shiquanhe **15** Cf
Shiragami–Misaki **17** FGd
Shirampur **19** IJk
Shirane–San (mt.) **17** Ff
Shiranuka **17** HIc
Shīrāz **21** Ecd
Shirbin **22** Cg
Shire (riv.) **26** Cc
Shiretoko–Hantō **17** Ib
Shiretoko–Misaki **17** Ib
Shir–Kuh (mt.) **21** Ec
Shiroishi **17** Gef
Shiwpuri **20** Ec
Shizuishan **16** Cc
Shizukawa **17** GHe
Shizunai **17** GHc
Shizuoka **16** IJcd
Shkodra **11** Cb
Shkumbini (riv.) **11** CDc
Shoshone Mountains **33** Bbc
Shoshong **26** Bd
Shreveport **32** Bb
Shrewsbury **7** Ee
Shuangcheng **16** Gab
Shuangyashan **16** Ha
Shuiji → Laixi **16** Fc
Shumlul, Ash– **21** Dd

Shuoxian **16** Dc
Shuqayq, Ash– **21** Cf
Shurayk, Ash– **25** Dc
Shushtar **21** Dc
Shwebo **19** Cd
Shweli (riv.) **16** Af
Siahan Range **20** BCc
Sialkot **20** DEb
Siam → Thailand (Ind. St.) **19** De
Siantan, Pulau– (i.) **18** Cd
Siapa (riv.) **37** Cb
Siargao (i.) **18** Gbc
Šiaškotan, ostrov– (i.) **14** Ie
Siau, Pulau– (i.) **18** Gd
Šiauliai **13** Bd
Siazan **21** DEa
Sibaj **13** Ed
Sibenik **6** BCe
Siberia (phys. reg.) **13** GOc
Siberut, Pulau– (i.) **15** Dj
Sibi **20** Cc
Sibillini, Monti– **10** Dc
Sibirjakova, ostrov– **13** Gb
Sibirtsevo **17** Cb
Sibiu **6** FGd
Sibolga **18** Ad
Sibu **18** Dd
Sibut **25** Bd
Sibutu Islands **18** Ed
Sibuyan (i.) **18** Fb
Sicasica **39** Ba
Sichuan (prov.) **16** BCd
Sicily (reg.) **10** DEef
Sicuani **39** Aa
Sideby **4** Ec
Sidérokastron **11** Ec
Sideros, Ákra– **11** Gf
Sidhi **19** Hj
Sîdi Barrâni **25** Ca
Sidi–Bel–Abbès **24** BCa
Sidi Ifni **24** Ab
Sidley, Mount– **42** grid square no.3
Sidon **22** Ef
Sidra, Gulf of– **24** Da
Sidrah, As– **24** Dab
Siedlce **5** Hb
Sieg (riv.) **5** Ac
Siegburg **5** Ac
Siegen **5** ABc
Siemiatycze **5** Ib
Siêmréab **18** IJe
Siena **10** Cc
Sieradz **5** Gc
Sierpc **5** GHb
Sierra Blanca **33** Cc
Sierra Blanca Peak **33** Cc
Sierra Colorada **40** Bab
Sierra Leone (Ind. St.) **23** Ae
Sierra Mojada **34** Bb
Sifnos (i.) **11** Fe
Sıgaçık **22** Ac
Sighetul Marmaţiei **6** FGc
Sighişoara **6** Gc
Sigli **18** Ac
Siglufjörður **4** map no.1
Signy Island **42** grid square no.1
Sigüenza **9** Db
Siguiri **24** ABc
Sigulda **4** Fd
Sihote–Alin (mts.) **14** Ge

Siirt **21** Cb
Sikar **20** DEc
Sikaram (mt.) **20** CDb
Sikasso **24** Bc
Síkinos (i.) **11** Fe
Sikkim (State) **19** Ac
Siktjah **14** Fb
Sil (riv.) **9** Ba
Sila, la– (mt.) **10** Fe
Silchar **19** Bd
Šile **22** Bb
Silesia (phys. reg.) **5** EFc
Silgarhi **19** Hi
Silifke **22** Ded
Siliguri **20** Gc
Siling Co (l.) **19** ABb
Silistra **11** Gab
Silivri **11** GHc
Siljan **4** Cc
Šilka (riv.) **14** Ed
Silkeborg **4** Bd
Sillajhuay, Cordillera de– (mts.) **39** Bab
Sillon de Talbert (cap.) **8** Bc
Šilovo **12** Fc
Silvassa **20** Dde
Silver City **33** Cc
Silverton **29** Ge
Silves **9** Ad
Simanggang **18** CDd
Šimanovsk **14** Fd
Simão Dias **38** Dc
Simav **22** Bc
Simav (riv.) **22** Bc
Simbirsk **13** DEd
Simelue, Pulau– (is.) **15** Di
Simeri Crichi **10** Fe
Simferopol **13** Ce
Simhan, Gebel– (mt.) **21** EFf
Simi (i.) **22** Ad
Šimkent (Čimkent) **13** FGe
Simla **20** Eb
Şimleu Silvaniei **6** Fc
Simojärvi **4** Fb
Simonstown **26** Ae
Simplon (p.) **10** Ba
Simpson Desert **29** Fcd
Simrishamn **5** Ea
Simušir (i.) **14** Ie
Sinabang **18** Ad
Sinaia **6** Gd
Sinai Peninsula **25** Db
Sinan **16** Ce
Sincelejo **37** Bb
Sind (riv.) **19** Gj
Sind (phys. reg.) **20** Cc
Sındırgı **11** Hd
Sindri **19** Ik
Sinelnikovo **12** Ed
Sines **9** Ad
Singapore (Ind. St.) **15** Di
Singaraja **18** Ef
Singatoka **28** map no.6
Singen **5** Be
Singida **26** Cb
Singitic Gulf **11** EFcd
Singkang **18** EFe
Singkawang **18** CDd
Singkep, Pulau– (i.) **18** BCe
Sinj **6** Ce
Sinjah **25** Dc
Sinkat **25** Dc
Sinkiang (Aut. Reg.) **15** Cef

Sinnicolaul Mare **6** Ecd
Sinnüris **22** Ch
Sinop **22** Eab
Sintana **6** Ec
Sintang **18** Dde
Sint Maarten / Saint Martin **35** Db
Sint Niklaas **8** EFb
Sintra **9** Ac
Sinüiju **14** Ff
Siófok **6** CDc
Sion **10** Aa
Sioux City **32** Ba
Sioux Falls **32** Ba
Sioux Lookout **31** Fcd
Siping **16** Fb
Siple, Mount– **42** grid square no.3
Siple Station **42** grid square no.3
Sipora, Pulau– (i.) **18** Ae
Siquijor **18** Fc
Siracusa **10** Ef
Sirajganj **20** Gd
Sir Edward Pellew Group **29** Fb
Siret (riv.) **6** Hc
Siret **6** GHc
Sirhän, Wädï as– (w.) **21** Bc
Sirina (i.) **11** Ge
Sirino, Monte– **10** Ed
Siros (i.) **11** Fe
Sirsa **20** DEc
Sirtica (phys. reg.) **24** Da
Sisak **6** Cd
Si Sa Khet **19** DEef
Sisimiut / Holsteinsborg **31** Jb
Sistan (phys. reg.) **20** Bb
Sisteron **8** Fe
Sitapur **20** Fc
Sithonia (pen.) **11** Ec
Sitia **11** Gf
Sitio da Abadia **39** Da
Sitka **31** Bc
Sittang (riv.) **19** Ce
Sittwe (Akyab) **19** Bde
Sivaki **14** Fd
Sivas **22** Fc
Sivaš, ozero– **12** Dd
Siverek **21** Bb
Sivrihisar **22** CDc
Siwah **25** Cb
Siwälik Range **19** Hlij
Siwan **19** Ij
Siwa Oasis **25** Cb
Sixth Cataract **25** Dc
Sjælland **4** BCe
Sjöbo **5** Da
Skadovsk **12** Dd
Skagerrak (str.) **4** ABd
Skagway **30** EFd
Skåne (phys. reg.) **4** Ce
Skanör–Falsterbo **5** Da
Skara **4** Cd
Skardu **20** Eab
Skarżysko–Kamienna **5** Hc
Skawina **5** GHcd
Skegness **7** Ge
Skellefteå **4** Eb
Skellefteälven (riv.) **4** Db
Skelleftehamn **4** Eb
Skhíza (i.) **11** De
Skhoinoúsa (i.) **11** Fe

Skíatos (i.) **11** Ed
Skibbereen **7** Bf
Skien **4** Bd
Skierniewice **5** Hc
Skikda **24** Ca
Skirakawa **17** Gf
Skíro (i.) **11** Fd
Skive **4** Bd
Skjoldungen **31** KLb
Skole **5** Id
Skópelos **11** Ed
Skopin **12** EFc
Skopje **11** Dbc
Škotovo **17** Cc
Skövde **4** Cd
Skovorodino **14** Fd
Skvira **6** Ib
Skye, Island of– **7** Cc
Slagesle **5** Ca
Slamet, Gunung– (mt.) **18** Cf
Slancy **4** Gd
Slatina **6** Gd
Slautnoje **14** JKc
Slave Coast **24** Cd
Slave River **31** Dbc
Slavgorod **13** Gd
Slavjanka **17** Bc
Slavjansk **13** Cd
Slavjansk na–Kubani **12** Ed
Slavonia (phys. reg.) **6** CDd
Slavonska Požega **6** CDd
Slavonski Brod **6** Dd
Slavuta **6** Ha
Sławno **5** Fa
Sleaford **7** Fe
Sliema **10** Efg
Sligo **7** Bd
Slite **4** Dd
Sliven **11** Gb
Slivnica **11** Eb
Sljudjanka **14** Dd
Slobodka **6** Ic
Slobodskoj **12** Hb
Slobodzeja **6** IJc
Slobozia **6** Hd
Słonie **5** Hb
Słonim **12** Cc
Slough **7** Ff
Slovakia (Ind. St.) **3** EFc
Slovakia (phys. reg.) **5** GHd
Slovenia (Ind. St.) **6** Bcd
Slovenské Rudohorie **5** GHd
Słubice **5** Eb
Slučʹ (riv.) **6** Ha
Sluck **12** Cc
Slunj **6** Bd
Słupsk **5** Fa
Småland (phys. reg.) **4** Cd
Smederevo **6** Ed
Smederevska Palanka **6** Ed
Smela **12** Dd
Smith Strait **41** grid square no.1
Smithton **29** map no.1
Smøla (i.) **4** Ac
Smolensk **13** Cd
Smólicas (mt.) **11** Dc
Smoljan **11** Fc
Smorgon **4** Fe
Snæfellsjökull (gl.) **4** map no.1
Snag **31** ABb
Snake River **33** Bb

Snake River Plain **33** Bb
Sneek **8** Fa
Sniardwy, Jezioro– **5** Hlb
Snieżka (mt.) **5** EFc
Snigirevka **12** Dd
Snøhetta (mt.) **4** Bc
Snowdon (mt.) **7** DEe
Snowdrift **31** DEb
Snowy River **29** Hf
Snyder **33** Cc
Soalala **26** map no.1
Soasiu **18** Gd
Sobat (riv.) **25** Dd
Sobral **38** CDb
Sochaczew **5** GHb
Soči **13** Ce
Society Islands **28** Bc
Socna **24** Db
Socompa, Paso de– (p.) **39** Bb
Socorro [Col.] **37** Bb
Socorro [U.S.] **33** Cc
Socorro, Isla– (i.) **34** ABc
Socotra (i.) **25** Fc
Socuéllamos **9** Dc
Sodankyla **4** Fb
Soddu **25** Dd
Söderala **4** Dc
Söderhamn **4** Dc
Söderköping **4** Dd
Södertälje **4** Dd
Soest **5** Bc
Sofala, Baía de– **26** Cd
Sofia **11** Eb
Sofijsk **14** Gd
Sôfu Gan (i.) **27** BCa
Sogamoso **37** Bb
Soğanlı (riv.) **22** Db
Sognefjorden (b.) **4** Ac
Sögüt Gölü **22** Bd
Soissons **8** Ec
Soitué **39** Jc
Sokal **5** Jc
Söke **22** Ad
Sokodé **24** BCd
Sokol **13** Dd
Sokółka **5** Ib
Sokolo **24** Bc
Sokolov **5** Dc
Sokoto (riv.) **24** Cc
Sokoto **24** Cc
Sol, Costa del– **9** CDd
Solåpur **15** Ch
Soledade **37** Cc
Soligalič **12** Fb
Soligorsk **12** Cc
Solikamsk **13** Ecd
Sol–Ileck **13** Ed
Solingen **5** Ac
Sollefteå **4** Dc
Sóller **9** Gc
Solling (mts.) **5** Bc
Solnečnogorsk **12** Eb
Solo → Surakarta **18** Df
Sologne (phys. reg.) **8** DEd
Solomon Islands **27** CDc
Solomon Islands (Ind. St.) **27** Dc
Solomon Sea **27** Cc
Solothurn **5** Ae
Solta (i.) **11** Bb
Soltau **5** Bb
Solvyčegodsk **12** Ga

Solway Firth (b.) **7** DEd
Solwezi **26** Bc
Soma **22** Ac
Somalia (Ind. St.) **23** Ge
Sombor **6** Dd
Sombrerete **34** Bb
Sombrero, El– **37** Cb
Somcuţa Mare **6** FGc
Somerset **29** Ga
Somerset (co.) **7** Ef
Somerset Island **31** Fa
Someş (riv.) **6** Fc
Somme (riv.) **8** Ec
Somport, Puerto de– (p.) **9** Ea
Son (riv.) **20** Fd
Sønderborg **4** Be
Søndre Strømfjord **31** JKb
Sondrio **10** Ba
Songea **26** Cc
Songhua Hu **16** Gb
Songhua Jiang → Sungari **17** Aab
Songjiang **16** Fd
Songkhla **15** Di
Songnim **16** Gc
Songo **26** Cc
Sonhat **19** Hk
Sonid Youqi **16** Db
Son La **19** Dd
Sonneberg **5** Cc
Sonora (riv.) **34** Ab
Sonoyta **34** Aa
Sonsón **37** Bb
Sonsonate **35** ABb
Sonsorol Islands **27** Bb
Son Tay **19** Ed
Sopot **5** Ga
Sopron **6** Cc
Sorbas **9** Dd
Sorel **32** Da
Sorgues **8** Fef
Soria **9** Fef
Sørøy **5** Ca
Sorocaba **39** Db
Soročinsk **12** Hc
Soroki **6** Hlb
Sorol Atoll (i.) **18** IJc
Sorong **18** He
Soroti **25** Dd
Sørøya (i.) **4** Ea
Sorraia (riv.) **9** Ac
Sorrento **10** Ed
Sør Rondane **42** grid square no.2
Sorsatunturi (mt.) **4** Gb
Sorsele **4** Db
Sorsogon **18** FGb
Sort **9** Fa
Sortavala **4** Gc
Sortland **4** Ca
Sosnovka **12** Hb
Sosnowiec **5** Gc
Šostka **12** Dc
Sosva **12** Jb
Sotteville–lès–Rouen **8** Dc
Souanké **26** Aa
Soudan **29** Fbc
Souflíon **11** FGc
Souk–Ahras **10** ABf
Sŏul → Seoul **14** Ff
Soure **38** Cb
Sousel **38** Bb

Sousse **24** Da
Souterraine, La– **8** DEd
South Africa (Ind. St.) **23** Ehi
Southampton **7** EFf
Southampton Island **31** Gb
South Andaman (i.) **19** Bf
South Australia (State) **29** EFde
South Bend **32** Ca
South Carolina (State) **32** CDb
South China Sea **16** DEf
South Dakota (State) **33** CDb
South East Cape **29** Hg
Southeast Pass **28** map no.3
South East Point **29** Hf
Southend–on–Sea **7** Gf
Southern Alps **27** De
Southern Cross **29** BCe
Southern Indian Lake **31** Fc
Southern Uplands (mts.) **7** DEd
Southern Urals (mts.) **12** Ic
South Geomagnetic Pole (1975) **42** grid square no.4
South Georgia (i.) **40** Ec
South Island **27** De
South Korea (Ind. St.) **15** Ef
South Magnetic Pole (1980) **42** grid square no.4
South Orkney Islands **36** Fj
South Platte (riv.) **33** Cb
South Point **28** map no.3
South Pole **42** grid square no.1
Southport **7** Ee
South Ronaldsay (i.) **7** EFb
South Sandwich Islands **36** Hli
South Saskatchewan (riv.) **33** BCa
South Shetland Islands **36** Dj
South Shields **7** Fd
South Uist (i.) **7** BCc
Southwest Cape **27** De
Southwest Pass (str.) **28** map no.3
Southwold **7** GHe
Sovetsk [Russia] **12** Bbc
Sovetsk [Russia] **12** Gb
Sovetskaja Gavan **14** GHe
Sôya–Misaki **17** GHb
Soyo **26** Ab
Sož (riv.) **12** Dc
Sozopol **11** GHb
Spain (Ind. St.) **3** Ccd
Spalding **7** Fe
Spanish Town **35** Cb
Sparks **33** Bc
Sparta **11** Ee
Spartanburg **32** Cb
Spartha, Cape– **11** Ef
Spartivento, Capo– [It.] **10** Be
Spartivento, Capo– [It.] **10** Ff
Spassk–Dalni **14** Ge
Spencer, Cape– **29** Ff
Spencer Bay **31** Fb
Spencer Gulf **29** Fe
Spey (riv.) **7** Ec
Spezia, La– **10** Bb
Spilimbergo **10** Da
Spišská Nová Ves **5** Hd
Spittal an der Drau **5** De

Spitzbergen (i.) **41** grid square no.3
Split **6** Ce
Spokane **33** Bb
Spoleto **10** Dc
Sporades, Northern– (is.) **11** EFd
Spree (riv.) **5** Dbc
Spremberg **5** Ec
Springbok **26** Ade
Springfield [Il.–U.S.] **32** BCb
Springfield [Ma.–U.S.] **32** Da
Springfield [Mo.–U.S.] **32** Bb
Springfield [Or.–U.S.] **33** Ab
Springfontein **23** Ehi
Springlands **37** Db
Springs **26** BCd
Springsure **29** Hc
Spurn Head **7** Ge
Squamish **33** Ab
Squillace, Golfo di– **10** Fe
Sredinny Hrebet (mts.) **14** IJd
Sredna Gora (mts.) **11** Fb
Srednekolymsk **14** Ic
Srednerusskaja vozvyšennost **13** Cd
Sredni Ural (mts.) **12** IJb
Šrem **5** Fb
Sremska Mitrovica **6** Dd
Srepok (riv.) **19** Ef
Sretensk **14** EFd
Srikakulam **20** FGe
Srī Lanka (Ceylon) (Ind. St.) **15** Ci
Srinagar **20** DEb
Srivardhan **20** De
Środa **5** Fb
Stade **5** Bb
Stadlandet (pen.) **4** Ac
Staffa (i.) **7** Cc
Stafford **7** Ee
Stahanov **12** Ed
Stalowa Wola **5** Ic
Standerton **26** BCd
Stanke Dimitrov **11** Eb
Stanley **36** Eh
Stanovoje Nagorje **14** EFd
Stanovoy Range **14** FGd
Stanthorpe **29** Id
Starachowice **5** Hc
Staraja Russa **12** Db
Stara Pazova **6** DEd
Stara Zagora **11** Fb
Starbuck Island **28** Bc
Stargard Szczecinski **5** Eb
Starica **12** DEb
Starnberg **5** Cde
Starnberger See **5** Cde
Starogard Gdański **5** Gb
Starokonstantinov **6** Hb
Starominskaja **12** Ed
Start Point **7** Ef
Stary Oskol **12** Ec
Stassfurt **5** CDbc
Staunton **32** CDb
Staurós **11** Ec
Stavanger **4** Ad
Stavropol **13** De
Stavropol → Togliatti **13** Dd
Stefanie, Lake– **25** Df
Stefansson Island **31** Ea
Stege **5** Da
Steinkjer **4** BCbc

Stelvio, Passo dello– **10** Ca
Stendal **5** Cb
Stenhouse Bay **29** Ff
Stepanakert → Harkendi **21** Dab
Stephenville **32** Fa
Sterling **33** Cb
Sterlitamak **13** Ed
Stettin **5** Eb
Stettiner Haff (g.) **5** Eb
Stewart **31** BCc
Stewart Island **27** De
Steyr **5** Ede
Stikine (riv.) **31** BCc
Stikine Ranges **31** BCbc
Stilis **11** Ed
Stilo, Punta– (cap.) **10** Fe
Stintu Gheorghe, Bratul– (riv.) **6** Id
Štip **11** Ec
Stirling **7** DEc
Stirling Range **29** Be
Stjørdal **4** Bc
Stockerau **5** EFd
Stockholm **4** Dd
Stockport **7** Ee
Stockton **33** ABc
Stockton on Tees **7** EFd
Stoēng Trêng **19** Ef
Stojba **14** Gd
Stoke–on–Trent **7** Ee
Stokes, Cerro– **40** Ac
Stolac **11** BCb
Stolbovj, ostrov– (i.) **14** Gb
Ston **11** Bb
Stonehaven **7** EFc
Stonehenge (:) **7** EFf
Stony Tunguska (riv.) **14** Cc
Stora Lulevatten (l.) **4** DEb
Store Bælt (str.) **4** Be
Storfjord (b.) **4** Ac
Storlien **4** Cc
Storm Bay **29** map no.1
Stornoway **7** CDb
Storsjön (l.) **4** Cc
Storuman **4** CDb
Strakonice **5** Dd
Stralsund **5** Da
Strängnäs **4** Dd
Stranraer **7** Dd
Strasbourg **8** Gc
Stratford–upon–Avon **7** Fe
Straubing **5** Dd
Streaky Bay **29** Ee
Strehaia **6** Fd
Stresa **10** Bb
Streževoj **13** GHc
Stříbro **5** Dc
Strimonikós Kólpos **11** EFc
Strofádhes, Nísoi– **11** De
Stromboli (i.) **10** Ee
Strömstad **4** BCd
Strömsund **4** Cc
Stronsay (i.) **7** EFb
Struga **11** Dc
Struma (Strymón) (riv.) **11** Ec
Strumica **11** Ec
Stry **6** FGb
Strymón → Struma (riv.) **11** Ec
Strzelecki Creek **29** FGd
Stubbekøbing **5** Da
Stupino **12** Ebc

Stura (riv.) **10** Ab
Stura di Demonte (riv.) **10** Ab
Sturge Island **42** grid square no.4
Sturt Desert **29** map no.1
Stuttgart **5** BCd
Styria (phys. reg.) **5** Ee
Suao **16** Ff
Šubarkuduk **13** Ee
Subotica **6** Dcd
Suceava **6** Hc
Sucre **39** Ba
Sucunduri (riv.) **37** Dc
Sudak **12** DEe
Sudan (phys. reg.) **24** CDc
Sudan (Ind. St.) **23** EFd
Sudbury **31** GHd
Sudd (phys. reg.) **25** CDd
Suddie **37** Db
Sudety (mts.) **5** EFc
Sueca **9** Ec
Sueco, El– **34** Bab
Suez **25** Dab
Suez, Gulf of– **25** Db
Suez Canal **25** map no.2
Suffolk (co.) **7** Ge
Suffolk **32** Db
Suğla Gölü **22** Dd
Suhar **21** Fe
Suhe–Bator **14** Dde
Suhiniči **12** DEc
Suhl **5** Cc
Suhona (riv.) **13** Dc
Suhumi **13** CDe
Suiá–Missu (riv.) **38** Bc
Suide **16** CDc
Suifenhe **16** Hb
Suihua **16** Ha
Suining **16** BCd
Suir (riv.) **7** Ce
Suita **17** Dg
Šuja **12** Fb
Sujfun (riv.) **17** Bbc
Sukabumi **18** Cf
Sukadana **18** CDe
Şukhayrah, Aş– **24** CDa
Sukhothai **19** Cde
Sukkertoppen / Maniitsoq **31** Jb
Sukkur **15** Cg
Sukumo **17** Ch
Sula, Kepulauan– **18** FGe
Sulaimäniya **21** CDb
Sulaimän Range **20** CDbc
Sula Sgeir (i.) **7** Cc
Sulawesi (Celebes) (is.) **18** EFe
Sulayyil, As– **21** De
Sulina **6** IJd
Sulina, Bratul– (riv.) **6** Id
Sulitjelma **4** CDb
Sulitjelma (mt.) **4** Db
Sullana **37** ABc
Sulmona **10** Dc
Sultan dağları (mts.) **22** Ccd
Sultanpur **19** Hj
Sulu Archipelago **18** EFcd
Sulūq **24** DEa
Sulu Sea **18** EFd
Šumadija (phys. reg.) **6** Ed
Sumatra (i.) **15** Dij
Sumba, Pulau– (i.) **15** DEjk
Sumba Strait **18** EFf

Tam - Teo

Tambao 24 BCc
Tambej 13 FGb
Tambelan Islands 18 Cd
Tambo 29 Hcd
Tambo (riv.) 37 Bd
Tambov 13 Dd
Tambura 25 Cd
Tamchaket 24 ABc
Tamdybulak 13 Fe
Tâmega (riv.) 9 Bb
Tamel Aike 40 Ab
Tamil Nadu (State) 20 Efg
Tamïyah, Jabal– (mt.) 21 Cde
Tampa 32 Cc
Tampere 4 EFc
Tampico 30 Ig
Tamsag–Bulak 14 Ee
Tamsweg 5 De
Tamworth 29 Ie
Tana [Kenya] (riv.) 25 De
Tana [Nor.] (riv.) 4 Fa
Tana, Lake– 25 Dc
Tanabe 17 Dh
Tanacross 31 Ab
Tanafjorden 4 Ga
Tanágra 11 Ed
Tanahbala, Pulau– (i.) 18 Ae
Tanahgrogot 18 Ee
Tanahjampea, Pulau– (i.) 18 Ff
Tanahmasa, Pulau– (i.) 18 Ade
Tanakpur 19 Hi
Tanami 29 DEbc
Tanami Desert 29 Eb
Tanana (riv.) 31 Ab
Tananarive → Antananarivo 23 GHgh
Tanaro (riv.) 10 Bb
Tanch'ŏn 17 Ad
Tanda 19 Hj
Tandag 18 Gc
Tandalti 25 Dc
Tandil 39 Cc
Tandjungkarang 18 Cef
Tandjungpinang 18 CDd
Tane–ga–Shima (i.) 16 Hd
Tanew (riv.) 5 Ic
Tanezrouft (phys. reg.) 24 BCb
Tanga 23 FGf
Tanganyika, Lake– 26 BCb
Tanggu 16 Ec
Tangier 24 Ba
Tang La (cap.) 20 Gc
Tangra Yumco (l.) 20 Gb
Tangshan 16 EFc
Tanimbar, Kepulauan– 27 Bc
Tanjung 18 Ee
Tanjungbalai 18 ABd
Tanjung Cina 18 Bf
Tanjungkarang 18 BCef
Tanjungpandan 18 Ce
Tanjungredeb 18 Ed
Tanjungselor 18 Ed
Tanna, Île– (i.) 28 map no.4
Tannu–Ola (mts.) 14 Cd
Tanout 24 Cc
Tansing 19 Hij
Ţanţā 25 Da
Tanzania (Ind. St.) 23 Ff
Tao'an 16 Fa
Tao'er He (riv.) 16 EFa

Taongi Atoll 27 Db
Taormina 10 Ef
Taoudenni 24 Bb
Taouz 24 Ba
Tapa 4 Fd
Tapachula 34 Cc
Tapajós (riv.) 38 Bb
Tapaktuan 18 Ad
Tapauá (riv.) 37 Cc
Tapirapeco, Sierra– (mts.) 37 Cb
Tapti (riv.) 20 Dd
Tapul Group 18 EFc
Taquari Novo (riv.) 38 Bc
Tara 13 Gd
Tara (riv.) 11 Cb
Tarakan 18 Ed
Taraklı 22 Cb
Taraklija 6 Id
Tarama–Jima (i.) 16 FGf
Tarancón 9 Dbc
Taranto 10 Fd
Taranto, Gulf of– 10 Fd
Tarapacá 37 BCc
Tarapoto 37 Bc
Tarare 8 Fe
Tarascon 8 Ff
Tarata 39 ABa
Tarauacá 37 Bc
Tarauacá (riv.) 37 Bc
Taravao 28 map no.2
Taravao, Isthmus of– 28 map no.2
Tarazona 9 DEb
Tarbagataj, Hrebet– (mts.) 13 He
Tarbela 20 Db
Tarbert 7 Cc
Tarbes 8 Df
Tarcoola 29 Ee
Taree 29 Ie
Tareja 14 BCb
Tarfaya 24 Ab
Tärgovište 11 Gb
Tarhankut, mys– 12 Dd
Tarhūnah 24 Da
Tarif 21 Ee
Tarifa 9 Cd
Tarifa, Punta de– (cap.) 9 BCd
Tarija 39 Bb
Tarim (riv.) 22 Ce
Tarim 21 Df
Tarïn Kowt 20 Cb
Tarko–Sale 13 Gc
Tarlac 18 Fa
Tarma 37 Bd
Tarn (riv.) 8 Df
Tárnaby 4 Cdb
Tarnobrzeg 5 Hlc
Tarnów 5 Hcd
Taroom 29 Hld
Tarquinia 10 Cc
Tarragona 9 Fb
Tarraleah 29 map no.1
Tarrasa 9 FGb
Tarso Emisu (mt.) 25 BCb
Tarsus 22 Ed
Tartagal 39 Bb
Tartu 4 Fd
Ţarţūs 22 Ee
Tarutau, Ko– (i.) 19 Cg
Tarutung 18 Ad

Tašauz → Dašhovuz 13 Ee
Tasejeva (riv.) 14 Cd
Tasikmalaya 18 Cf
Taškent 13 Fe
Taşköprü 22 DEb
Taşköy 22 EFb
Taš–Kumyr 13 Ge
Tasman (State) 29 map no.1
Tasman Peninsula 29 map no.1
Tasman Sea 27 CDde
Tăsnad 6 Fc
Tassili–n–Ajjer (mt.) 24 Cb
Tassili Oua–n–Ahaggar (plat.) 24 Cbc
Taštagol 13 Hd
Tata 6 CDc
Tatakoto Atoll 28 Cc
Tatar Autonomous Republic (Aut. Rep.) 13 DEd
Tatarbunary 6 IJd
Tatarsk 13 Gd
Tatar Strait 16 Jab
Tateyama 17 FGg
Tathlïth 21 Cf
Tatta 20 Cd
Tatui 39 Db
Tau 28 map no.5
Taubaté 39 Db
Taujsk 14 Hcd
Taukum (phys. reg.) 13 Ge
Taunggyi 19 Cd
Taungup 19 Be
Taunton 7 Ef
Taunus (mt.) 5 ABc
Tauragė 12 Bb
Taurus Mountains 22 CEd
Tautira 28 map no.2
Tavas 22 Bd
Tavda (riv.) 13 Fd
Tavda 13 Fd
Taveuni Island 28 map no.6
Tavira 9 Bd
Tavričanka 17 Bc
Tavşanli 22 Bc
Tavua 28 map no.6
Tawau 18 Ed
Tawitawi Group (is.) 18 EFcd
Ţawkar 25 Dc
Tawzar 24 Ca
Taxila (r.) 20 Db
Tay (riv.) 7 Ec
Taymä 21 Bd
Tay Ninh 19 Ef
Taytay 18 EFb
Taz (riv.) 13 Hc
Taza 24 Ba
Tāzirbū, Wāḥāt al– 24 Eb
Tazovski 13 Gc
Tbilisi 13 De
Tchibanga 26 Ab
Tchien 24 Bd
Tczew 5 Ga
Teano 10 Ed
Tébessa 24 Ca
Tecer dağları (mts.) 22 FGc
Tecuci 6 Hd
Tedžen 13 Ff
Tedžen (riv.) 13 Ff
Tees (riv.) 7 EFd
Tefé 37 Cc
Tefé (riv.) 37 Cc

Tefenni 22 Bd
Tegal 18 Cf
Tegucigalpa 30 Jh
Tehauntepec, Golfo de– 34 Cc
Tehauntepec, Istmo de– 34 Cc
Tehaupoo 28 map no.2
Tehrän 21 DEb
Tehuacán 34 Cc
Tehuantepec 34 Cc
Teifi (riv.) 7 Def
Tejkovo 12 EFb
Tejo (riv.) 9 Bc
Tekeli 13 Ge
Tekirdağ 22 Ab
Tektjur 14 Gc
Tel (riv.) 20 Fd
Tela 35 Bb
Telares, Los– 39 Bb
Telavi 21 Ea
Tel Aviv–Yafo 22 DEfg
Telegraph Creek 31 BCc
Telemark (phys. reg.) 4 ABd
Telen (riv.) 18 Ede
Telén 39 Bc
Teleno (mt.) 9 Ba
Teles Pires, Rio– (riv.) 38 Bc
Teles Pires o São Manuel, Rio– (riv.) 38 Bb
Tell Atlas (mts.) 24 BCa
Telok Anson 19 Dh
Telposiz, gora– (mt.) 13 EFc
Telsen 40 Bb
Telšiai 12 Bb
Téma 24 Bd
Tematangi Atoll 28 Bd
Tembilahan 18 Be
Temerloh 19 Dh
Temirtau → Akmol 13 Gd
Temnikov 12 Fc
Tempio Pausania 10 Bd
Temple 32 Bb
Temrjuk 12 Ed
Temuco 39 Ac
Tena 37 Bc
Tenali 20 Fe
Tenasserim (phys. reg.) 19 Cef
Tenasserim (riv.) 19 Cf
Tenda, Col di– (p.) 10 Ab
Ten Degree Channel 19 Bfg
Ténéré (phys. reg.) 24 Dbc
Tenerife (i.) 24 Ab
Ténès 24 Ca
Tengchong 19 Ccd
Tengiz, ozero– 13 Fd
Tengréla 24 Bcd
Tengxian 16 Ec
Teniente Matienzo 42 grid square no.1
Tenke 26 Bc
Tenkodogo 24 BCc
Tennant Creek 29 Eb
Tennessee (State) 32 Cb
Tennessee (riv.) 32 Cb
Tenojoki (riv.) 4 Fa
Tenosique 34 Cc
Tenryū 17 EFg
Tenryū–Gawa (riv.) 17 EFg
Tenterfield 29 Id
Teófilo Otoni 39 Da
Teotihuacán 34 Cbc

Tol - Tub

Tolitoli **18** EFd
Tolmezzo **10** Da
Tolo, Gulf of– **18** Fe
Tolosa **9** DEa
Toltén **39** Ac
Tolú **37** BBc
Toluca de Lerdo **34** BCc
Tom (riv.) **13** Hd
Toma, La– **39** Bc
Tomakomai **17** GHc
Tomari **14** He
Tomaševka **5** IJc
Tomašpol **6** Ib
Tomaszów Lubelski **5** IJc
Tomaszów Mazowiecki **5** Hc
Tombador, Serra do– (mts.) **38** Bc
Tomb–e Bozorg **21** EFd
Tombôco **26** Ab
Tombouctou **24** Bc
Tombua **26** Ac
Tomé **39** Ac
Tomelilla **5** Ea
Tomelloso **9** Dc
Tomini **18** Fd
Tomini, Teluk– **18** Fde
Tommot **14** Fd
Tomorit (mt.) **11** Dc
Tom Price **29** Bc
Tomsk **13** Hd
Tomtabacken (mt.) **4** Cd
Tonalá **34** Cc
Tondano **18** FGd
Tønder **5** Ba
Tone (riv.) **17** Gg
Tonekäbon **21** Eb
Tonga Islands (Ind. St.) **28** Acd
Tongatapu Group **28** Ad
Tongchuan **16** CDc
Tonghe **16** Ga
Tonghua **16** FGb
Tongjiang **16** Ha
Tongliao **16** Fb
Tongoa (i.) **28** map no.4
Tongsa Dzong **19** Jj
Tongzi **16** Ce
Tónichi **34** Bb
Tonk **20** Ec
Tonkin (phys. reg.) **19** DEd
Tonkin, Gulf of– **19** Ede
Tonle Sap (l.) **19** Df
Tonneins **8** CDe
Tonopah **33** Bc
Tonota **26** Bd
Tons (riv.) **19** Hj
Tønsberg **4** Bd
Toora–Hem **14** Cd
Toowoomba **29** Id
Topaklı **22** Ec
Topeka **32** Bb
Topki **13** Hd
Topliţa **6** Gc
Topol'čany **5** FGd
Topozero, ozero– **4** Gb
Torat–e–Heydariyeh **21** FGbc
Torbalı **11** Gd
Torbay **7** Ef
Toréz **12** Ed
Torgau **5** Dc
Tori–Shima (i.) **17** Gi

Tormes (riv.) **9** Bb
Torneälven (riv.) **4** EFb
Torneträsk (l.) **4** DEa
Torngat Mountains **31** Ic
Tornio **4** Fb
Tornionjoki (riv.) **4** EFb
Toro **9** Cb
Toro, Cerro del– (mt.) **39** ABb
Toro, Punta– (cap.) **35** map no.1
Törökszentmiklós **6** Ec
Toronto **31** GHd
Toropec **12** Db
Tororo **25** Dd
Torre del Greco **10** Ed
Torrelavega **9** CDa
Torremolinos **9** Cd
Torrens, Lake– **29** Fe
Torrens Creek **29** GHc
Torrente **9** Ec
Torreón **30** Hg
Torrés, Îles– **28** map no.4
Torres Strait **27** Cc
Torrijos **9** Cc
Torrington **33** Cb
Torsby **4** Cc
Tortona **10** Bb
Tortosa **9** Fb
Tortosa, Cabo de– (cap.) **9** Fb
Tortue, Ile de la– (i.) **35** Cab
Tortuga, Isla la– (i.) **37** Ca
Toruń **5** Gb
Torżok **12** DEb
Tosashimizu **17** Ch
Tosa–Wan **17** Ch
Toscana (reg.) **10** BCbc
Toscano, Arcipelago– **10** BCc
Tossa **9** Gb
Tostado **39** Bb
Tosya **22** Eb
Totana **9** Ed
Totma **12** Fab
Totness **37** Db
Totoya (i.) **28** map no.6
Tottori **16** Hc
Toubkal, Jebel– (mt.) **24** Ba
Touggourt **24** Ca
Touho **28** map no.4
Toul **8** FGc
Toulon **8** FGf
Toulouse **8** DEf
Toungoo **19** Ce
Touraine (phys. reg.) **8** Dd
Tourcoing **8** Eb
Touriñan, Cabo– (cap.) **9** Aa
Tournon **8** Fe
Tours **8** Dd
Towada **17** Gd
Townshend, Cape– **29** Ic
Townsville **29** Hb
Towuti, Danau– **18** Fe
Toyama **16** Ic
Toyama–Wan **17** Ef
Toyohashi **16** Id
Toyooka **17** Dg
Toyota **17** Eg
Tozanlı (riv.) **22** Fb
Trabzon **21** BCa
Trafalgar, Cabo– (cap.) **9** Bd
Trail **33** Bb
Trajan's wall **6** Hld

Tralee **7** ABe
Tranås **4** Cd
Trang **19** Cg
Trani **10** Fd
Transantarctic Mountains **42** grid square no.4
Transcona **33** Da
Transkei (hist. reg.) **26** Be
Transvaal (prov.) **26** BCd
Transylvania (phys. reg.) **6** FGc
Transylvanian Alps (Southern Carpathians) **6** FGd
Trapani **10** Df
Trasimeno, Lago– **10** Dc
Tras–os–Montes (phys. reg.) **9** Bb
Trat **19** Df
Traunstein **5** Dde
Traverse City **32** Ca
Travnik **6** Cd
Trbovlje **6** Bc
Trebbia (riv.) **10** Bb
Třebíč **5** Fd
Trebinje **11** Cb
Trebišov **5** Hd
Třebová **5** Fd
Tree Pagodas Pass **19** Cef
Treinta y Tres **39** Cc
Trélazé **8** Cd
Trelew **40** Bb
Trelleborg **4** Ce
Tremiti, Isole– **10** Ec
Tremp **9** Fa
Trenčín **5** Gd
Trenque Lauquen **39** Bc
Trent (riv.) **7** Fe
Trentino–Alto Adige (reg.) **10** Ca
Trento **10** Ca
Trenton **32** Dab
Tréport, Le– **8** Dbc
Tres Arroyos **39** BCc
Três Casas **37** Cc
Tres Esquinas **37** Bb
Três Lagoas **39** Cb
Tres Lagos **40** ABb
Tres Picos, Cerro– (mt.) **39** Bc
Tres Puntas, Cabo– **40** Bb
Três Rios **39** Db
Tres Virgenes, Las– (mt.) **34** Ab
Treungen **4** ABd
Treviso **10** Db
Tricase **10** Ge
Trichur **20** Ef
Tridentine Alps **10** Ca
Trier **5** Ad
Trieste **10** Db
Trikala **11** Dd
Trikhonis, Limni– **11** Dd
Trincomalee **15** Ci
Trindade, Ilha da– (i.) **36** Gef
Třinec **5** Gd
Trinidad (i.) **37** CDa
Trinidad [Bol.] **39** Ba
Trinidad [U.S.] **33** Cc
Trinidad, Rio– (riv.) **35** map no.1
Trinidad and Tobago (Ind. St.) **36** DEbc

Trinity (riv.) **32** Bb
Tripoli [Leb.] **22** Ee
Tripoli [Lib.] **24** Da
Tripolis **11** Ee
Tripura (State) **19** Bd
Tristan da Cunha (is.) **23** ABi
Trivandrum **15** Ci
Trnava **5** FGd
Trogir **10** Fc
Troglav (mt.) **6** Ce
Troia **10** Ed
Troick **13** Fd
Troicko–Pečorsk **13** EFc
Trois–Rivières **31** Hld
Trojan **11** Fb
Trojansky prohod **11** Fb
Trollhättan **4** BCd
Trollheimen (mt.) **4** Bc
Trombetas (riv.) **38** Ba
Tromelin (i.) **23** map no.1
Tromsø **4** DEa
Tronador (mt.) **40** Ab
Trondheim **4** Bc
Trondheimsfjorden–(b.) **4** Bc
Troödos, Mount– (Olympus) **22** De
Trotus (riv.) **6** Hc
Trouville–sur–Mer **8** CDc
Trowbridge **7** EFf
Troy (r.) **22** Ac
Troy [Al.–U.S.] **32** Cb
Troy [N.Y.–U.S.] **32** Da
Troyes **8** Fc
Trucial Coast **21** EFe
Trudovoje [Kaz.] **13** Fd
Trudovoje [Russia] **17** Cc
Trujillo [Hond.] **35** Bb
Trujillo [Peru] **36** BCd
Trujillo [Sp.] **9** Bc
Trujillo [Ven.] **37** BCb
Truk Islands **27** Cb
Truro [Can.] **31** Id
Truro [U.K.] **7** Df
Truskavec **6** FGb
Trutnov **5** Fd
Trysil (riv.) **4** Cc
Trzcianka **5** EFb
Tsaratanana (mt.) **26** map no.1
Tsau **26** Bcd
Tshabong **26** Bd
Tshela **26** Ab
Tshikapa **26** Bb
Tshuapa (riv.) **26** Bb
Tsinan (Jinan) **15** Df
Tsingtao (Qingdao) **16** Fc
Tsu **16** Id
Tsugaro–Kaikyō **16** IJb
Tsumeb **23** Dg
Tsuruga **16** Ic
Tsuruoka **17** Fe
Tsushima **17** Ae
Tsushima (is.) **16** Gd
Tsushima–Kaikyō **17** Agh
Tsuyama **16** Hcd
Tual **18** Hf
Tuamoto Archipelago **28** BCcd
Tuapse **13** Ce
Tuban **18** Ef
Tubarão **39** Db
Tübingen **5** Bd
Ṭubruq **24** Ea

Wac - Woo

Waco **32** Bb
Waddenzee **8** Fa
Waddington, Mount– (mt.) **31** Cb
Wad Madanī **25** Dc
Wafra **21** Dd
Wager Bay **31** FGb
Wagga Wagga **29** Hf
Wagin **29** Be
Wagrowiec **5** Fb
Waha **24** DEb
Wahiawa **28** map no.1
Wahpeton **32** Ba
Waialua **28** map no.1
Waidhofen an der Ybbs **5** Ee
Waigeo, Pulau– (i.) **18** Hde
Waikabubak **18** Ef
Wailuku **28** map no.1
Waimea **28** map no.1
Waingapu **18** Ff
Wajh, Al– **21** Bd
Wajima **17** Ef
Wajir **25** DEd
Wakasa–Wan **17** Dfg
Wakayama **16** Id
Wake Island **27** Db
Wakhan (phys. reg.) **20** Da
Wakkanai **16** Ja
Walachia (phys. reg.) **6** FHd
Wałbrzych **5** Fc
Walcheren **8** Eb
Wałcz **5** Fb
Wales (reg.) **7** DEef
Walgett **29** Hde
Walgreen Coast **42** grid square no.3
Walikale **25** Ce
Walker Mountains **42** grid square no.3
Wallaroo **29** Fe
Walla Walla **33** Bb
Wallis Islands **28** Ac
Walls **7** Fa
Walpole, Île– (i.) **28** map no.4
Walsall **7** Fe
Walsenburg **33** Cc
Walvis Bay **26** Ad
Wamba (riv.) **26** Ab
Wamba **25** Cd
Wanaaring **29** GHd
Wangaratta **29** Hf
Wangiwangi, Pulau– (i.) **18** FGef
Wangpan Yang **16** Fd
Wangqing **16** GHb
Wangxian **15** Df
Wanning **16** Dg
Warangal **20** EFe
Warburton, The– (riv.) **29** Fd
Warburton Mission **29** Dd
Ward, Mount– **42** grid square no.1
Wardha **20** Ed
Wardha (riv.) **20** Ede
Waren [Ger.] **5** Db
Waren [Indon.] **27** Bc
Warmbad **26** Ad
Warnemünde, Rostock– **5** CDab
Warragul **29** Hf
Warrego Range **29** GHcd
Warrego River **29** Hd
Warri **24** Cd

Warrnambool **29** Gf
Warsaw **5** Hb
Warta (riv.) **5** Gc
Warwich **7** Fe
Warwick **29** Id
Wasatch Range **33** Bbc
Wāshim **20** Ed
Washington (i.) **28** ABb
Washington **32** Db
Washington (State) **33** ABb
Washington → Teraina **28** ABb
Washington, Mount– **32** Da
Wasifiya, El– **25** map no.1
Wäsiṭah, Al– **22** Ch
Waspán **35** Bb
Watampone (Bone) **18** EFef
Waterford **7** Ce
Waterloo [Bel.] **8** Fb
Waterloo [U.S.] **32** Ba
Watertown [N.Y.–U.S.] **32** Da
Watertown [S.D.–U.S.] **32** Ba
Waterville **32** Ea
Watford **7** Ff
Watheroo **29** Be
Watrous **31** Ec
Watsa **25** CDd
Watson Lake **31** Cbc
Wauchope **29** Ie
Waukara, Gunung– (mt.) **18** EFe
Waukarlycarly, Lake– **29** Cc
Wausau **32** BCa
Wave Hill **29** Eb
Wäw **25** Cd
Wawa **32** Ca
Wäw al Kabïr **24** Db
Waycross **32** Cb
We, Pulau– (i.) **18** Ac
Weda **18** Gde
Weddell Sea **42** grid square no.1
Weed **33** Ab
Weiden im der Oberpfalz **5** CDd
Weifang **16** EFc
Weihai **16** Fc
Wei He (riv.) **16** Cd
Weimar **5** Cc
Weinan **16** CDd
Weipa **29** Ga
Weishan Hu (l.) **16** Ecd
Weisse Elster (riv.) **5** Dc
Weissenfels **5** Cc
Wejherowo **5** Ga
Welkom **26** Bd
Wellesley Islands **29** FGb
Wellington [Austl.] **29** He
Wellington [N.Z.] **27** De
Wellington, Isla– (i.) **40** Ab
Wells **33** Bb
Wells, Lake– **29** Cd
Wels **5** Ed
Welshpool **7** Ee
Wenchang **16** Dg
Wenshan **16** BCf
Wentworth **29** Ge
Wenzhou **16** Fe
Werder **25** Ed
Werra (riv.) **5** Bc
Werribee **29** Gf
Werris Creek **29** Hle
Wesel **5** Ac
Weser (riv.) **5** Bb

Wessel, Cape– **29** Fa
Wessel Islands **29** Fa
West Bengal (State) **20** Gd
West Cape **27** De
Westerland **5** ABa
Western Australia (State) **29** BDcd
Western Carpathians (mts.) **5** FHd
Western Dvina (riv.) **12** BCb
Western Ghats (mts.) **20** DEef
Western Malaysia (State) **18** BCd
Western Sahara (Dep.) **23** Ac
Western Samoa (Ind. St.) **28** Ac
Western Sayans **14** BCd
Westerwald (mt.) **5** ABc
Westfalen **5** ABc
West Falkland (i.) **40** Bc
West Ice Shelf **42** grid square no.2
West Nicholson **23** EFg
Weston **18** Ecd
Weston–super–Mare **7** Ef
West Palm Beach **32** CDc
Westport [Ire.] **7** Be
Westport [N.Z.] **27** De
Westray (i.) **7** Eb
West Siberian Plain **13** FHcd
West Virginia (State) **32** CDb
West Wyalong **29** He
Wetar, Pulau– (i.) **18** Gf
Wewak **27** Cc
Wexford **7** CDe
Weyburn **31** Ed
Weymouth **7** EFf
Whalsay (i.) **7** Fa
Whangarei **27** De
Whasington, Mount– **32** Da
Wheeler Peak **33** Bc
Wheeling **32** CDab
Whiehorse **30** EFc
White Bay **31** Jc
Whitehaven **7** Ed
White Nile (riv.) **25** Dc
White River [Ar.–U.S.] **32** Bb
White River [Nb.–U.S.] **33** Cb
White Volta **24** Bd
Whitney, Mount– **33** Bc
Whyalla **29** Fe
Wichita **32** Bb
Wichita Falls **33** CDc
Wick **7** Eb
Wickham **29** Bc
Wicklow **7** De
Wicklow Mountains **7** Ce
Widgiemooltha **29** Ce
Wieliczka **5** Hcd
Wieluń **5** Gc
Wiener Neustadt **5** EFe
Wienerwald (mts.) **5** EFd
Wieprz (riv.) **5** Ic
Wiesbaden **5** ABc
Wiese, ostrov– (i.) **13** Gb
Wight, Isle of– **7** Ff
Wigtown **7** Dd
Wilcannia **29** Ge
Wildspitze (mt.) **5** Ce
Wilhelmshaven **5** ABb
Wilkes Land **42** grid square no.4

Willemstad **35** Db
William Creek **29** Fd
Williams Lake **31** Cc
Willis Group **29** Ib
Williston **33** Cb
Williston Lake **31** Cc
Willmar **32** Ba
Willow **30** CDc
Wilmington [De.–U.S.] **32** Dab
Wilmington [N.C.–U.S.] **32** Db
Wilson, Mount– **33** Cc
Wilson's Promontory **29** Hf
Wiluna **29** BCd
Winchester **7** Ff
Windhoek **23** Bf
Windorah **29** Gd
Wind River Range **33** BCb
Windsor [U.K.] **7** Ff
Windsor [U.S.] **31** Gd
Windward Islands **28** Bc
Windward Passage **35** Cab
Winisk **31** Gc
Winneba **24** BCd
Winnemucca **33** Bb
Winnipeg **31** Fcd
Winnipeg, Lake– **31** Fc
Winnipegosis **31** Ec
Winnipegosis, Lake– **31** EFc
Winona **32** Ba
Winslow **33** Bc
Winston–Salem **32** CDb
Winterthur **5** Be
Winton **29** Gc
Wisconsin (State) **32** BCa
Wiślany, Zalew– (lag.) **5** Ga
Wisłok (riv.) **5** Hd
Wismar **5** Cb
Withe Sea **13** Cc
Witputz **26** Ad
Wittemberg **5** Dc
Wittenberge **5** Cb
Wittenoom **29** Bc
Wittlich **5** Ad
W.J.Van Blommestein Meer **37** Db
Wkra (riv.) **5** Hb
Włocławek **5** Gb
Włodawa **5** Ic
Włoszczowa **5** Ghc
Woking **7** Ff
Woleai Atoll **27** Cb
Wolf Point **33** Cb
Wolfsberg **5** Ee
Wolfsburg **5** Cb
Wolin (i.) **5** Eb
Wollaston, Islas– **40** ABc
Wollaston Lake **31** Ec
Wollaston Peninsula **31** Dab
Wollongong **29** Ie
Wołomin **5** Hb
Wołów **5** Fc
Wolu **18** Fe
Wolverhampton **7** Ee
Wönsan **16** Gc
Wonthaggi **29** GHf
Woodland **33** Ac
Woodroffe, Mount– **29** Ed
Woods, Lake of the– **32** Ba
Woodstock **31** Id
Woodward **33** CDc
Woomera **29** Fe

Yus - Zyw

Yushan (mt.) **16** Ff
Yutian **20** Fa
Yuyao **16** Fde
Yvetot **8** Dc
Yzeure **8** Ed

Z

Zabajkalsk **14** Ede
Zabib **21** Cg
Zábol **21** Gc
Zabrze **5** Gc
Zacapa **35** Bb
Zacatecas **34** Bb
Zadar **6** Bd
Zafir, Az– **21** Cef
Zafra **9** Bc
Żagań **5** Ec
Zagora **24** Ba
Zagorsk → Sergiev Posad **13** Cd
Zagreb **6** Bd
Zagros Mountains **21** DEc
Zagyva (riv.) **6** Dc
Zähedän **21** FGd
Zaḥlah **22** EFef
Ẕahrän, Aẕ– **21** DEd
Zaire (riv.) **26** Ab
Zaire (Ind. St.) **23** DEf
Zaire → Lualaba (riv.) **26** Bb
Zaječar **6** EFe
Zajsan **13** He
Zajsan, ozero– **13** He
Zakopane **5** Gd
Zalaegerszeg **6** Cc
Zaláu **6** Fc
Zaleščiki **6** GHb
Zalṭan **24** DEb
Zambezi (riv.) **26** Cc
Zambezi **26** Bc
Zambia (Ind. St.) **23** EFfg
Zamboanga **18** Fc
Zambrów **5** Ib
Zamora **9** BCb
Zamora de Hidalgo **34** Bbc
Zamosć **5** Ic
Żanatas **13** FGe
Záncara (riv.) **9** Dc
Zanjän **21** Db
Żannetty, ostrov– **14** IJb
Zante (i.) **11** De

Zante **11** De
Zanthus **29** Ce
Zanzibar **23** FGf
Zaoqing **16** Df
Zapadna Morava **6** Ee
Zapala **39** ABc
Zaporožje **13** Ce
Zaqāzīq, Az– **25** Dab
Zara **22** Fc
Zarasai **4** Fe
Zárate **39** Cc
Zaraza **37** Cb
Zard Küh (mt.) **21** DEc
Zarghunshahr **20** Cb
Zaria **24** Cc
Zarkovski **12** Db
Zarqā, Az– **22** Ff
Zarqa, El– **22** CDg
Żary **5** Ec
Zarzaïtine **24** CDb
Zaskar Mountains **20** EFb
Żaškov **6** IJb
Žatec **5** Dc
Zavidovići **6** Dd
Zavitinsk **14** FGd
Zavolžje **12** Fb
Zavolžsk **12** Fb
Zawi **23** EFg
Zawilah **24** Db
Zbaraž **6** GHb
Zbąszyń **5** EFb
Zborov **6** Gb
Zbruč (riv.) **6** Hb
Żdanov → Mariupol **12** DEd
Żd'ar nad Sázavou **5** EFd
Zdolbunov **6** Ha
Zduńska Wola **5** Gc
Zeehan **29** map no.1
Zefat **22** Ef
Zeitz **5** Dc
Zeja **14** Fd
Zeja (riv.) **14** Fd
Zélaf **22** Ff
Želanija, mys– **13** FGb
Zelenoborski **4** GHb
Zelenodolsk **12** GHb
Zelenogorsk **4** Gc
Żelenogorsk–Ilimski **14** Dd
Zelenogradsk **4** Ee
Zelenyi (i.) **17** Jc
Żeleznogorsk **12** DEc
Żeltyje Vody **12** Dd
Zëmio **25** Cd

Zemun, Belgrade– **6** Ed
Zenica **6** CDd
Zeravšan (riv.) **13** Ff
Zernograd **12** Fd
Zézere (riv.) **9** Ac
Žezkazgan (Džezkazgan) **13** Fe
Zgierz **5** Gc
Zgorzelec **5** Ec
Zhangguangcai Ling (mts.) **17** IJbc
Zhangjiakou **16** DEb
Zhangye **16** Bc
Zhangzhou **16** Ef
Zhanjiang **15** Dgh
Zhaodong **16** FGa
Zhaotong **16** Be
Zhejiang (prov.) **16** EFe
Zhengzhou **15** Df
Zhenhai **16** Fde
Zhenjiang **16** EFd
Zhenyuan **16** Ce
Zhijiang **16** Ce
Zhob (riv.) **20** Cb
Zhongba **15** Cfg
Zhongwei **16** BCc
Zhongxian **16** Cd
Zhoushan Qundao **16** Fde
Zhucheng **16** EFc
Zhumadian **16** Dd
Zhuolu **16** DEb
Zhuzhou **16** De
Žiar–nad Hronom **5** Gd
Žibä' **21** Bd
Zibo **16** Ec
Ziel, Mount– **29** Ec
Zielona Góra **5** Ebc
Ziftá **22** Cg
Żigansk **14** EFc
Zigong **16** Be
Ziguinchor **24** Ac
Żigulevsk **12** Gc
Zihuatanejo **34** Bc
Zile **22** Eb
Zilfi, Az– **21** CDd
Żilina **5** Gd
Zillah **24** Db
Zima **14** Dd
Zimbabwe (r.) **26** Cd
Zimbabwe (Ind. St.) **23** EFgh
Zimnicea **6** Ge
Zinder **24** Cc
Zipaquirá **37** Bb

Žirje (i.) **6** Be
Žirnovsk **12** FGc
Ziro **19** Bc
Žitny Ostrov (phys. reg.) **5** Fde
Žitomir **13** Bd
Zittau **5** Ec
Zlatica **11** EFb
Zlatograd **11** Fc
Zlatoust **13** Ed
Zlatoustovsk **14** Gd
Zlin **5** Fd
Żlobin **12** CDc
Złocieniec **5** Fb
Złotoryja **5** EFc
Złotów **5** Fb
Zmeiny, ostrov– **12** Dd
Žmerinka **6** Hib
Znamenka **12** Dd
Znojmo **5** EFd
Žohova, ostrov– **14** Ib
˜Žoločev **6** Gb
Zolotonoša **12** Dd
Zomba **26** Cc
Zonguldak **22** Cb
Zorritos **37** Ac
Zouar **25** Bbc
Zouïrât **24** Ab
Zrenjanin **6** Ed
Zudañez **39** Ba
Ẕufár (phys. reg.) **21** EFf
Zug **5** Be
Zugspitze (mt.) **5** Ce
Zújar (riv.) **9** Cc
Zujevka **12** Hb
Žukovka **12** Dc
Zumba **37** Bc
Zumbo **26** Cc
Zunyi **16** Ce
Županja **6** Dd
Zürich **5** Be
Zürichsee **5** Be
Zuwärah **24** Da
Zvishavane **26** BCd
Zvolen **5** Gd
Zvornik **6** Dd
Zwickau **5** Dc
Zwiesel **5** Dd
Zwolle **8** Ga
Żyradów **5** Hbc
Zyrjanka **14** HIc
Zyrjanovsk **13** He
Żywiec **5** Gd